INTERNATIONAL NUCLEAR DIPLOMACY AND INDIA

U.N. GUPTA

ATLANTIC
PUBLISHERS & DISTRIBUTORS (P) LTD

Published by

ATLANTIC

PUBLISHERS & DISTRIBUTORS (P) LTD

B-2, Vishal Enclave, Opp. Rajouri Garden,
New Delhi-110027
Phones : 25413460, 25429987, 25466842

Sales Office
7/22, Ansari Road, Darya Ganj,
New Delhi-110002
Phones : 23273880, 23275880, 23280451
Fax : 91-11-23285873
web : www.atlanticbooks.com
e-mail : info@atlanticbooks.com

ISBN 81-269-0692-8

Printed in India
at Nice Printing Press, Delhi

Preface

The present generation of people and the new States are unable to grasp as to why the USA that dropped the atom bombs on Hiroshima and Nagasaki in 1945 is so much opposed to proliferation of nuclear technology and occurrence of nuclear wars. It is interesting that there is no developed and functional nuclear law segment in public international law. Nuclear law has not, as of 2006, crossed the take-off status; it is not in a nascent stage either, since it appears that the States have developed a consensus to operate without any nuclear law and to interact by way of nuclear diplomacy. The reasons for this are to be found in the games of power politics that are sanctioned and are allowed by contemporary international law. The concepts of State sovereignty and right to wage war in self-defence or for enforcement of international law are treated to be part of laws of peace. When a war takes place, the International Court of Justice has recognized that use of nuclear weapons is not prohibited. This position is coupled with the law of United Nations Organization Charter, which recognizes five 'superpowers' to be in one-to-one status with the law of the Charter. In this matter of fact, the nuclear powers, which mean five superpowers that are the permanent members of UN Security Council, have immense diplomatic power edge over all other States of the world. The nuclear diplomacy is a matured phenomenon since 'balance of terror' has ruled it for about fifty years now and has prevented nuclear powers from using ferocious nuclear weapons against other States, just as any nuclear law would otherwise like this to be. Actually, 'nuclear diplomacy' is the present 'nuclear law'. How this has developed since 1945, when atom bombs were dropped over Hiroshima and Nagasaki, and what are the actual relationships between haves and have-nots of nuclear technology and weaponry are the subject matter of this book. Of course, for a clearer understanding, a sociological approach for anatomy of main State actors in nuclear field, that is, the five superpowers, and countries like North Korea, Iran, Pakistan, India and Iraq, and how these have been involved in or have been drawn into this nuclear diplomacy has been preferred.

Crystallization of a 'Nuclear Law' has been sidelined by the preliminary step taken for 'nuclear disarmament' by the pacifists, non-nuclear States and the United Nations Organization since 1945. Instead, the Cold War rivalry prompted the Big Powers to compete unhindered in the development of state-of-the-art nuclear weaponry alongwith nuclear powered submarines and outer space carriers of nuclear warheads. Side by side, the conventional weapons that developed into 'weapons of mass destruction' are not less blind or indiscriminate killers than atomic bombs and nuclear artillery. This had put all the laws of war into a wastebasket. The only positive international law on nuclear matters is in the form of a passive resolution of General Assembly that sets an obligation on all States not to use weapons of mass destruction including nuclear weapons in a conflict. However, the 'balance of terror' recognized both by USA and earlier USSR in self-interest helped the development of a nuclear diplomacy effective enough to prevent world wars, an objective which was pursued by international law and the United Nations also. The book emphasizes on and brings out the role of good as well as of bad in international nuclear diplomacy in preventing nuclear wars and the use of 'weapons of mass destruction'. Nuclear wars are prevented by compulsions of diplomacy and not by any law or supra-State authority, which this book examines. Since prohibition or non-proliferation of nuclear technology goes into the details of various processes and instruments, it is common to describe the various mechanical devices in books for proper understanding of the subject of nuclear non-proliferation. Nuclear disarmament and non-proliferation do not cover development of nuclear energy for industrial or civil use. The principles involved for making a nuclear weapon or nuclear reactor are simple but gadgets required for preparing components and complete working devices are hi-tech. These components and technology are sold or acquired in world black-market. A chapter, second, has been added in the book to understand or inform the readers about the basics of related nuclear science and technology.

International nuclear diplomacy has been preoccupied with maintenance of hegemony of nuclear States by preventing other States from acquiring nuclear technology and expertise. This has led to one-sided developments, since nuclear technology has also civil energy production utility particularly when carbon energy resources of the world are fast dwindling. This has led to various acrimonious situations since upto a certain point nuclear expertise is common to nuclear weapons and nuclear civil reactors. India has also been caught in this state of affairs. This aspect has been given detailed attention in the book.

India had to become a nuclear State both for self-defence and for supplicating its energy needs. There were compulsions and obstructions from international nuclear diplomacy. The strange thing is that while nuclear diplomacy has been outside of Charter of United Nations for five Big Powers, other States including India have to adopt their nuclear policies under the Charter. However, by the year 2006, the world recognizes and accepts the Indian points of view on the score and this is a successful achievement of diplomacy on the part of India. The book analyses particularly the efforts of India and also of some other States to survive in the jungle of international diplomacy and nuclear diplomacy, this is done both chapter-wise and specifically.

I had occasions to give lectures as Professor of Law on several portions of the book from time to time, particularly on those related to disarmament, on the role of UN General Assembly or non-alignment movement in developing or controlling nuclear diplomacy as also on the Indian nuclear policies. These lecture notes have immensely helped me in motivation for writing and also in fixing the contents of this book.

I am thankful to the Atlantic Publishers and Distributors (P) Ltd., particularly to Dr. K.R. Gupta, who undertook to publish this book of national interest.

I acknowledge my feelings for my wife, Shashi Gupta, who not only provided me much needed moral support and time for writing the book, but also helped me out of physical ailments at the same time.

U.N. GUPTA

Abbreviations

ABM	Anti Ballistic Missile (Treaty)
BARC	Bhabha Atomic Research Centre (India)
BWR	Boiling Water Reactors
CEP	Circular Error of Probability
CNTBT	Comprehensive Nuclear Test Ban Treaty
CTBT	Comprehensive Test Ban Treaty
CWC	Chemical Weapons Convention
DRDO	Defence Research and Development Organization (India)
DPRK	Democratic People's Republic of Korea
EU	European Union
FA	Framework Agreement (North Korea)
FBR	Fast Breeder Reactors
GRL	Goods Review List (Iraq)
GA	General Assembly (United Nations)
GATT	General Agreement on Tariffs and Trade
GLCM	Ground Launched Cruise Missile
HCI	Humanitarian Coordinator for Iraq
Hi-tech	High Technology
IAEA	International Atomic Energy Agency
ICBM	Intercontinental Ballistic Missile
ICJ	International Court of Justice
IDC	International Data Centre
INVO	Iraq Nuclear Verification Office
ISG	Iraq Survey Group

ITER	International Thermonuclear Experimental Reactor
KEDO	Korean Peninsula Energy Development Organization
KT/Kt	Kiloton
LOC	Line of Control
MW	Megawatt
NATO	North Atlantic Treaty Organization
NIEO	New International Economic Order
NPT	Nuclear Non Proliferation Treaty
NSG	Nuclear Suppliers Group
OPEC	Oil Producing and Exporting Countries
PHWR	Pressurized Heavy Water Reactors
PNE	Peaceful Nuclear Explosion
Pu	Plutonium
SALT	Strategic Arms Limitations Treaty
SC	Security Council (United Nations)
SEATO	South East Asia Treaty Organization
SLBM	Submarine Launched Ballistic Missile
U	Uranium
UK	United Kingdom
UN/UNO	United Nations Organization
UNCTAD	United Nations Conference on Trade and Development
UNMOVIC	United Nations Monitoring, Verification and Inspection Commission
UNOCHA	United Nations Office for the Coordination of Humanitarian Affairs
UNOHCI	UN Office of the Humanitarian Coordinator for Iraq
USA/US	United States of America
USSR	Union of Socialist Soviet Republics
WMD	Weapons of Mass Destruction
WTO	World Trade Organization

Contents

1

Diplomacy of Nuclear Fundamentalism

Diplomacy and Law for Nuclear Bombs

The world and we are alarmed and obsessed with the likely devastating effect of nuclear war on mankind and on earthly environment. No State or statesman wants a nuclear war to take place. International law regulates the law of warfare and maintenance of peace among States. But, international law upto the end of twentieth century neither prohibited nor regulated nuclear weapons as instruments of warfare. The International Court of Justice has been specific on this matter and has clarified the position of customary as well as conventional international law on this matter: nuclear weapons are not *per se* illegal. There is no rule in international law that prohibits a State from its sovereign right of using any weapon when its very survival or existence is in jeopardy. It is clear that there can be a law that prohibits both a nuclear war and application of nuclear weapons by the States in a war. However, till now such a law is yet to evolve. What has evolved is the move for voluntary disarmament of nuclear weapons possessed by the States, and the Charter of the United Nations is for it. The move for disarmament presumes the right of States to possess nuclear weapons and it is very much short of declaring illegal any nuclear war and nuclear bombs. Then the question is as to what has prompted the States from keeping their nuclear weapons under cover. Commonly, there appears to be some kind of law-and-order situation that restrains States against nuclear warfare. The answer to the enigmatic situation is that nuclear technology and war machinery are being regulated by the wisdom of international diplomacy in absence of international law in this field. In hard reality, nuclear weapons are regulated not by international law but by diplomacy of States. Again, some distinction is apparent between international diplomacy and nuclear diplomacy. Latter is somewhat independent of former. International diplomacy takes place within the ambit of international law, while nuclear diplomacy is pure power politics within the realm of nineteenth century sovereign powers of States.

INTERNATIONAL DIPLOMACY AND NUCLEAR DIPLOMACY

International Diplomacy

Nuclear diplomacy is a part of general international diplomacy operating among nuclear powers *inter se* and also with respect to other non-nuclear States with differing purposes. International diplomacy in ultimate analysis is a negotiated crafty endeavor to achieve by peaceful maneuvers those advantages over an adversary State which nations till Second World War generally used to wrest by actual war followed by a treaty of peace. International diplomacy takes place within the bounds of international law. It is understood that the States interact in multifarious ways and for many reasons, not necessarily for *inter se* superiority: viz., they interact for acquiring industrial raw materials, indigenous industrialization, transfer of technology, food to stave away starvation, petrol or latest arms among scores of other reasons. International diplomacy is regulated by international law. War is a coercive diplomacy but it is not a solution of multitude of the problems faced or aspired by the States now. Instead, diplomacy is the required interrelated science of inter-departmental discipline for the successful satisfaction of the needs of modern nations. Many times diplomacy looking for peace in the present is part of the future hostile designs. It was said that preparation for war begins in peacetime. After Bandung Conference of 1955, China extolled peace and coexistence among States with differences in ideologies and conflicting interests, to which India was also a party, while China prepared for war against India. The war took place in 1962, with India remaining ignorant of the designs of China till the end of the war and suffered humiliating defeat. In diplomacy of war, time is gained both for acquiring superiority in arms and for developing allies; there may be lies told in order to cover comparatively weak position or for national good. There is the diplomacy of prompting a weak enemy to fire the first shot in order to make compulsion to enter into a defensive war a good excuse.[1] Indian public and media took the peaceful overtures of Pakistan in early 2005 as somewhat distrustful if not fully deceptive. Yet, taking itself to be overwhelmingly superior in war-power, India reciprocated with caution. Under the Charter of UNO defensive wars are permitted and aggressive wars are prohibited, this brings in wide scope for diplomacy for 'inviting' war, war or proxy war. Moreover, the people of a State believe in defending their country and aggression on its territory, and this ensures both internal and international support. This means that even the powerful States use diplomacy to compel the inimical States to fire the first shot or commit aggression. This was how in 1971 India fought a defensive war against Pakistan and divided it into two States. Again, Pakistan has indulged into the diplomacy of provoking India to fire the first shot since late 1990 onwards by sponsoring terrorism in Indian State of Kashmir and elsewhere in India. India has been in reply using diplomacy to get Pakistan designated as a 'rogue' State by the USA, the best friend of Pakistan, because Pakistan has links with the 9/11 terrorist attacks on USA led by Osama bin Laden terrorist outfit. This somewhat prevented a nuclear attack on India by Pakistan around the years 2002-2003 because of restraints on Pakistan from USA.

Diplomatic Moves of Nuclear States

Since 1945, the nuclear States have achieved by diplomacy what earlier required a real war among States. It is a fact that nuclear weapons make a State heady and nuclear reactors boost further the economy of developed States. Both of them require a high technology and economic base for their sustenance. The less developed States seek nuclear reactors for their energy needs, more so when coal and petrol resources are limited and are becoming scarce and increasingly costly. For good or superfluous reasons both nuclear weapon and nuclear reactor supplier States are pursuing high-grade international diplomacy and their old time politics. A reference to some elements of such diplomacy is interesting as well as helpful for understanding the nuclear diplomacy and politics of contemporary times. It is also to be understood that while 'nuclear diplomacy' is not regulated by present-day international law the 'international diplomacy' and politics have to be within the ambit of international law:

(1) Waging 'peace' or 'cold war' is diplomacy often practised by States for avoiding armed confrontation. The relationships between China and India since 1962 and between Pakistan and India since 1971 have been of 'cold war' type. Cold War between the West and the East power blocs (1945-91) has been assessed in diplomacy as "perpetual war for perpetual peace". It was a situation of "peace through strength." Here 'peace' referred to bargaining of a goal by threats of using force. Threat of war short of actual war had been in 1950s used as 'diplomacy of brinkmanship' by USA against expansionist designs of Soviet Russia, leading to cautious inactivity or negotiated peace on the part of both. Bi-lateral negotiations on disarmament by the two States for strategic arms limitation or reduction of nuclear arms had been diplomatic move for avoiding a real mutually destructive war by show-off, comparing and matching their respective armaments on negotiating table rather than on battle-field.

(2) International terrorism is both diplomacy and politics when patronized by States. The terrorism patronized, if not sponsored by Pakistan in the Indian State of Kashmir, has been a politics calculated to make Kashmir an international issue and to compel India to discuss the future of Kashmir with Pakistan, while India treats the accession of Kashmir a closed matter, a non-issue on conference table. Now nuclear terrorism has also developed in the world.

(3) Emphasis on human rights of free speech and freedom of movement alongwith right to property by the West for 45 years since 1945 was to underrate diplomatically the totalitarian communist form of governments of 'Iron Curtain' both internationally and for enlightenment of the 'dumb and voiceless' people living in such States.

(4) There are politician States in international community just as individual politicians are in democratic societies, which persist to force their objectives even by molding the basic political order, e.g., (a) the oil diplomacy of developed States scattered all over the world in the oil-rich Middle East is international politics that influences adversely the economic and sovereign rights of the States of the region over their natural resources. (b) The USA has the pastime 'one man army' pursuit and interest in managing world affairs to its advantage, particularly in so far as that would keep the States of any region away from communism. Under this politics, the USA likes to play the role of patron or 'big brother' wherever there is a State victim of international aggression and when diplomacy or politics requires, it takes over the burden of restoring the boundaries of such a victim State upholding the mandate of the UN Charter.[2] The diplomacy of giving of long-term 'soft' loans or 'political favoritism' with visible or invisible strings attached has been helpful to USA in this activity of managing world affairs since 1950s. The USA gave free aid, grants, loans and military supplies to its allies under NATO, CENTO or SEATO and loans, etc, to undeveloped non-communist States as well. The West collaborated with international financial institutions that depend on funds contributed by the US, like World Bank, with generous contributions for the development of underdeveloped States but at the same time controlled the decisions and operations of the institutions to fit into its international diplomacy. USA has often used 'dollar diplomacy' to prevent expansion of communism, ease inter-State tensions, pacify aggressive States, to find solution to long-standing international feuds, to justify US actions in international arena, for gaining allies or maintaining favorable opinion of international community. The 'dollar diplomacy' has often taken the form of aid for reconstruction and rehabilitation of people of States ravaged by US bombings or economic aid to partners of US fight against international terrorism. To a much-limited extent though, Soviet Russia[3] had and China has also played this helping-hand diplomacy as part of their

doctrinaire international politics of increasing the number of communist States, of course, to the annoyance of the West.

(5) The 'Big Five' powers have entrenched politics of maintaining perpetual hegemony over other members by way of 'veto power' under the Charter of United Nations. This politics has kept the concept of 'collective security' in a suppressed position.

(6) The advocacy by the USA of the principle of self-determination since the First World War was diplomacy directed against European empire systems all over the world and for opening these areas for international trade as against the policy of 'imperial preference' in colonies. This objective was achieved as a price for US participation in the two World Wars, both enemies and allies lost their empires. The empires of Turkey, Germany, Italy, England, Belgium, Holland, Spain or Portugal have been broken down by this diplomacy of 'self-determination' either by Treaties of Peace after the two world wars or by signing of the Charter of United Nations.

(7) Again, the West ardently favours democratic form of government over totalitarian governments as a doctrinaire approach in general. In conflicts between autocrats and patriots it prefers patriots. But it tolerates favourable dictatorship more than indifferent or hostile democracies when diplomacy so requires. It has also been said that Soviet Russia regarded and communist China regards democracy as a transitionally 'favourable civil rule over people' till the working class of people wrest the government. The two power blocs had accordingly, during cold war era, developed their diplomacy towards each other and towards new 135 or so States since 1945. But now Soviet Russia is no more and Communist China is competing in world trade. The new international trade system of 'global free trade' under the World Trade Organization (WTO) has created a new alternative to world conflicts, which sidelines the UNO also.

Diplomacy and Media

International diplomacy requires a lot of propaganda within international community since there are generally some inherent abnormalities or hidden motives in the moves of diplomacy. There must be States around that will listen, sympathize, agree and regroup. The propaganda is made at international conferences, the world platform provided by General Assembly or Security Council of United Nations, by international policy statements, receptions, dinners to foreign dignitaries, visits of Presidents, Prime Ministers or Ministers of Foreign Affairs to other States, soliciting support through media reports or by direct radio broadcasts or television telecasts. This kind of 'public opinion' is used in order to unnerve, to bring pressure, to confuse, to isolate politically or to condemn the opposing State. During the cold war period, communism condemned capitalism and eulogized Marxism from the point of view of common man, farmer or factory worker; the propaganda was directed to expand communist totalitarian system of government in new States of post Second World War period by internal revolution against constitutional government without recourse to war with the West opposed to expansion of communism. Similarly, the West had made tremendous propaganda directed both to the peoples of 'Iron Curtain' and to new uncommitted States praising political freedom of people in 'democracies', pleasures of private property, the 'rule of law' and 'free' governments as distinguished from a system based in silent obedience to ruling oligarchy. As a result of such propaganda, there were more asylum seekers from communist States than *vice versa*. Powerful States, like the USA, China, Russian Federation, care for their status in international community and have 'social' or 'commercial' causes apart from strategic alignments, and for that these build their image by propaganda. There are other international causes also for soliciting world attention: Arab alignment against Israel in Palestine, China desiring retrieving Taiwan,[4] North Korea trying to unite South Korea, Anglo-American oil interests in the Middle East, Islamic fundamentalist targeting USA or India, among others. Diplomacy is constantly at work on such issues using international propaganda as its instrument.

NUCLEAR-STATUS STATES

Nuclear Diplomacy

The nuclear diplomacy is an additional item of international diplomacy in the hands of nuclear powers. It has had two wings. First, the nuclear bombs in the hands of power conscious States produced nuclear fundamentalism, maintaining an exclusive elite club crossing the rigidity of ideological compulsions or inhibitions and a nuclear colonialism. Secondly, the knowledge of immense general destructive impact of nuclear explosions on mankind and environment led to nuclear deterrence against war among big powers possessing nuclear bombs; and, as a corrective of the situation, this further led to a broad-based humanism and movement for nuclear and general disarmament of States.

Nuclear diplomacy in its origin is linked with war among States. It had its starting point in the race for winning the Second World War by Hitler and by the Allied powers. Hitler's Germany had by few months failed to produce atomic bomb by the time it had to surrender in 1945. Hitler lagged behind in this race but the scientists of United Kingdom and of USA working jointly aided by Einstein and other scientists of the American Universities produced the atom bomb. The Allied powers dropped two atom bombs, one at Hiroshima and another on Nagasaki and brought the Second World War to a close. The victorious powers exalted on the destructive power of atomic bomb on enemy, not knowing and realizing the evil consequences of nuclear explosions on people other than enemies. The scientists were elated by their success in foreclosing the Second World War by few weeks. The military strategists and the US-UK governments, after the war was over, discovered in nuclear bombs a potential instrument of international diplomacy. The democratic and capitalist West was troubled and irked by the installing of puppet totalitarian communist governments in the States of Europe liberated from Nazi occupation and placed under "Iron Curtain". Winston Churchill had in March 1946 urged the Anglo-American alliance to protect the Christian civilization from the menace of USSR, to break the 'Iron Curtain' and to liberate the people of States enslaved by the Soviet tyranny. The USA, on its part under the 'Truman Doctrine', had shown its determination[5] to "free people to maintain their free institutions and their national integrity against aggressive movements that seek to impose upon them totalitarian regimes". This doctrine became part of a US broad-based and long-drawn diplomacy of 'containment' of Soviet expansionist designs. The nuclear deterrence of the West was soon set against ideological expansion of communist Soviet Russia. The American 'brink of war' diplomacy supported by nuclear weapons and mutual defense pacts, like NATO,[6] did desist USSR from expanding its ideological colonialism. In its origin, the 'nuclear diplomacy' within its own limited range was an important ingredient of the conflict between 'Free States' of 'West' and the totalitarian States of 'Iron Curtain' called 'East', the term 'East' being used with reference to the geography of Europe. Though there was a keen desire to ban nuclear war and to work for nuclear disarmament since 1946, the nuclear weapons and nuclear war remained legal. If the nuclear States have not used nuclear weapons in their wars since then, it is the result of nuclear diplomacy and not of the sanctions of international law. The nature and contents of nuclear diplomacy have supplanted international law in the use of nuclear weapons and have successfully prevented nuclear wars. These make the study of 'check and save' politics of big powers interesting.

NUCLEAR FUNDAMENTALISM

The atomic bombs of 1945 proved to be more than a new destructive weapon developed by the USA and UK jointly in the laboratories of USA. The new weapon had boosted the ego of the Big Two in international relations and in their conduct. When USA hesitated to exchange of nuclear information, or share nuclear technology or nuclear weapons with war shattered Britain, latter chose to become another nuclear power by 1953 in its own right after testing atomic bombs at Woomera Range in Australia. These two were not willing to share the secrets of atom bombs with Soviet Russia, the third of the Big Three of the Second World War. Rather nuclear bombs[7] were treated as a weapon of contemporary diplomacy, that is, it was used by the West to keep Soviet Russia within control and prevent it from expanding communism and the Iron Curtain. It is a normal instinct of powerful States to continue to remain powerful and alongwith this to deny or prevent acquisition of equally or more destructive weapons by the probable adversaries. However, the Big Two had become Big Three in 1949, when Soviet Russia also produced and tested its atom bomb, and, till early 1960s there was internal race for supremacy in quality and quantum of nuclear weapons of both strategic and tactical nature among the Big Three. France became a nuclear power in 1960, when it tested its nuclear bomb in Sahara Desert. China, a *de facto* State, became the fifth nuclear power in 1964. Nuclear fundamentalism came into existence or crystallized as a tendency after Cuba confrontation between USA and Soviet Russia of 1961-62 and the perfection of inter-continental ballistic missiles (ICBM) by 1965. The two power blocs by the turn of events of the time became convinced of total mutual annihilation and destruction through a nuclear war irrespective of the question as to which of them initiated the war. As a consequence to such realization, the Big Three powers produced in 1963 the Treaty Banning Nuclear Weapon Tests, their unity for the purpose was a strange phenomenon in the era of 'cold war'. The basic aim of the treaty was to close the race by non-nuclear States for nuclear arms through research and development or otherwise, and to make it a part of the movement for general and complete disarmament under international control in accordance with the objectives set in the Charter of UNO. It was believed by the Big Three that development of nuclear bombs necessarily requires explosion tests in atmosphere or under water, which the Treaty prohibited; France, the fourth big power, did not sign the Treaty. Underground nuclear tests were not prohibited and the Big Three continued with development of their nuclear programmes in this way. For mutual limitations nuclear tests in outer space were also prohibited; at that time only USA and USSR had developed space entry technology through ballistic missiles. The Nuclear Test Ban Treaty is applicable only to those States that sign and ratify it. It is not applicable to non-signatories with the result that two important States, France and China, continued their nuclear development plans by testing their devices in atmosphere till 1980. India and Pakistan had not signed the Treaty but had conducted their nuclear tests underground. It may be mentioned that the USA, UK, Russia, France and China,[8] all are permanent members of Security Council and have veto right, while India and Pakistan are not permanent members.[9] This makes vital difference relating to equal rights in world politics and international law, since nuclear bombs have no use other than in a war and Chapter VII of the Charter of United Nations regulates war of aggression. Nuclear fundamentalism is now the attitude of the five permanent members of the Security Council, which prevents and does not tolerate acquisition of nuclear arsenal and nuclear technology by other States of the world. The ground adopted for this attitude is that other States can be immature or 'rogue' States. Somehow, while India and Pakistan are tolerated but not accepted as nuclear powers for the purposes of Treaty on the Non-Proliferation of Nuclear Weapons, 1968, and the projected Comprehensive Nuclear Test Ban Treaty, 1994, the eighth nuclear State, North Korea, is in the category of States to be divested of nuclear bombs and nuclear technology as early as possible by the fundamentalists of nuclear club. The nuclear fundamentalism is evasive on the question of disarmament. Such States are agreed not to agree on general or nuclear disarmament in so far as these may affect them.

Nuclear Colonialism

In general 'colonialism' refers to exercise of political power over alien people in far-flung regions of the world for the benefit or wishes of 'imperialist' or 'colonial' power. The colonialism in post Second World War era may be for satisfaction of national ego, for aggrandizement of territories, for development of free markets or unplanned free economy, for obtaining industrial raw materials cheaply or for playing international politics against enemies. Before advent of UNO, 'colonialism' included exercise of sovereignty over the alien nation but now 'neo-colonialism' is an epithet of discredit and denunciation involving an indication of curtailment of 'free wish' of the victimized sovereign State. The term 'nuclear colonialism' is to be understood in the context of defense pacts under which nuclear powers station their nuclear bombs on the military bases situated in the territories of non-nuclear States. The avowed purpose is the common defense and mutual aid to 'develop their individual and collective capacity to resist armed attack', recognizing that armed attack against one or more members of the pact shall be considered an attack against all members of the pact.[10] It may be mentioned that the Nuclear Non-Proliferation Treaty of 1968 prohibits any nuclear State Party to the Treaty from transferring to any recipient State whatsoever nuclear weapons or other nuclear devices, directly or indirectly, without making any distinction between peace and wartime. However, in case of NATO the nuclear weapons[11] in the custody of USA are to be handed over to allied forces out of the storage depots located in the territories of member States at a time of alert. The non-nuclear States that are members of the NATO train their troops in the use of such nuclear weapons and have preset plans for their use. It is understandable that the US-led NATO command has full control over the military forces of host States. Such States cannot make use of the nuclear weapons mentioned at their discretion when they think that they may need them for their defense. This is a kind of nuclear colonialism. Economic collaboration and eliminating conflicting economic policies help economically weaker section of the pact members and at the same time increases in multifarious ways their dependence on developed superpowers. In order to get out of this nuclear colonialism both Britain and France developed their own nuclear bomb that these can use independently, of course, outside the areas covered by NATO pact. The States of Europe had worked for their economic independence by forming European Union (EU), taking full advantage of General Agreement on Tariffs and Trade (GATT). A similar situation of neo-colonialism and nuclear colonialism had arisen within

'Iron Curtain' or Warsaw Pact States. Communist China, outside iron curtain, not only claimed ideological purity and superiority of Maoist communism over revisionist communism of Soviet Russia but also developed its own nuclear bomb in 1964 in order to fight an impending war against nuclear USA with reference to Taiwan matter. Both USA and Soviet Russia were growing into nuclear fundamentalists and China preferred to be a nuclear power in place of depending on USSR for a shield or 'nuclear umbrella' against nuclear USA. This happened though USSR was natural and ideological ally of Communist China. Similarly, it can be said that in absence of any 'nuclear umbrella' from USA and USSR, fearing the results of a crucial defensive war with Pakistan-China alliance, India also ventured to become a nuclear power in 1970s and onwards. The diplomacy of 'peace through strength' is antidote to the spread of nuclear colonialism in specific cases.

Nuclear Deterrence

Power as such is a heady thing that leads to uncalled-for decisions and often to tyranny. To exercise power for the sake of using it is the weakness of autocrats. History of international relations confirms that after accumulating military power, the States or kings on local issues have sought excuses for war against the neighboring States or kings, if not for the fulfillment of the desire to conquer the world. Hitler is an example of this obsession. It was debated from human angle in 1950s whether it was at all necessary for the USA to have dropped atomic bombs over Hiroshima and Nagasaki in August 1945 when it was known that Japan had militarily collapsed and the end of war was foreseeable. Another side of the avoidable use of nuclear bombs was that the results of the atom bombs dropped on Japan territory confirmed the inhuman destructive power of nuclear bombs for the wisdom of future generations. However, taking both sides to be true it can be said that a heavy price was paid by the then nearly a century old Japanese war mania. Nuclear deterrence period started when the USSR became second nuclear power in September 1949. Prime Minister Churchill had thereafter insisted on British nuclear bomb and by October 1953 Britain was an established another nuclear power independently of USA. Though Soviet Russia had become a nuclear power, still till 1957 the USA and UK debated and waited for the right moment and excuse to finish USSR with their nuclear bombs. Churchill held the view that Soviet advance and seizure of Western Europe had been forestalled by American nuclear deterrence. In the meantime, the USA had made a 20-year pact with Canada and ten States of Western Europe for establishment of North Atlantic Treaty Organization (NATO) on 4 April, 1949, for mutual defense, by going for a swift massive rearmament of Western Europe[12] against suspected or rather imminent Soviet aggression. The USA developed tactical nuclear artillery for use against Soviet army in 1952-54 and placed it in NATO armory on the belief that this meant last word against Soviet advancement in the area. For strategic devastation of Soviet Russia the USA had Strategic Air Command, had acquired and equipped with nuclear bombs hundreds of overseas bases for big bombers encircling major portion of European part of industrialized Russia. In January 1954, the USA launched a series of atomic energy powered submarines, which could without need of frequent refueling remain at sea and devastate Soviet navy. The only thing then lacking with the West was ballistic rocket missile but in December 1955 it was announced by US that by 1957 or 1958 this deficiency would be met.

To counter this, the USSR took the help of delaying diplomacy for negotiating disarmament of nuclear weapons. But by the time thus gained, Soviet acquired hydrogen bomb by August 1953. It also developed a fleet of long-range bombers capable of targeting US establishments with atom and hydrogen bombs. However, strategic planners of both sides did not regard bombers as the solution of the problem of power-balance or victory over each other and the race was on for rockets that were powerful enough to hit targets several thousands kilometers away. Soviet Russia declared on 26 August 1957 that it had perfected an ICBM that could hit with nuclear warheads targets several thousands of miles away. It proved the claim by launching the first 184 pounds earth-satellite called 'Sputnik', which orbited earth about 500 miles above at 18,000 mph speed for several weeks before it burnt itself in atmosphere when it fell back after losing speed. Soon USA also developed its ICBM capacity when on 31 January 1958 it put 'Explorer' satellite into earth orbit. Britain, France, Germany and China also developed similar space missiles later by 1960.

The pattern of war diplomacy of Big Powers vitally changed after 1957 when it became clear that 'heavy bombers would decide the war' concept had become obsolete with the coming up of the era of nuclear warheads carrying missiles. Approaching enemy bombers gave latitude of several hours' notice with efficient radar systems[13] available to both sides for taking counter-measures of defense or retaliation but this warning time for ICBM is never more than 15 minutes. With the possession of missiles with nuclear warheads the power of ultimate destruction of enemy was mutual. Each superpower had the means of destroying and annihilating the other after suffering first onslaught. The question raised at the time was whether the statesmen would follow the path of mutual suicide that would also bring alongwith it a sort of universal death syndrome. In the Cuban stand-off of 1962 between USA and USSR in which shipments of missiles and bombers by the USSR to Cuba were interdicted by the so-called US 'quarantine' measures, President Kennedy was on the verge of starting a nuclear war on USSR but Khrushchev[14] regarded the steps of President Kennedy as immature and childish and settled the matter by removal of bases and missiles from Cuba. It was regarded as a failure of statesmanship on the part of Kennedy for the US action taken in self-preservation by opting for a full-scale atomic war. Realization had matured by early 1960s that in the West and the East conflict a nuclear war was not going to be a method for settlement of the question whether totalitarianism of Soviet pattern or capitalism under democratic system of the West was the better ideal. War among superpowers was a positive instrument of mutual suicide and also of human evolutionary mutations. A 'balance of terror' had set in and the wars of the future, as in Vietnam, became 'proxy wars' conducted by the superpowers by conventional weapons.

The low-key but pertinent nuclear question mark is whether nuclear status is a deterrent to international conflicts. The prevention of Soviet political system proliferation by nuclear status of USA by mid-1950s had given rise to importance and relevance of one-sided nuclear status and thereafter all big powers—UK, France and China, worked hard to acquire nuclear status. Where both parties to a conflict possess nuclear arms, the realization or fear of co-annihilation works against furtherance of the conflict and not the nuclear status. This has been witnessed in Cuban missiles crisis of 1962 between USA and Soviet Russia, projected attack on Taiwan for its incorporation by China set against USA, the projected Pakistan war on India in 2002 by ballooning Kashmir issue, and US threat to make pre-emptive nuclear strikes on North Korea for posing nuclear dangers in the Korean Peninsula. However, proxy wars or non-war conflicts with conventional arms do take place in order to avoid use of nuclear weapons of war: that is to say that nuclear deterrence has now been circumvented. There has been advent of global or international terrorist non-state entities obsessed with ideologies as prime movers, like *Al Qaeda*. These entities, possessing most sophisticated weapons, use human suicide bombs and having prospect of acquiring of nuclear 'rogue' bombs, do not care for nuclear status of any State. The US 9/11 incident sufferances could trigger broadside wars in Afghanistan and Iraq but US nuclear deterrence did not work any magic. Retribution at individual and State level will not cleanse the world of terrorism or nuclear weapons programmes.

THE DISARMAMENT MIRAGE

Opposition to Nuclear Armaments

It was observed earlier that the knowledge of immense destructive impact of nuclear explosions on mankind and environment led to awakening of inherent deterrence against nuclear war among big powers. As a corrective of the problem this knowledge led to a broad-based humanism alongwith a movement for nuclear and general disarmament of States. It may be mentioned that in 1950s a number of scientists, intellectual leaders and statesmen of the world had without success made appeals for cessation of nuclear tests. Among them were Bertrand Russell, Indian Prime Minister Nehru and Dr. Albert Schweitzer. The maker of America's initial atom bomb J. Robert Oppenheimer was dismissed from the position of US representative in Atomic Energy Commission in 1954 for opposing on considerations of humanity, the development of hydrogen bomb by USA; while Einstein, who had inaugurated the atomic age, died in 1955, widely expressing his disillusionment that atomic energy would herald a new era for human welfare. The US atomic scientist Ralf E. Lapp had emphasized that there were no 'defenses' against hydrogen bomb attack on USA, since the radioactive fallout of each one megaton nuclear bomb would kill all the residents within 1,00,000 squire miles of the target and would render this an area of 'no-entry' and uninhabitable for more than two weeks. Now, both sides have air launched nuclear cruise missiles (ALCMS), strategic nuclear delivery vehicles (SNDV), submarine/sea launched ballistic missiles (SLBMS), intercontinental ballistic missiles (ICBM) with independently fractionated multiple-warheads, long-range and short-range low height cruise missiles and artillery with nuclear warheads. The devastating effect of these instruments of war on humanity and natural environment when extensively used in a war is within the knowledge of the leaders of nuclear superpowers. There will be no victors but only vanquished masses of people after a full-scale nuclear war. Nuclear disarmament is a remedy but this militates against the concept of State sovereignty and has so far proved to be a mirage.

Nuclear Disarmament

The capacity of man for self-destruction was evident to the statesmen and physicists of post Second World War. There were to be no 'victors' and no 'vanquished' after the next war. Einstein had warned that after the third world war, which will be a nuclear war, sticks and rock bits would be used to fight the next wars. The question till early 1960s was how to prevent the Big Powers from their continued annual testing of nuclear devices. It was all through felt that the logic of choice was between life and death but the military strategists and patriots of nuclear States were earnestly obsessed with considerations of 'national security' and went on fabricating new nuclear and conventional weapons. Defensive strategies were discussed but the West found that England, France and Japan in any case would be first casualties of nuclear war with Soviet Russia; none of strategies were therefore held workable. Since USSR was lagging behind in nuclear weapon race, it was pushing nuclear tests and was refusing halting of nuclear tests. In this sticky situation USA also worked hard to maintain its qualitative and quantitative nuclear weapon and long-range air force superiorities. 'Disarmament for peace' was a formula inherited from the experiences of the first total war, the First World War. The diplomacy of the period between the two World Wars was to prepare for victory in a war while preaching for disarmament. When the United Nations Organization was formed in 1945 with the principle of collective security, the Big Powers were to be the pillars of collective security; these tried to be individually stronger and stronger in order to ensure peace in the world. The Charter of United Nations, however, did not venture into the task of disarmament beyond the consideration[15] of 'general principles governing disarmament and regulation of armaments', entrusting[16] the Security Council with the formulation of plans for 'establishment of a system for the regulation of armaments' and assigning to the Military Staff Committee[17] the function of advising and assisting the Security Council in the matter of 'regulation of armaments and possible disarmament'. The composition of the Military Staff Committee, limited to five permanent members of Security Council indirectly means that there must be prior agreement among the five Big Powers for mutual disarmament but these may consider peremptorily the disarmament of other States of the world when deemed necessary. The latter situation will not be a proposition for 'general disarmament'. As for nuclear disarmament, the General Assembly constituted the Atomic Energy Commission in January

1946 for submitting proposals to Security Council on peaceful uses of atomic energy and for controlling and eliminating atomic weapons. The Security Council had established a Commission on Conventional Armaments on 13 February 1947. Further, the Security Council had adopted[18] on 12 August 1948 a 'statement of principles' that made disarmament 'contingent' upon (a) agreement on armed forces for the United Nations as contemplated under Article 43 of the Charter, (b) a system of control of atomic energy and agreement for international supervision, and (c) effective enforcement against violation (of the agreements). The Atomic Energy Commission was asked accordingly, to work for securing a foolproof system of complete security. These principles of 1948 would have left USA and UK alliance as sole nuclear weapon States. The USSR, not yet a nuclear power, retaliated by proposing in General Assembly in September 1948 for one-third reduction of all armed forces and complete prohibition of nuclear weapons. Rejecting this, the General Assembly laid emphasis on methods of collecting[19] and verifying armament information as first step towards disarmament. Soviet attitude was against a verification system and USA was opposed to any ban on nuclear armaments, and thereafter stalemates in working out various details relating to disarmament prevailed on negotiation tables. On 19 December 1951, the two Commissions were amalgamated into the Disarmament Commission in order to prepare a draft treaty for the regulation, limitation and balanced reduction of all armed forces and armaments to a level adequate for defense of States but not sufficient for aggression. The States were to make necessary disclosures and submit to verifications and also to 'effective international inspection' where necessary. The Disarmament Commission became victim of cold war and did not achieve anything. Further, after the 'balance of terror' had taken over as damper of war mania diplomacy in early 1960s the vision of general disarmament became a matter of history and bilateral efforts to reduce or balance nuclear weapons by USA and USSR became the object of diplomacy till the 'Star War' race emerged in 1983.

Bilateral Disarmament Efforts

As mentioned earlier, nuclear disarmament has little meaning unless the five nuclear powers agree to its terms and conditions. Such an agreement is only a dream not to become reality due to games of world-power politics. In a narrowed down bilateral approach the USA and USSR have since 1970s tried on several treaties for limitation on use and reduction of armaments. Prominent of these are:

1. Treaty on Limitation of Anti-Ballistic Missiles System (ABM Treaty), 1972;
2. Interim Agreement on Limitation of Strategic Offensive Arms Treaty (SALT-I), 1972;
3. Treaty on the Limitation of Underground Nuclear Weapon Tests, 1974;
4. Treaty on Limitation of Strategic Offensive Arms (SALT-II), 1979;
5. Treaty on Elimination of Intermediate-Range and Short-Range Missiles, 1987;
6. Strategic Arms Reduction Treaty (START-I), 1991;[20] and
7. Strategic Arms Reduction Treaty (START-II), 1993.[21]

Now, after 1998 there are three more nuclear powers. Of these, India feels nearly threatened by nuclear Pakistan and remotely threatened by nuclear China. While China has long-range missiles capable of covering whole of India, Pakistan has missiles with nuclear warheads capable of hitting around 2000 Km inside India. If both Pakistan and China were to align against India, which is not likely to take place now, India has no option but to be extensively remain prepared for a defensive nuclear war. There is no scope for bilateral disarmament treaty between India and Pakistan so long as Pakistan has an eye on Kashmir. Nuclear North Korea is a problem in the East Asia Pacific region, since it wants to unite with the separated South Korea State and has long-drawn hostility towards Japan. Because of its location and international diplomacy, nuclear North Korea is suspected or despised by China, Russian

Federation and USA alike and these three nuclear powers want North Korea to be disarmed of its nuclear arsenal. Negotiations of bilateral kind between North Korea on one hand and six other States on the other are in the process, but are in a 'balance of terror' between USA and North Korea.

NUCLEAR LAW OR NUCLEAR DIPLOMACY ?

Nuclear Weapons Law

As the fact of matter is so far the indigenous manufacture, possession and probable use of nuclear weapons in a war are within sovereign rights and powers of the States. Sovereignty is an attribute of independent States under international law and the Big Five nuclear powers that are permanent members of UNO are not willing to give it up. There is no direct law that prohibits the use of nuclear weapons in a war, though some remote conventions and agreements do exist which prohibit use of such weapons by signatory States that produce certain defined bad effects or evil consequences.

ICJ on Nuclear Law

The International Court of Justice had examined the legality of nuclear weapons in international law in an Advisory Opinion sought by UN General Assembly[22] in 1994 on the query: "Is the threat or use of nuclear weapons in any circumstances permitted under international law?" The International Court gave the opinion that the provisions of Second Hague Declaration of 1899, the regulations under The Hague Convention IV of 1907 or the Geneva Protocol of 1925 do not specifically prohibit nuclear weapons. Negatively, ICJ affirmed that there is no international customary or treaty law, which 'authorizes' use of 'any' weapon, nuclear or general, in a war. Moreover, the threat or use of any weapon in a war has never been dependent on any authorization process at any time under international law and this would apply to nuclear weapons also. It means that a nuclear State is free to decide if at all or when and in what manner to use its nuclear weapons. The ICJ expressed its opinion that if the developments of the last fifty years are taken into account it is clear that public opinion has been against the threat or use of nuclear weapons and no nuclear State has taken recourse to these weapons in the wars that they have fought. There have been attempts under the Charter of UNO for concluding Convention prohibiting the use of nuclear weapons totally. The ICJ pointed it out that there is in existence an obligation on the part of nuclear States to pursue in good faith and to bring to conclusion the negotiations that would lead to regulation of armaments and possible nuclear disarmament. This obligation obviously does not as such extend to prohibition of nuclear weapons or their use. Also, the ICJ observed that it cannot be said with finality whether the threat or use of nuclear weapons by any State would be unlawful in the extreme situation of self-defense and self-preservation when the very survival of this State is at a stake.

Examining the subject matter of Advisory Opinion further, the ICJ observed that there are humanitarian laws of war and of weapons used in war. These laws though do not prohibit nuclear weapons, but do seek protection of civilian populations and make distinction between combatants and non-combatants. Obviously, violation of such humanitarian laws by use of nuclear weapons would expose the leaders and military officers to war crimes after the war is over. The ICJ also pointed out that under the law of neutrality rights of neutral States require that the effects of war or any international armed conflicts should not overreach to the territories of neutral states whereas in a nuclear war the devastating nuclear radioactive fallout cannot be so contained. Therefore, nuclear weapons would always violate the laws of neutrality. The ICJ noted the spirit of times, *opinio juris,* in that the UN General Assembly had in 1961 adopted the resolution[23] advising the member States to make a Convention that prohibits the use of nuclear weapons in any circumstances, which in other words would be banning of nuclear weapons. As mentioned earlier by the provisions of the Charter, such a Convention must have the approval of Security Council if the General Assembly is to adopt it as its resolution. This brings in the diplomacy of nuclear fundamentalism as obstacle for conclusion of desired or projected Convention.

UN General Assembly on Nuclear Law

The UN General Assembly at its 55th session in the year 2000 considered the Advisory Opinion of ICJ and observed[24] that according to the International Court there exists for the members "an obligation to pursue in good faith and to bring to a conclusion negotiations leading to nuclear disarmament in all its aspects under a strict and effective international control." The matters of nuclear disarmament, banning nuclear war and banning the nuclear weapons by international law at present rest at this point.

What to Think?

When the fate of human civilization is at stake at the stupidity, whim, astuteness or good judgment of nuclear powers which number to eight in 2005, wisdom requires that one should know the conflicts in international politics and interests of nuclear powers that may bring the feared nuclear holocaust. The matters have become complicated because nuclear fission reactors are sources of much needed requirement for electricity both for nuclear and non-nuclear States. While international control is being sought for production, possession and use of nuclear weapons through 'peace and security' considerations, nuclear reactors are commercial or world trade commodity. Non-nuclear States are obviously resenting any monopoly of nuclear powers on greater, free and easy availability of nuclear reactors on the ground that the dividing line between nuclear reactors and nuclear weapons is thin. As such, a study of the dividing line between nuclear reactors and nuclear weapons is necessary and is pursued ahead as next topic.

ENDNOTES

1. Attack by Japan on USA during the Second World War was of this nature.
2. The US-UK led unilateral action ignoring UNO or violating Charter of UNO for ousting regime of President Saddam Hussain in Iraq in

2003, is looked upon more as part of Anglo-American oil diplomacy for protecting their oil interests in the Middle East against nationalization process in the region rather than their devotion for democracy.

3. Since 1954 USSR offered loans to 'underdeveloped' States, viz. Afghanistan, Cuba, Ethiopia, Guinea, India, Indonesia, Iraq and United Arab Republic that were outside the 'Iron Curtain'.
4. The "Red People's Liberation Army" of Mao Tse-tung in 1949 had after a civil war driven the (Nationalist) Kuomintang regime of Chiang Kai-Shek to the island of Formosa, later Taiwan, which was the residual territory of China. Since 27 June 1950 the Nationalist Government and Taiwan have been under military protection of USA against 'Red' mainland China.
5. On 12 March 1947 President Truman had asked Congress to sanction $ 400 million aid to save Greece and Turkey from Soviet expansions.
6. Signed on 4 April 1949, the North Atlantic Treaty Organization by USA, Canada and 10 States of Europe was a pledge of 'mutual defense against Soviet aggression'.
7. Of the nuclear bombs the Hydrogen bomb is theoretically 1000 times more powerful than plutonium atomic bomb. USA perfected hydrogen bomb by May 1951, Soviet Russia by August 1953 and Britain by May 1957.
8. In 1971 communist government on mainland of China was given recognition and this new (nuclear power) government henceforth represented China in UNO including the Security Council in place of Nationalist (Chiang Kai-Shek) government.
9. North Korea is the eighth State to acquire nuclear bombs and production technology. Israel has nuclear technology but has not produced nuclear bombs.
10. For example, see Articles 3 and 5 of North Atlantic Treaty Organization.
11. According to 'The Nuclear Data Handbook' following nuclear weapons can be used by allied powers of NATO: Genie air-to-air rocket; B-28 thermonuclear bomb; Honest John missile; Nike-Hercules missile; 8" artillery fired atomic projectile; B-43 nuclear bomb; 155 mm. Artillery fired atomic projectile; Pershing IA missile; B-61 thermonuclear tactical bomb; and Lance missiles.
12. Greece and Turkey were also admitted to NATO in February 1952.
13. America called it DEW-line (Distant Early Warning) of radar stations. Soviet Russia had similar system.

14. Khrushchev was 'boss' of Soviet Union, being Secretary of Communist Party Central Committee and Chairman of Council of Ministers of Soviet Union.
15. Article 11: Charter of United Nations.
16. Article 26: Charter of United Nations.
17. Article 47: Charter of United Nations.
18. It was not a decision of Security Council and was not subject to veto, actually Soviet bloc had opposed the 'Statement of Principles".
19. This is wider than voluntary disclosure, though it includes such disclosure.
20. State of Soviet Russia collapsed in 1991 before ratifying the START-I. The new State, Russian Federation, is legally not automatically bound by any of the above-mentioned treaties.
21. The successor State of Soviet Russia, the Russian Federation, signed the treaty in January 1993 but ratified START-II in the year 2000.
22. G.A. Resolution 49/75K: of 15 December 1994.
23. G.A. Resolution 1653: of 1961.
24. G.A. Resolution 33X: of 2000.

2

Nuclear Scare – The Hardcore of Matter

The nuclear scare in international politics is real. A nuclear bomb on explosion produces tremendous heat and radioactivity that destroys immediately all matter within its area of incidence and as time passes it mutilates humans, environment and vegetation for generations. All those States that have enemies possessing nuclear weapons plan to keep away from nuclear confrontation. On diplomatic front, we know USA and Soviet Russia were enemies of highest order but for about fifty years fearing nuclear war, they avoided direct conflict; now Soviet Russia with communist ideology is extinct. Taiwan became a bone of contention between China and the USA, both are nuclear powers, but China has been deferring invasion of the island. Militarily, over-running of Taiwan is not a big proposition for China but the US protection to Taiwan has kept China unnerved, fearing a nuclear war with the USA. Recently in late 2003, nuclear bombs again played important role when the USA wanted to finish off North Korea[1] by making pre-emptive nuclear strike, if necessary, regarding it to be an 'end game of cold war', and for the reason of North Korea being one of the 'axis of evil'. North Korea finding itself in a deadly trap retaliated and warned USA that it will not hesitate to drop those nuclear bombs that it possesses on USA through its long-range missiles.[2] The result was that USA after verifying and confirming the nuclear capabilities of North Korea did not risk retaliatory nuclear devastation of its own people and property by initiating an 'Iraq 2003 type of pre-emptive war' on this country. This was a stand-off between two States achieved since the year 2003 on the basis of nuclear diplomacy of North Korea.[3] Further, Pakistan is adamant to annex Kashmir part of India and has declared its policy that it will use nuclear weapons against India if there is any war. India has not reciprocated in similar confrontational terms and has announced 'no first use' of nuclear weapons against Pakistan or any other country.

Now various inquisitive technical inquiries arise in the minds of common intelligentsia, though not amounting to confusion, for grasping the meaning of several media news reports, like, '8000 radioactive uranium rods in the 5-MW research Yongbyon atomic reactor', enrichment of uranium as alternate to plutonium in nuclear bomb-making, or how these alongwith plutonium relate to a nuclear bomb. Before everything else laymen, one like me, also want to know about the related interesting international media reports—the link between radioactivity, uranium and plutonium, in simple or least possible scientific language, not for the purpose of producing nuclear bomb but for understanding what mischief a State can do when it is violating the Non-Proliferation Treaty of 1967. Media reports that just as there are peddlers[4] of machine guns, armed vehicles, smart bombs, battle tanks, anti-tank missiles, supersonic jetfighters, now there are peddlers dealing with equipments, techniques, and blueprints for making atom bombs, uranium fuel rods, centrifuge system[5] for enrichment of uranium to weapon grade[6] alongwith missile systems for targeting the nuclear bombs accurately. Under the domestic law, when a law is made for maintenance of essential supplies, it spells out the essential commodities and so on, in a similar manner when international treaty law prohibits nuclear proliferation, it is worthwhile to understand the items, their working modes and the commercial transactions of which come under the purview of treaty. This inquiry is the underlying objective of this chapter.

COMMONSENSE ABOUT NUCLEAR SCIENCE

Nuclei of Elements

Nuclear science and Scientists tell the students that atom is the smallest or ultimate first part of an element and the elements in the world are in all around 103 in number. An atom combines with its brother forming a molecule for stability. Atom in turn has a nuclei composed of three parts. First, the 'proton'[7] that is positively charged central piece, second is 'electron'[8] that is negatively charged and exists in the form of a cloud, and both of them are present in equal numbers in the nuclei of an element and this 'number' is the identification mark of the element and is called its 'atomic number'. Both proton and electron being in equal numbers make the nuclei of all atoms neutral. In addition to these two parts in the nuclei of elements, helium and hydrogen nuclei being exceptions, there is the third part referred to as 'neutron'. Each neutron[9] is neutral, since it is composed of one proton and one electron. Total number of protons and neutrons in the central part of nuclei of an atom determines the chemical nature of any element and this total number is called the 'atomic weight' of the element. Each electron in the nuclei cloud of an element has a separate circular at random orbit and revolves around the nuclei. For example, hydrogen has one electron, oxygen has 8, lead has 82 or uranium has 92 electrons and therefore as many circular orbits for each of the electrons around the nuclei. The electronic cloud of the rotating electrons increases with the atomic number of the nuclei. The chemical nature of the element is determined by the interactions of the outer electron in the nuclei with other elements. It is interesting that the holding together or binding force of the nuclei of an element depends on the positive electric charge of the protons in the nature of magnetic pull that keeps the electrons revolving and prevent them from straying away. This binding force that keeps protons and electrons intact in an atom can become marginal or less than marginal in certain circumstances leading to the danger of imbalance and destruction of the nuclei giving rise to the formation of isotopes[10] of the same element or even new elements altogether. This happens when the protons diminish by process of radiation[11] as alpha (α) rays or electrons escape as beta (β) rays or neutrons break into protons and electrons or escape the nuclei as gamma (γ) rays. The break-up of neutron is accompanied with fission (breaking down) or fusion (joining up), leading to formation of new elements or isotopes[12] of the same element and isobars.[13] In this process when the atoms of a radioactive element are present in good quantity a chain nuclear reaction is caused and tremendous heat, light and radiations are emitted both by fission and fusion of atoms and in these we are interested here in connection with nuclear explosions.

Thermonuclear Reactions

The nuclei of an atom is light and is not stable; two or more light nuclei could get fused together, resulting in a more stable nuclei of a higher atomic weight. The nuclear reaction that involves the combination or fusion of two light nuclei into formation of a heavier element is called 'nuclear fusion.'[14] But how this can be done? Science tells us that atomic nuclei are positively charged that repel each other and so in normal course their union is difficult. However, it has been found by scientists that at very high temperatures, the nuclei may develop sufficient energy to overcome the repelling forces and to fuse two nuclei. This happens at a temperature of about 10 million centigrade, which is reached by the fission of U-235, and this high temperature also prevails on the sun. The high temperature of the sun is explained to be due to a series of nuclear reactions involving Carbon-Hydrogen-Nitrogen cycle.[15] Hence, in the furnace of the sun new elements are being continuously formed by fusion starting from hydrogen nuclei and all known elements are present in the form of gases on the sun. Similarly, when nuclear bomb explodes, air is sucked in and the gases present in the atmosphere fuse together, giving rise to new elements which rise above into the sky in the form of electrically charged cloud composed of several elements and compounds, just as on catching fire or on exploding a drum of petrol emits or raises a cloud of smoke composed of new chemicals or compounds.

Radiations

It is found that the nuclei of gases, particularly hydrogen, helium, oxygen and nitrogen when they get rarified in open by speedy motion as is the nature of gas form or are heated to high temperatures, these gases become prone to the loss of electron. All these gases have atomic numbers ranging from one to eight. At the other extreme, the nuclei of elements with atomic numbers 83 to 94 are heavy and have dense cloud of electrons orbiting in circular orbits. As mentioned, the nuclei have number of electrons equal to its atomic number. Because of the heaviness of the nuclei, there is chain reaction within and normally radioactive emissions called radiations[16] take place in normal situation, which slowly reduce the atomic number. Becquerel first discovered radioactivity and it is a spontaneous production of energy by certain minerals. The minerals containing radioactive elements create hot surroundings, which is several degrees temperature higher than normal. Radon, radium, thorium, uranium and plutonium are some of such elements within the above-mentioned atomic numbers. The radioactive substances show energy changes within the element include both emission and absorption, and the energy transformation associated with radioactivity[17] of such elements is extremely large as compared to normal chemical changes such as burning of coal or ignition of petrol. After transformation, all radioactive elements get degenerated ultimately into non-radioactive lead, like this: Radioactive Plutonium –94 to Neptunium –93 to Uranium –92 to Paladium –91 to Thorium –90 to Actinium –89 to Radium –88 to Fr – 87 to Radon-86 to Atinium –85 to Polonium-84 to Bismuth –83 finally to non-radioactive Lead –82. The transitional products of fission are themselves radioactive elements and become stable after emitting one or more electrons.

Fission

Within a radioactive element, like thorium or uranium, a nuclear reaction[18] takes place when the radioactive nuclei captures or absorbs any roving neutron, whereby the atomic mass goes beyond 'critical mass' and the nuclei breaks for acquiring a stable condition, giving out extra alpha or beta radiations. Even some neutrons are also emitted as gamma rays. The ^{92}Uranium$_{238}$ is stable as such but beyond a mass of about 5 kg, depending upon shape, nature of surroundings and presence of Uranium-235 in traces as impurity (upto 0.7 per cent), it becomes critical. When hit by a neutron U-235 absorbs it and becomes 92/U-239 ($^{92}U_{239}$) with an electron to spare and on next hit by a neutron it becomes converted to a new element 93/Np-239 ($^{93}Np_{239}$). As this new element neptunium is highly radioactive and unstable and emits electron, it is transformed into a stable element 94/Pu-239 ($^{94}Pu_{239}$), which is plutonium.[19] Scientists explain the phenomenon of fission in U-238. When the uranium nucleus captures a neutron it becomes very 'hot' and the oscillation processes of the heated matter changes and in no time the nucleus breaks into two parts, which separate with outflow of tremendous energy. Uranium without emission of energy on split will create barium and krypton; the combined atomic numbers of these two equal that of the uranium nucleus. However, the products vary with every split, since the two products plus the emitted energy equal the nuclei plus the colliding and captured neutron[20]. It is calculated that one pound of uranium undergoing fission produces as much heat energy as is produced by burning about 1,500 tons of coal. Further, the absorption of neutron for fission differs from element to element: Thorium and U-238 undergo fission only on absorption of fast moving neutrons; while U-233, U-235 and plutonium are always in a state of high excitation and these rapidly capture moving neutron of any energy to undergo fission. Irradiating thorium to higher atomic number by fusion processes produces U-233. India is depending on this U-233 for fuel for its nuclear reactors by indigenous production. After fission there are secondary products also which evaporate to escape identification from the normal products while the latter are still very hot.[21]

When two or more blocks of Uranium -238 are brought together and if the 'critical mass'[22] is exceeded, fission starts creating heat along with vigorous radiations from breaking of neutrons. Uranium -235 and Plutonium -239 are similar and are quicker than U-238 in attracting and capturing stray neutrons and in setting fission chain. In controlled circumstances this chain fission is used for generating electricity in atomic reactors. But, for a position of safety the Uranium-238,

Uranium -235 or Plutonium-239 is kept in its sub-critical size. For fission, it is necessary that neutrons should not escape from the lump of material, which they do in case of sub-critical mass but not in case of super-critical size of the lump.

A non sub-critical mass of U-238, U-235, U-233 or Pu-239 becomes critical by vigorous or sudden change in resting conditions. Such changes are (1) motion of high speed, (2) nearby explosions or (3) surrounding high temperature, among others. The sun glows because of continuous nuclear fissions taking place in its permanent nuclear chain reaction fission furnace whereby hydrogen is by fusion transformed into nitrogen, carbon, oxygen and other elements, which in turn lose or gain neutrons to form other elements. Sun has all the elements known to us in gas form. Similar is the position in the core of earth where, of course, on a downward scale, intense heat is generated by breaking up of elements and formation of new elements by nuclear fusion or fission.[23] Of course, accepting the natural phenomenon the underground nuclear explosions are also permitted by international law set by Non-Proliferation Treaty also. Help is taken of this method of fission in producing hydrogen bomb and short range nuclear artillery. Centrifuge system that rotates the radioactive element at a very high velocity and with tremendous centrifugal force, was sold by a Pakistani peddler for a cost of 50 million US dollars for converting U-234, the spent fuel in atomic reactors into bomb grade Pu-239 in 1980s and 1990s. When the atomic bomb explodes there is no residue of uranium or plutonium mass but only heat which melts everything within a radius, clouds of new elements are formed out of sucked in air elements, this dust is loaded with beta and neutron radiations which kill the living flora and animals including humans wherever they fall before losing the radioactivity, and that loss of injurious radioactivity takes a couple of months.

THE NUCLEAR MERCHANDIZE

The alleged infamous peddler of nuclear merchandize, i.e., technology, machinery, materials and contraptions, A.Q. Khan of Pakistan, had been since 1980s selling for price nuclear equipment, blueprints for processing raw uranium for use in reactors as fuel, processing this fuel additionally for making U-235 atom bomb, gas centrifuge systems, reprocessing machinery for converting spent-fuel and by-products of fission in nuclear reactors into plutonium for making nuclear bombs, blueprints for making nuclear bombs and so on to Iran, Libya, Nigeria and Iraq. He had been bartering against sophisticated missile systems the same to North Korea. By the barter transactions, while North Korea became a nuclear power, Pakistan acquired capability to hit Indian targets with nuclear bombs by these acquired missiles and missile technology. Bush administration officials of the United States were seriously and earnestly investigating[24] in 2004 both of these kinds of transactions of A.Q. Khan. As broker or purchaser of nuclear machinery for making nuclear bombs from black market, the peddler visited several countries of Europe. His visits to Sudan, Mali, Nigeria and Niger have been regarded as significant because all these States have known or untapped uranium deposits. He is estimated to have made transaction worth more than 150 million US dollar till 2003 to enrich himself or Pakistan. Much of the exploits of Khan came to light when Iran and Libya opened their territories for dismantling by IAEA of their nuclear bomb-making facilities under the nuclear Non-Proliferation Treaty. Of course, nuclear reactors for production of electricity are peaceful and are exempted from NPT obligations. A somewhat coordinated glimpse into all these nuclear contraptions of merchandize is needed for enlightenment of persons like us on what masterly mysteries of Nature and God have been tapped by humans for their material comfort, better life or for achievement of their nefarious and inhuman ambitions in the field of international politics.

Procuring Uranium

Uranium as an element was discovered in 1930s alongwith its radioactive qualities. There are several radioactive elements, Radium is used for X-rays, which have wide application, Radon has medicinal properties. That uranium isotope can be used for heat generation was the discovery of researches by

European emigrant scientist-professors, including Einstein, who had settled in the USA in 1930s. There was no demand for uranium in the market till 1945 except for work in research laboratories. Its commercial and military use potential became known after atom bombs were dropped in Hiroshima and Nagasaki in August 1945.

With scientific progress, while radioactive elements radium and radon among others have medicinal uses, thorium and uranium are used for nuclear reactors for producing electric energy. Uranium is also used for making nuclear bombs. Plutonium, an another radioactive element is unstable, is made from uranium in laboratory, and is better suited than uranium for making nuclear bombs.[25]

Uranium in traces is found scattered all over the world, particularly on sea beaches. In addition, a small fraction of uranium is also found in concentrated mineral ores. It is at some places extracted from 'open-cast pits' but generally it occurs in small concentrated units in underground mines of other minerals. Uranium is very quickly oxidized and does not occur in nascent form, since due to radioactive emissions it is gradually reduced to lower elements. Major uranium producers are Australia, Canada, China, Kazakhstan, Namibia, Niger, Russia, and Turkmenistan. Some States like India, Sudan, Mali and Nigeria also have uranium deposits. Indian uranium ore has around .7% metal yield. From the raw minerals, uranium is converted into metal form; only thereafter it becomes or is made suitable for use in an actual nuclear reactor or weapon. Natural uranium metal has to be processed or enriched into U-238 and then into U-235 for fission or producing heat; Plutonium (Pu-239) is produced from U-235 by enrichment processes. Both U-235 and Pu-239 are used for nuclear bombs. Uranium-235, the essential fissionable component of the uranium, cannot be separated from natural Uranium-238 by chemical means; the atoms of these two isotopes have to be separated from each other by physical means. For nuclear bombs, U-235 should have at least 90% proportion in a U-238 bloc. For this enrichment, the USA, Britain, France and Russia have developed various secret processes. Academic scientists and encyclopedias refer to some less secretive processes that were developed by 1945 before atom bomb had become a reality. At that time of history, researches on nuclear fission were conducted in the Universities of the USA and not in defense establishments and so there was little secrecy.[26] Popularly known processes for separation of these two isotopes of uranium for explosion grade are two:

(1) The centrifuge process, and

(2) The electromagnetic process.

(1) *The Centrifuge Process.* The centrifuge process involves high velocity rotation of the uranium mineral or its gaseous uranium hexafluoride preparation in metal tubes with separators by which the heavier isotope is spun to the outside, as in crude oil separation into petrol, kerosene oil, etc., or a cream from milk separator[27]. When uranium by centrifugal force is diffused through barriers, or filters molecules of uranium containing the lighter isotope, Uranium-235 passes through the filter earlier than those containing the heavier isotope U-238. A third category of uranium called enriched mixture of U-238 and U-235 collects on the end side of the centrifuge tube separators. Media has reported that Pakistan has been selling the centrifuge system to North Korea, Iran and Libya in two models. The P-1 model is used to process uranium ore into gas, a step towards enrichment[28] of uranium, by separation of natural uranium and fissionable uranium as mentioned above. This produces basic nuclear fuel, which is subsequently turned into rods that are used for fission in a nuclear power reactor or a nuclear weapon, depending on the grade of U-235 produced. The second model sold by Pakistan is of advanced centrifuge design, known as P-2 that is capable of producing highly enriched uranium,[29] U-238 enriched to 90% of U-235 or more level, to be used for nuclear weapons exclusively. In general, the gas centrifuge system is used to process uranium, which then can be used for nuclear fuel for reactors or for bombs or missile warheads, depending on the level of enrichment.[30] India has since mid-1980s hundreds of gas centrifuges working in three of its reactors producing

U-233 from thorium, U-235 from U-238 and plutonium Pu-239 from U-235 both as recycled or enriched nuclear fuel for reactors and for nuclear defensive minimum deterrence preparedness.

(2) *The Electromagnetic Process*. Magnetic field is employed by a 'mass spectrograph' to bend a current of uranium ions; the heavier ions (uranium-238) bend at a larger radius than the lighter ions (uranium-235), allowing the two separated currents of ions to be collected in separate receivers. This process is much superior to gas centrifuge process and produces larger quantities of nuclear fuel at less cost. The production of large quantities of Uranium-235 is accomplished through a super mass spectrograph, called 'calutron' in USA. It is also used for converting U-238 into plutonium (Pu-239) via U-235; both of them U-235 and Pu-239 are of weapon grade fuel for nuclear explosions. The making of plutonium involves the transmutation of Uranium-238 into Pu-239 in a reactor pile. Scientists explain that when a nucleus of U-238 is hit by a neutron it absorbs it and becomes 92/U-239 ($^{92}U_{239}$) with an electron to spare and on next hit by a neutron it becomes neptunium 93/Np-239 ($^{93}Np_{239}$). As this new element neptunium is highly radioactive and unstable and emits electron, it is transformed into a stable element 94/Pu-239 ($^{94}Pu_{239}$), which is plutonium.[31] The P2 centrifuge of Dutch origin promoted by Pakistan and the 'calutron' of USA ensure this transmutation.

Next step in production of nuclear bomb consists in reducing of the fissionable products of the fuel production plants to pure metal, thereafter fabricating the metal to required shapes and finally in providing them with protective shield or casing that prevents neutrons from escaping and thereby makes storage for long time possible. The shielded or encased metal is known as 'core' for reactors or bombs. For reactors the core is made of aluminum plated uranium rods usually 1.1/2 inch thick and 4 inch long, while for nuclear bomb or missile warhead it is fabricated into different desired shapes and sizes.

Nuclear Reactor

Acquisition or indigenous development of nuclear reactors for civil use is permitted under the nuclear Non-Proliferation Treaty, which came into effect in 1970. The countries which are not Nuclear Weapon States are allowed to develop nuclear power and are also allowed to make their own fuel. India is not a signatory of the NPT; it is a nuclear weapon State and makes its own nuclear power reactors alongwith fuel cores for these, but significantly without obtaining materials prohibited by NPT from other States.

Nuclear reactors have such details over which law, politics and diplomacy have worked for transfer of technology, equipment or materials under international controls of IAEA or Nuclear Suppliers Group:

(a) Nuclear reactor is a device for the burning of nuclear fissionable matter or fuel for useful purposes, like producing steam for power generators. The nuclear reactor is at the same time devised[32] to dampen the harmful explosive effect of the fission chain reaction. Natural Uranium-238 is safer for reactors than U-235 (highly reactive), since the latter requires more intricate moderators and shields.

(b) The atomic reactor requires the fuel uranium in thickly aluminum plated rods usually 1.1/2 inch thick and 4 inch long.

(c) The fuel rods are stored and inserted in moderators: it may be specially purified graphite bloc with special holes in which the rods are fitted, or it may be a tank full of heavy water[33] in which the rods are securely suspended as rod-units, the latter is called a 'swimming pool' type reactor.[34]

(d) In between every two rods or rod-units there are 'control panels/rods' generally made of cadmium and steel which absorb or do not let those neutrons flying out of the rods to pass through them. These rods are adjustable: raising them exposes the rods to each other that increases fission between adjacent rods and lowering them likewise reduces the fission.

(d) The fuel rods and the moderators are suspended in a coolant liquid[35] which is an alloy of sodium and potassium, that is continuously pumped in and out of the chamber. The coolant liquid gets heated to a high temperature and is forced into a cooling radiator in which water turns into steam and the steam in turn is used to generate electricity by rotating the wheels of generators.

(e) All these contraptions are enclosed in a shield made of special concrete of about 8 ft. thickness. This protective chamber prevents heat, G-rays, neutrons, etc. from escaping out and injuring people working around. Remote controls and robots manage the whole work.

Nuclear or Atomic Bomb

It has turned out for information of intelligentsia that there are two methods for exploding a nuclear core: The trade dealings in instrumentation, machinery and parts for these have been subject-matter of violations of NPT obligations and lead to international scandals:

(1) *N-Bombs: Of Explosion Methods*. This method alongwith specialized contraptions requires hi-tech detonators, nuclear core of specific shapes, catalysts and fission boosters.

  (a) The core contains either of U-235 or Pu-239 of slightly sub critical mass in order that this may undergo fission readily. These two isotopes are chosen, since only these consistently emit neutrons for fission in abundance.

  (b) Several pieces of sub-critical fission material are kept together in the core separated from each other by using proper insulating materials between the pieces that would avoid neutrons of one from reaching other piece.

(c) In order to turn sub-critical mass of the core to a critical mass, the contents of the core are combined extremely quickly or suddenly by means of detonators.

(d) Thereafter the released neutrons of the critical mass of the core set a chain reaction of fission and the nuclear explosion results. The fission boosters ensure explosion within appointed time.[36]

(2) *N-Bombs: Of Implosion Method.* Implosion type nuclear weapon devices are generally for use as missile nuke warheads.

(a) The core of an implosion-type atomic bomb consists of a sphere or a series of concentric shells of fissionable material surrounded by a jacket of high explosives.

(b) The explosive belt is simultaneously detonated. This outer-belt explosion causes implosion of the fissionable material core by putting the core under enormous pressures.[37] Being compressed into a smaller size, the nuclei in the core get more tightly packed and the chances of an emitted neutron's striking a nucleus are increased to a point of certainty and that immediately sets chain reaction for fission.

(c) An important aid for certainty and accuracy in achieving criticality of fuel for fission is the use of a tamper. This tamper is a jacket of beryllium oxide or some other substance that surrounds the fissionable material and reflects back some of the escaping neutrons into the fissionable material, where they can thus cause more fissions. Also, the use of beryllium makes it possible to fabricate smaller and lighter nuclear weapons. Surrounding the core with a neutron reflector reduces the minimum amount of plutonium or highly enriched uranium required to sustain a chain reaction or "critical mass". Beryllium is used as an effective neutron reflector.

(d) In addition, special devices for a "boosted fission" are required; these are fusion materials, such as deuterium or tritium, and are added into the fission core. A few grams of tritium mixed with roughly equal amounts of deuterium inside a warhead "boost" the yield of the fission explosion several times, and this leads to reductions in the size and weight of the weapon. The fusion material boosts the fission explosion by supplying neutrons into the fission core in superabundance. The booster makes it possible to make low, medium and high yield nuclear bombs—for tactical or strategic use in a war.

(e) For accuracy of timing for implosion, polonium is used in conjunction with a catalyst beryllium to ensure that the chain reaction leading to a nuclear explosion in the core is initiated at the correct moment.[38] Polonium with atomic number 84 and atomic weight 210 is a radioactive metallic substance.

The Hydrogen Bomb

It is essentially a fusion bomb as distinguished from fission nuclear bomb. The fusion of hydrogen isotopes and other gases of air into elements of higher atomic numbers is achieved by hydrogen bomb on explosion. The devastating energy released by the hydrogen bomb is a by-product, that is, the resistance to forced fusion. To explain, the nuclear fusion is a nuclear reaction involving the combination or fusion of two lighter (unstable) nuclei to form a heavier (but stable) one. All nuclei are positively charged but electrons of equal negative charge are needed to make the atom neutral. Nuclear fusion requires application of sufficient external energy to overcome the mutually repulsive forces of two nuclei, which are positive, and as is known two positive charges repel each other. This energy for fusion is provided by a primary fission of U-235 or

Pu-239 nuclei in the form of an explosive chain reaction that produces very high temperature of the order of 10 million degrees centigrade which provides sufficient energy to overcome the repulsive forces of hydrogen isotopes, namely, Proton (H-1), Deuteron (H-2) and Triton (H-3), and the resistance to their fusion into heavier stable nuclei is the explosion of the hydrogen bomb.

It is said that hydrogen bomb is about 1000 times more devastating in effect covering a larger area than a general nuclear fission bomb for the weight of U-235 or Pu-239 used up for causing the explosions. The current generation of weapons is of 200 to 750 kiloton yields as against 15-21 kiloton Hiroshima and Nagasaki bombs.

The Nuclear Holocaust

The catastrophes associated with the use of nuclear bombs or nuclear holocaust have been highlighted by (a) those who are proud of the scientific achievement; mostly US and UK nuclear scientists of 1940s and their governments which dropped the atom bomb in Japan in 1945; (b) negatively by the pacifists who want that the catastrophic nuclear wars should be prohibited and disarmament of nuclear bombs should take place; and, (c) by those also who justify the balance of terror as a national policy and accept the right to use this weapon in order to avoid a war and emphasize that in a war against them, they would not hesitate to use nuclear weapons. Now in our period of the history of international law and politics, the nuclear diplomacy of States should proceed with the knowledge of the nature and extent of devastation that the nuclear explosions are most likely to cause.

On the other hand, enthusiastic scientists also belittle their atomic or nuclear bombs by comparing these with earthquakes or volcanic eruptions. They tell us that the 1815 volcanic eruption at Sumbawa in Indonesia was equivalent to 60,000 Hiroshima type atom bombs. The eruption of volcano in 1980 at Mount St Helens in Washington State of USA equaled 500 Hiroshima size atom bombs. The recent 26 December 2004 earthquake of Sumatra in Indonesia which killed 2,00,000 human beings around South-East Asia coasts, including India and Somalia by Tsunami tidal waves was said to equal 8,000 Hiroshima atom bombs.

Scientists now state it after observations that sudden enormous amount of energy is released on fission of nuclear bomb, and the nuclear bombs are exploded not on impact on earth but are timed to explode at a calculated height in air for maximum effect. Technically, the fission method bomb requires abundant air supply by suction, particularly when it is hydrogen or thermonuclear bomb.

The damaging effects of nuclear explosion are thus visualized by the observers of Hiroshima and Nagasaki nuclear bombings and the scientists:

First, thermal energy in the form of heat of about 10 million degrees centigrade temperature is suddenly released. This is in the form of a circular base of fire flame going upto 20 to 30 thousand feet. The high temperature by itself directly melts and evaporates human and material things lying within that circular base. Surrounding air is sucked into the fire flame for oxygen leading to various kinds of nuclear fusion and chemical reactions in circular zones of their impact. Studies[39] describe various zones depending on the size of nuclear bomb that may be from 1 kiloton to 50 kiloton or more TNT explosive power yield. There is diminishing effect of heat of the impact of the explosion with increase of distance on the ground viz.:

1. Vaporized Area, where nothing remains to be seen.
2. Total Destruction Area without vaporization.
3. Severe Blast Damage Area, where strong buildings and structures remain less damaged but other directly exposed things are severely or badly damaged.
4. Severe Heat Damage Area, where inflammable things and structures catch fire due to intense heat, people directly exposed also die, upto 50% humans die due to exposure to heat or lack of oxygen.

Second, the nuclear explosions, which suck dust and other ground materials up into the fireball, create 'convection air currents'; alongwith there are fusion effects of high temperature also. The sucked up matter being extremely hot rises high up into the air, sucking in more air and creating the characteristic mushroom-shaped cloud of an atomic explosion, which rises even beyond the height of Mt. Everest. As the hot matter reaches cool area of atmosphere, strong stormy winds ranging to 600 kmph speed rush in to the site of explosion from areas several kms away. The stormy winds thus generated cause a lot of severe damage on the ground.

Third, the detonation, as is usual, immediately produces a strong 'shock wave' that moves outward in all directions from the blast to distances of several miles. The shock wave gradually loses its force as it moves away. Such a shock wave destroys buildings for several kms from the location of the burst. The strength of the shock wave is measured in terms of overpressure, that is, the difference between the pressure immediately on the shock wave front and the pressure before explosion. The overpressure wears off as the distance increases from the explosion centre. An overpressure of 0.35 kg per sq cm (5 kg per square inch) is sufficient to flatten buildings and normal structures and to cause human fatalities. For 1-megaton bomb the devastating overpressure is calculated to continue upto a distance of 12 km.

Fourth, 'radiations' are released[40] from radioactive substances in the form of beta and gamma rays alongwith moving neutrons from the vaporized materials. These flash outwards from the place of burst directly killing the living beings. People may also be indirectly exposed to such radiations when inside buildings leading to casualties from death to remote genetic mutations, depending on the extent of body exposure. The radiations emanate due to Strontium-90 or Plutonium-239 ions. Vaporized matter of mushroom-shaped cloud condenses into fine particles much of which are radioactive. This is called radioactive debris or nuclear fall-out. A major portion of the radioactivity released from a nuclear explosion is in the form of electromagnetic radiations that cover the entire spectrum range, that is, from X-rays to thermal radiations. The X-rays are absorbed by the medium surrounding the exploding weapon and heat the atmospheric gases to create expanding dust bubbles of high temperature.[41] Atmospheric wind currents carry these bubbles to the upper reaches of troposphere or stratosphere. Scientists tell that when this radioactive fallout finally settles on earth it contaminates water and landmass in forms that are highly injurious to living creatures, which even kill fish in seawaters. This radioactivity continues to subsist for several weeks till Strontium-90 or Plutonium-239 ions degenerate into lower non-radioactive elements. The effects of radioactive fallout on humans and living beings have been described by several studies. Apart from direct injuries the radioactive fallout is injurious to our future generations as well when it rises beyond acceptable or toleration limits for radioactive radiations. Every nuclear explosion adds to the already existing radioactive poison in the global atmosphere. It is now believed that increase in global radioactivity reduces the lifespan of exposed persons and the dose causes unseen mutations in the genes of human beings. The result is that defective children are likely to be born in later generation in the area of increased radiations. The fallout from nuclear fission invariably contains Strontium-90, which is easily absorbed by plants and other vegetation consumed by humans or cattle. "Strontium-90 is a terrible poison – a poison that did not exist in the world, except for a few stray atoms in uranium and thorium minerals, a few years ago. One teaspoonful of this poison, distributed equally among all the people of the world, would kill all of them within a few years. When a single super bomb is detonated, about thousand times, this amount is thrown up into the air. It is fortunate that only a small part of it gets into the bodies of human beings".[42] The poisonous strontium takes about six weeks, after which it fades out as spent substances. Further, the radiations from nuclear explosions also cause long-term damage to the biodiversity of the environment. The soil and the ecosystem are also affected. A large-scale global nuclear war can lead to long-term climatic changes caused, apart from radiations, by the smoke thrown up by burning matter of cities. This phenomenon is visualized as "nuclear winter".

Hiroshima and Nagasaki, August 1945

The scientists now treat the wartime explosions at Hiroshima and Nagasaki as the units of nuclear ferocity and the consequent devastation. For example, the devastation in South-East Asia coastal areas by the Tsunami tidal waves caused by the earthquake of 26 December 2004 on collision of under-sea Indian, Burmese and Australian plates meeting off Sumatra in Indonesia, is calculated to be 8,000 times more ferocious than the Hiroshima atom bomb. In turn, the potential ferocity of nuclear bomb is measured in terms of its explosive power as compared to 1,000 kiloton of TNT. The destructive power is based on the observed tolls at Hiroshima and Nagasaki. The first prototype atom bomb made in July-August 1945 was test fired in Trinity, New Mexico, in open and vacated desert with underground observation posts and it gave the basic idea of the results on nuclear explosion,[43] like a ball of fire, high vertical flame, petrifying of sand into rock and the rise of mushroom cloud. Later, on August 6 and August 9, 1945, two nuclear bombs were dropped at Hiroshima and Nagasaki respectively in war-theater of Second World War in Japan and these explosions gave vivid picture of devastation with prolonged fission radiation effects on human body and environment. Various authors, journalists, pacifists and protagonists of nuclear weapons of the period have given vivid accounts of the consequences of the two explosions while expounding their points of view.[44] Here, at this place the recount is only with reference to the consequences as related to the kiloton power of the nuclear bomb and related also to the terrain where these two bombs were dropped.

(a) The first atomic bomb was dropped by the United States on Hiroshima, an open city with surrounding lands in Japan, on 6 August 1945 at 8:15 in the morning. It used Uranium-235 and had the features of a 'gun-assembly bomb'. It released the force of 15 to 17 kilotons of TNT. It was air-burst 1,900 feet (680 metres) above the residential city and it completely devastated more than 10 square km of the city. The bomb outright destroyed 60,000 of the Hiroshima city's buildings and overall more than 67 per cent of the city's structures were destroyed or damaged. The population actually present was estimated at 350,000 at the time of explosion 66,000 were killed immediately and 69,000 were injured, but other 1,40,000 died by the end of the year[45] and not to mention about thousands who continued to suffer from radiation exposure.

(b) The second nuclear weapon dropped in actual war was Plutonium-239 bomb; it was to be dropped on city Kokura on August 9, 1945. But, the B-29 bomber spent 10 minutes hovering over Kokura without sighting the city due to bad weather; it then unloaded the bomb on Nagasaki Island at 11:02 a.m. local time, it had burst at 1,650 feet above the land. Good fate of people of Kokura was ill-fated day for Nagasaki. The Plutonium-239 bomb produced a blast of about 21 kiloton of TNT. It is estimated that 39,000 persons were killed, 25,000 injured and about 40 per cent of the city's structures were destroyed or seriously damaged. Some disappointed scientists of the decade felt that the bomb would have successfully produced several times more calamities and devastation at Kokura but the bomb could not show its full ferocity or capacity in terms of deaths and destruction of property at Nagasaki. The fault, it was emphasized, was not of the bomb for fewer people that had died and less property that was devastated since the island was small, living population was sparse, city was a factory area, the workers were yet to turn up in morning and the topography of Nagasaki had proved to be rather treacherous for the bomb. The Japanese surrendered to USA the next day, cutting short the Second World War by few days. This was taken to be an achievement by the Americans and other allied powers with thanks to the two atom bombs.

THE TWO 1945 EXPLODED BOMBS: FISSION RADIATIONS AND HUMANS

The two nuclear bombs, as predicted by physicists, first generated an enormous fireball after explosion. This in turn produced radiations in a wide spectrum: heat rays, light rays,

X-rays, neutrons, ionized radiation or gamma rays and strong electromagnetic fields.[46] Along with these:

(1) The bombs created an area of scorching heat: the temperature was 600°C upto a distance of 1 km from the Hiroshima bomb-centre and 1.5 km from the Nagasaki, the bomb-centre was death zone. A third-degree burn zone extended beyond 10 km that led to death within a week or else the tissue below the skin, such as muscle, was destroyed. Third-degree burn survivors, with more than 25 per cent of the body covered by burns, immediately went into shock and needed emergency treatment, which no one was around to provide.

(2) The intense spark light was created which caused too much damage to those people who looked directly at the light in the sky at the time of the explosion. To those who were not blinded, the damage to the eye was temporary and that lasted for a few hours or for a few days.

(3) The 'toxic ionizing radiation'[47] was also caused from the radioactive fallout that was carried by the winds after nuclear explosions to the troposphere or stratosphere and took time to settle.[48] The lethal, toxic and harmful effects of ionization radiation were two:

   (a) The 'acute effects' that result from rapid exposure and show up gradually within a few weeks. The Gamma rays and X-rays penetrate human tissues easily, creating moderate ionization along their paths. Biological damage is related to the degree of tissue ionization produced by penetrating radiation. At Hiroshima and Nagasaki, these toxins affected those who were in the cities at the time of the explosion, and also those who entered the two places even 100 hours after the blasts, and those who went near the contaminated hypocenter of explosion. These acute effects followed from the exposure of people to the fallout immediately after the explosion. Acute radiation sickness from severe exposure in Hiroshima and Nagasaki resulted in death within or around in two weeks' time alongwith severe pain; those who were exposed to a lesser degree died six to eight weeks later.[49] Further, the fallout from nuclear fission contained Strontium-90 that was easily absorbed by plants and other vegetation like cattle fodder. This Strontium-90 is a terrible poison for human beings and vegetation. Strontium-90 takes about six weeks when it fades out as spent force.

(b) Latent effects also arose from subsequent or delayed exposure or which resulted from prolonged exposure to relatively lower levels of radiations at Hiroshima and Nagasaki. These became noticeable after a longer period of time. According to the Radiation Effects Research Foundation at Hiroshima and Nagasaki, the incidence of cancer, particularly leukemia, increased in the period between 1950 and 1953. An increased number of people suffered from other kinds of cancer also later. Since the radiation mostly affects those cells in the human body that replicate most rapidly children and infants were more sensitive to radiation injury than adults; naturally the fetuses were the most vulnerable. The unborn children who were exposed to radiation quite likely suffered from intelligence quotient impairment, mental retardation and poor physical growth.

To consolidate, the discussed dangers of wartime nuclear explosion technology are not confined to actual use of nuclear bomb on enemy. The development and perfection of nuclear weapon know-how is through nuclear test explosions. If such experimental nuclear explosions were continued or are frequent and simultaneous by several States, the catastrophic effect on ecology and living beings will be the same as that after a nuclear war. As such, sane diplomacy requires the evolution of the art and science of finding solution both of nuclear experiments and international conflicts with possibility of the use of nuclear weapons. The discussions made so far show the evil nature of nuclear weapons both in substance and in effect. But are nuclear reactors used for mass production of electricity safe?

Radiation Leakage in Nuclear Reactors

The developed States of the West since 1960s are depending on nuclear reactors using U-233 or U-235 for continuous mass and durable production of electricity both for civilian and industrial use. In the past, the mass production of electricity has been through burning of coal or diesel oil, or hydroelectric power generators. The nuclear reactors are next in line. India has thermal power generating units using coal or diesel oil. Hydroelectric powers stations have reached their optimum potential. India is now facing terrible energy resource crunch to meet requirements of its industrial growth. To fill in the gap, more and more nuclear reactors, indigenously built or commercially supplied by foreign States, are being installed in India. However, the nuclear reactors are not foolproof safe. The reactors entail danger of radiation exposure through leakage, negligence or accident. The concerned States normally underplay the magnitude of disaster, the causes leading to radiation leakage and the causalties suffered in or around the reactors. The fear of radiation lurks even in and nearby thousands of nuclear reactors functioning around the world in addition to radiation from actual nuclear explosion. Of course, every scientifically known effort is made to insulate the radiations from the reactors, both for the operators and the nearby population. In this context, in India the Indian Atomic Energy Regulatory Board (AERB) prescribes the safe limits of radiation doses[50], that nuclear plant personnel and people living outside nuclear plants are allowed to receive. It keeps tabs on safety and radiation issues in nuclear facilities in the country. These facilities work under the Department of Atomic

Energy of the Government of India. According to the AERB, a nuclear facility worker may receive up to 100 millisievert (mSv) of radiation over a five-year period with an average of 20 millisievert a year, but the dose should not exceed 30 millisievert in a given year. At the international level, International Commission on Radiological Protection (ICRP) prescribes the working limits for radiations from reactors. The ICRP has stipulated the same five-year dosage but it is more liberal in allowing an annual dose limit of up to 50 millisievert. The life-term dose that a nuclear plant worker can receive is one sievert (1,000 millisievert).

It may be noticed that the International Nuclear Event Scale ranges from Level 1 (anomaly) to Level 7 (major accident or disaster). It was a minor 'incident' if it fell between Levels 1 and 2. Any event between Level 1 and Level 4 is categorized as 'incident' and events above Level 4 are called 'accidents'. There are four international mishap events related to nuclear reactors on record in this context:

(i) The 1979 accident took place at the Three Mile Island nuclear power station, near Harrisburg in USA. It released radiation 8.0 and 0.015 mSv within a 16 km and 80 km radius, respectively, considered to be less than the background annual radiation dose. The mishap event was classified as one of Level 5. There was no death.

(ii) The nuclear reactor disaster at Chernobyl in the Soviet Union on 29 April 1986, however, was devastating. Due to human and technical errors, the capacity of a unit of the reactor had suddenly increased during a scheduled shut down. There was considerable emission of steam with subsequent reaction, resulting in formation of nascent hydrogen that eventually exploded. The explosion damaged the reactor safeguard system that led to release of radioactivity and radioactive dust. The disaster led to more than 30 deaths, hundreds of hospitalization cases and the evacuation of thousands of nearby residents to safer places. The 'Chernobyl disaster' is recorded as a Level 7 event.

(iii) There was a serious incident at the Kalpakkam Atomic Reprocessing Plant (KARP) in India on 21 January, 2003, at which six workers were exposed to radiation levels, exceeding annually permissible limits, but it was not a case of dangerous exposure. Persons were engaged to work in this particular portion of the plant under special procedures.[51] There were no deaths. The report was that the incident was of "a little bit of over-enthusiasm", of "error in the technical judgment" of the employees, and of a snag in the safety and hazard warning equipment that had gone unnoticed. The doses that the workers had received had "exceeded the annual [prescribed] dose limit of 20 millisievert" but the authorities asserted that the exposures that took place were "much, much lower than the [prescribed] life-time dose limit of one sievert" (1,000 millisievert).

(iv) In Britain's Thorp Reprocessing Plant at Sellafield in April 2005 it was detected that about 83,000 liters of highly radioactive liquid had continued to leak unnoticed for about nine months. This leakage was due to several human oversights, engineering errors and automatic monitors that had failed. The liquid had accumulated in a safe pool. The company stressed that the leakage was contained and that the incident had not posed any radiation exposure threats.[52]

ENDNOTES

1. North Korea possessing weapons of mass destruction was regarded to be a threat to peace in Asia-Pacific and Korean Peninsula itself for having avowed policy of uniting the two Koreas.

2. Pertinently at technical level, North Korea announced for substantiating its counter-threat that it had 8000 radioactive uranium rods from the closed 5-MW research Yongbyon atomic reactor; which it had "shut down" under the bilateral deal Agreed Framework (A.F.) made with the USA in 1994. These were sufficient to produce 5 to 6 plutonium numbs. It had also acquired second

way technology for producing nuclear weapons through the enrichment of uranium. Subsequently, Pakistani nuclear scientist A.Q. Khan confirmed that he was shown three nuclear devices/ weapons and that he had as early as late 1980s negotiated North Korea for the sale of equipment for a second way of producing nuclear weapons through the enrichment of uranium, as opposed to use of plutonium: PTI news from New York, 'AQ says he saw 3 N. Korean N-bombs: Report' *The Times of India*, April 14, 2004.

3. This is a description of net situation irrespective of righteousness, morality and legality of the attitudes of the two sides, the USA and North Korea.
4. Roving salesmen or brokers.
5. Centrifuges are metal tubes that spin uranium hexafluoride gas, the raw material for uranium, in order to separate out the uranium $_{235}$ which is needed for making a nuclear reaction. In this way, uranium can be enriched to the level required for a nuclear power station and also to the higher levels which are needed for a nuclear bomb.
6. Media reports say that the "amount of highly enriched uranium needed to make a nuclear weapon varies with the degree of enrichment and the sophistication of the weapon. Higher the enrichment level, the less is the amount of uranium required to make a nuclear explosive device."
7. Proton is a sub-atomic particle, which has a unit positive charge and a mass equal to the mass of an atom of hydrogen.
8. Electron is a sub-atomic particle, which has a unit negative charge and a mass equal to 1/1840 of the mass of an atom of hydrogen. The electrons are a nuclei orbit in a circular path but the path is in one plane. Orbital of an electron is the region of space around the nucleus where the probability of finding the electron is maximum. The different electrons of an atom are distinguished by their quantum numbers. Electron is a Beta (b) particle.
9. Neutron is a sub-atomic particle which has no charge and has a mass almost equal to the mass of an atom of hydrogen. One neutron has 1 proton and 1 electron. Beta radiations involve breaking of a neutron, so when one b particle escapes by radioactivity one neutron decreases and one proton increases in the nuclei, making the nuclei unstable.
10. Isotopes are variants of the same atom, f.n. 12, below.
11. Radioactive rays are three:

    Alpha Rays (a-rays): are ejected out of the nuclei; consist of positively charged particles (these are deflected by electric and magnetic fields); each a-particle is a helium nucleus: it has +2 units of charge and 4 units of mass. Thus the new element formed on emission of a-particle has a mass number less by 4 units and atomic number less by 2 units [Thus $^{92}U_{238}$ minus one a-ray becomes $^{90}U_{234}$] and the $^{90}U_{234}$ is called an Isotope of uranium.

Beta Rays (b-rays): are also ejected out of the nuclei, are negatively charged, are mere electrons, are 100 times more penetrating than (alpha) a-rays, produce less luminosity, but have better photographic effect greater than of alpha rays. b-Particles are electron: The removal/emission of b-particle means breaking of a neutron into one proton and one electron and raising of atomic number by one and creation of new isotopes [Thus: $^{90}U_{234}$ minus one b-ray becomes $^{91}U_{234}$ and $^{91}U_{234}$ minus one b-ray becomes $^{92}U_{234}$.

Gamma (g) Rays: are produced as results of secondary effects of atomic disintegration; carry no charge and are neutral; Gamma (g) Rays are light rays of very short wavelength, they are highly penetrating, produce less luminosity and have less effect on photographic plate.

12. Isotopes of an element: These are atoms of the same element having the same atomic number but different mass numbers. Viz., $^{92}U_{238}$ or $^{92}U_{234}$ is the isotope of uranium, which are required as fuel for nuclear reactor or nuclear bomb respectively.

13. Isobars: These are atoms of different elements having the same mass numbers but, of course, different atomic numbers. These are produced by radioactivity effect: one a-ray or two b-rays escape or change result is the production of isotope of the parent element; while one beta-ray change results in production of an isobar that is an element with different atomic number.

14. Nuclear Fusion: (a) It is a nuclear reaction involving the combination or fusion of two lighter (unstable) nuclei to form a heavier (but stable) one. (All nuclei are positively charged but electrons provide equal negative charge to make the atom neutral). Nuclear fusion requires application of sufficient external energy to overcome the mutually repulsive forces of two nuclei which are positive and two positive charges and repel each other. Nuclear fission is reverse of nuclear fusion and releases energy.

    (b) The hydrogen bomb works on this principle: The fission of U-235 or Pu-239 nuclei in the form of an explosive chain reaction produces very high temperature of many million degrees centigrade which provides sufficient energy to overcome the repulsive forces of hydrogen isotopes, Proton (H-1), Deuteron (H-2) and Triton (H-3), and as next step their fusion into heavier stable nuclei is the explosion of a nuclear bomb.

15. This was enunciated by two scientists, Von Weizsacher and Hans Bethe, in 1932. They held that 45 mg of hydrogen through thermonuclear fusion produced as much energy as was produced by burning one ton coal.

16. Radiations are electro-magnetic waves and possess energy. Radiation spectrum—Radiowaves, Microwaves, Infra-red rays, visible light rays, ultra-violet rays, X-rays, alpha, beta & gamma rays, or cosmic rays. The electro-magnetic waves have:

    (a) wave-length (l) that is the distance between two adjacent cresses or troughs in a particular wave;

    (b) wave number, that is, the total number of waves which can pass through a space of one cm.

    (c) Frequency that is the number of waves or cycles which can pass through a point per second. – unit is Hz (Hertz) Frequency (¦) = velocity of light (c) / wave length (l) [velocity of light (c) = 3×10^{10} (10 raised to the power 10) cm per sec];

    (d) Energy (E):- of a radiation depends upon its frequency (¦). [E = h¦ (h is plank's constant = 6.52×10^{-10} (10 to the power –10); [or E = h . c / l (velocity of light/wave length)].

    Detection or measurement of Radiation:- There are several methods and instruments for this purpose. However, the Geiger-Mueller Counter and Scintillation Counter are usual for the work. Latter is superior to the former. Detection and measurement of radioactivity is based on extent of 'ionization' caused by the radiations when these pass through same medium.

17. The nuclei of radioactive substances are unstable: atoms of such elements continuously disintegrate forming atoms of new elements – that have different physical and chemical properties. The radioactive disintegrations unlike chemical activity cannot be reversed. Radioactive substances emit active rays different from light which:

    (a) penetrate solid matters,

    (b) ionize gases and

    (c) produce luminosity in substances, like zinc sulphide or barium platinocyanide.

18. A nuclear reaction in uranium will only take place if there are enough U-235 atoms present to allow this process to continue as a self-sustaining chain reaction. This much requirement by weight is known as "critical mass". However, every 1,000 atoms of naturally occurring uranium contain only upto seven atoms of U-235, with the remaining 993 being denser U-238.

19. Neptunium and plutonium are not found in natural form, since by emission of radioactivity they have not survived time. But, these can be produced in laboratory.
20. The names of scientists connected with this formulation are Hahn, Meitner and Frisch.
21. See, for interesting general account of nuclear processes: M.L. Oliphant "The Scientific Achievement" in *The Atomic Age*: Sir Halley Stewart Lectures, 1948, pp. 11-31. The contents of this and some other paragraphs of this chapter have been written on and after reading this lecture.
22. At the point in terms of weight at which one of the neutrons produced by a fission will, on average, meet another nuclei and will create another fission, critical mass has been achieved. Other related terms used by scientists are 'sub-critical' and 'super-critical'.
23. Earthquakes and nuclear explosions are recorded on Richter scale.
24. *BBC World News.co*, 'Bush Seeks Tougher Nuclear Curbs', Thursday, 12 February 2004, 'A.Q. Khan Visited Uranium-Rich Nations', *The Hindu*, Tuesday, April 20, 2004, *Associated Press News*: "Mr. Khan's network is suspected to have visited countries other than Libya, North Korea and Iran, seeking customers and materials for his black-market trade".
25. Plutonium has no other use. It is obtained by a complicated technology using centrifuge equipment in the processing plants.
26. Reference was or is made: M.L. Oliphant "The Scientific Achievement" in *The Atomic Age*: Sir Halley Stewart Lectures, 1948; Encyclopedia Britannica gives vivid details of nuclear research history; Frederick L. Schuman in Chapter XV, *International Politics*, & Victor Gollanz, *No More War*, 1958, which provide ready knowledge of nuclear scientific processes.
27. This contraption was perhaps initially called 'cyclotron' in USA.
28. *BBC World News. co*: 'Iran Uranium Plant Sparks New Row', April, 2004.
29. *BBC World News.* co, 'Iran's Nuclear Stance Criticized', Monday, 8 March, 2004.
30. *Washington Post*, 'U.N. Inspectors find Link to Iran Nuke Program', The Associated Press, 19 February 2004.
31. Neptunium and plutonium are not found in natural form, since by emission of radioactivity these have not survived. But, these can be produced in laboratory.
32. On the other hand, the nuclear bomb gives full play to the explosive effect of the fission chain reaction.

33. Quality-wise less, but an alternative to heavy water is a mixture of ordinary water and liquid paraffin.
34. The Indian nuclear reactor at Trombay in India is a 'swimming pool' type: It has 35 rods of U-235 that hang in a tank full of heavy water. The tank is 28′ × 10′ × 18′ size and has outer protective screen 8.5 ft thick. It was commissioned in August 1956.
35. It remains liquid even at very high temperatures and does not turn into gas or vapour.
36. Also see points (c) and (d) under *'The Implosion Method'*, below.
37. It may be to the magnitude of 10 million pounds per square inch, as described by scientists.
38. *BBC World News*.co: 'Iran Nuclear Omissions Worry UN' Tuesday, 24 February, 2004, 23:02 GMT.
39. T. Jayaraman 'Atomic Weapon Blast Zones' *Frontline*: Vol. 15, No. 15, July 18-31, 1998.
40. Ionizing radiation is radiation that produces ions in matter during interaction with other atoms in the fallout. The toxic effect of radiation is related to the ionization. The alpha particles, beta particles, neutrons, and positrons are examples of particulate ionizing radiation. Gamma rays and X-rays are electromagnetic ionizing radiations.
41. See, T. Jayaraman, 'The Horrors of a Nuclear War' *Frontline* Vol. 15, No. 15, July 18-31, 1998.
42. Victor Gollanz, *No More War*, 1958.
43. A description is given on, 'Manhayyan Project', *Encyclopedia Britannica, 2002*; T. Jayaraman, 'The Horrors of a Nuclear War' *Frontline* Vol. 15, No. 15, July 18-31, 1998.
44. For instance, Bertrand Russell, P.M.S. Blackett, Wilbur Smith among many other sane thinkers expressed concern over the impacts of nuclear age on future human thought and behaviors. Frederick L. Schuman in Chapter XV, *International Politics*, gives a vivid analysis of the 'madness' of nuclear age.
45. T. Jayaraman, 'The Horrors of a Nuclear War' *Frontline,* Vol. 15, No. 15, July 18-31, 1998.
46. The electromagnetic fields or electromagnetic pulse does not damage living organisms but causes damage to electronic and electrical equipments.
47. See f.n. 40, above.
48. T. Jayaraman, 'The Horrors of a Nuclear War' *Frontline,* Vol. 15, No. 15, July 18-31, 1998: The radioactive contaminants include

long-lived radioisotopes such as of Strontium-90 and Plutonium-239, they have direct lethal effects on humans for weeks after the explosion. The poisonous radiation substances consist of beta particles, gamma rays, neutrons or X-rays. In a 1-megaton nuclear explosion, large quantities of these can directly penetrate 4-6 km before they are fully absorbed or after some time their lethal toxic effects come within toleration ranges of living beings. But the toxic effects of radioactive fallout take a few months before these become harmless.

49. Victor Gollanz, *No More War*, 1958.
50. T.S. Subramanian "The Kalpakkam Incident", *Frontline*, Volume 20-Issue 17, August 16-29, 2003.
51. KARP is one of the three reprocessing facilities in the country along with at Trombay and Tarapore, T.S. Subramanian, The Kalpakkam 'Incident'; *Frontline*, Volume 20-Issue 17, August 16-29, 2003.
52. PTI news from London, 'Highly Radioactive liquid leaked at Sellafield in UK', *The Times of India*, Lucknow Ed., 30 May 2005.

3

Weapons of Mass Destruction (WMD)

Nuclear Weapons

The development, acquisition and possession of ferocious weapons of warfare in order to win a war or to diplomatically silence an enemy has been active diplomacy or a sovereign right of States. Nuclear bomb is the ultimate weapon, for the present, among the weapons of mass destruction (WMD). Alongwith this, the prevention of production of weapons of mass destruction from reaching the armory of hostile States is an additional instrument of diplomacy of this new century. As seen in this decade this diplomacy works both against potential enemies and for prolongation of hegemony of high-tech developed States in international politics. After witnessing the horrors of Second World War, humanism had made an entry in international legal order. Statesmen, pacifists and nations desire that people of the world should be free from destructions caused by more and more ferocious weaponry, including nuclear bombs. The process in this direction was, of course, already known as disarmament. The enigmatic question raised by the nations was whether nuclear and other destructive weapons should be destroyed first or should be banned first. Almost forty years had passed since 1945 with diplomacy at crossroads during which international community as such could not come to a decision and take any concrete step against obnoxious weapons. However, the end of cold war diplomacy after the demise of Soviet Russia in 1991 has given a pause to the situation and has brought some consensus since mid-1990s on the matter.

An Overview

The international community had, in the decade preceding 1995, witnessed hectic armed activities and international political upheavals: There had been a proxy war between Iraq and Iran in which the West-backed Iraq had used chemical weapons on Iraq territories, Soviet Russia had broken down, giving rise to ethnic strife in newly formed States, Yugoslavia was dismembered, went through several ethnic genocides that invited UN intervention, Iraq had annexed Kuwait in contravention of international law in 1990-1991 for about seven months, which had resulted in application of UN sanctions against Iraq. The action in Iraq for freedom of Kuwait had resulted in legally justified armed action but caused on civilian population of Iraq inhuman atrocities by a new set of weaponry short of weapons of mass destruction. USA and NATO had used napalm and cluster bombs and other weapons of indiscriminate destruction, such as landmines and booby traps, both in Yugoslavia and Iraq. The USA had been prepared to use, though it did not use, tactical neutron bombs as and when these might have been necessary. Coupled with all this, the end of cold war era (1945-1991), in which the constant fear of nuclear war was countered by a 'balance of terror', gave rise to the feeling in UN circles for a general disarmament of weapons strategic as well as non-strategic weapons of mass destruction, which are indiscriminate in causing damage. This fear extended both to conventional and nuclear weapons.[1]

From the very outset, i.e. since 1945, the United Nations was seized with the problem of control of nuclear weapons and 'regulation' of armaments to save the humanity and succeeding generations from the scourge of war. For this, it established a system for disarmament negotiations and for proper regulation, control and inspection of atomic energy facilities of the States. The General Assembly in 1946 unanimously adopted the resolution "Principles governing the General Regulation and reduction of Armaments" and adopted another resolution by which the International Atomic Energy Commission was created. Since then and by now, in the interest of the protection of humanity various bilateral or multilateral treaties have been agreed upon but these are binding only on the signatories. One can recall that the determination of US President Reagan of March, 1983, for proposed 'Strategic Defense Initiative' (SDI), popularly known as 'star war', for defense against Soviet nuclear ballistic missile attack on USA had created worldwide feeling of horror. The USA showed or claimed its capacity of destroying artificial satellites and upcoming Soviet nuclear missiles before these entered into the atmosphere of USA from outer space to hit the US targets. The USSR had retaliated by going for similar defense system, including destroying in outer space US strategic ballistic defense missiles. The thirtieth and thirty-first sessions of General Assembly (1995 and 1996), a diplomatic platform, amply gave vent to these international fears against ferocious weapons causing indiscriminate injuries[2] and various positive steps were taken then and in the years that followed against weapons of mass destruction both nuclear and conventional.

Weapons of Mass Destruction

The concept of 'weapons of mass destruction' (WMD) is composite of conventional and nuclear weapons which cause unnecessary, excessive and indiscriminate damage to human beings. Whatever be the weapon technology, the effect on the non-combatants is profound. The States, particularly of the modernized and high technology West, had devised conventional weapons and weapon delivery systems that equaled nuclear weapons in destructive power. The guided missiles, long range artillery, smart bombs, the land and watermines, AK-rifles, nerve gas and chemical bombs, biological bombs, cluster bombs, or napalm bombs, have made wars with conventional weapons many times more ferocious than the weaponry with which the Second World War was fought. This new conventional weaponry is now available not exclusively to the States that are controlled by international and traditional diplomacy but also to the lawless terrorist and poacher entities or groups. The terrorism with suicide bombings has both national and international dimensions and it is more devastating than the open war among the nations. State terrorism is an instrument of diplomacy that has now assumed the form of 'proxy war' among States, that is, a State may promote terrorism in another (hostile) State and sidetrack an overt war. State terrorism is peripheral and escapes direct UN censor, while war comes under jurisdiction of the Security Council of United Nations. The United Nations, through the General Assembly, has reacted against this modernization process of weapons and it has attempted to limit, regulate or prohibit the proliferation of such weapons, whether nuclear or conventional and whether the use of such weapons is by States or by terrorist groups. The UN watch machinery[3] on WMD, through the Secretary General closely follows all developments and trends with regard to weapons of mass destruction in all of their aspects. It solicits, collects and provides information to Member States and the international community on the weapons possessed by the States. The UN also supports and participates in multilateral efforts to strengthen the international norms on disarmament and non-proliferation of weapons of mass destruction related to WMD. As such the menace of WMD is being dealt with in cooperation with relevant intergovernmental organizations and specialized agencies of the United Nations system, like, the International Atomic Energy Agency (IAEA), the Organization for the Prohibition of Chemical Weapons (OPCW) or the Preparatory Commission for the Comprehensive Nuclear-Test-Ban Treaty Organization.

DISARMAMENT OF WMD

As part of the move for general disarmament in the world, the United Nations General Assembly had taken a firm stand in 1996, for "Prohibition of the Development and Manufacture of New Types of Weapons of Mass Destruction and New Systems of Such Weapons" on the report of the Conference on Disarmament.[4] Under this stand the 'Prohibition' extends to radiological weapons, lethal chemical weapons and other emerging new types of Weapons of Mass Destruction (WMD), nuclear or conventional, that have characteristics comparable in destructive effect to those of weapons of mass destruction as earlier identified in the definition of weapons of mass destruction adopted by the United Nations in 1948. It has called upon "all States, immediately to give favourable consideration to those recommendations of the Conference on Disarmament". This resolution of General Assembly has been taken by the West to create a positive obligation on the States and to being in the nature of consensus development against proliferation of WMD. A resolution of General Assembly that lays down general obligation of States on the subject matter of the resolution assumes virtually the nature of an enacted law. During the years since 2001, the USA and other allied powers, that had unilaterally taken armed action in Iraq without the backing of Security Council, have cited this GA Resolution as justification for pushing Iraq against the wall. The US doctrine of taking pre-emptive nuclear action against the nations coming under 'axis of evil' also takes into account this 1996 resolution of GA as a part of international law against those States which do not already possess nuclear weapons and try to acquire or possess them in violation of NPT, etc.

Proliferation of Nuclear Matter

Matters of fission control are alarming and complicated, since more than 50 States, apart from nuclear States, possess lethal nuclear fission materials. Some of them are producers of nuclear raw material as their natural resource. Many of them are operating civil nuclear reactors for energy by importing nuclear fuel but are preserving the spent uranium based waste from which plutonium can be obtained by recycling processes. As we know, plutonium can be enriched to produce nuclear weapons. A gloomy specter for pursuers of nuclear disarmament was drawn by the US Institute for Science and International Security (ISIS) in a briefing[5] for the world press in early September 2005. It was claimed that several States of the world possess nuclear fissionable material worth making more than 3 Lakhs (0.3m) nuclear bombs. Some States are preserving and not destroying 180 tons of nuclear uranium waste from reactors and this can be enriched to make 75,000 nuclear bombs. There are another 140 tons (the figure will be 286 tons by 2010) of Neptunium ($^{93}Np_{239}$) and Americium ($^{95}Am_{241}$) accumulated nuclear waste from reactors in 2005, which can produce 5000 nuclear bombs. The Director of ISIS, David Albright, further stated that 35 States had accumulated 1830 tons of Plutonium ($^{94}Pu_{239}$) that can produce 2.25 Lakhs (0.225m) nuclear bombs.

Widening Concept of WMD

The term WMD has since 2000 become a convenient concept in order to incorporate more and more weapons out of the list of conventional weapons for prohibition. Earlier in 1991, the General Assembly had adopted a resolution[6] entitled "Transparency in Armaments", which requested the Secretary-General to establish and maintain a worldwide non-discriminatory 'Register of Conventional Arms'. This is to include data on international arms transfers as well as any information provided by Member States on military holdings; procurement through national production and their relevant present and future policies with respect to such specified weapons. Thus far, by 2004, 164 Member States have reported to the Register one or more times. The Register comprises of seven categories of major conventional arms, namely battle tanks, armored combat vehicles, large caliber artillery systems, combat aircraft, attack helicopters, warships (including submarines) and also missiles and missile-launchers. The Register has been in operation with effect from calendar year 1992. The Register captures the great bulk of the global arms trade in the categories of conventional weapons. Some of these conventional weapon systems are now regarded to be WMD because these are supposed or known to cause 'indiscriminate mass deaths'. Missiles, the carriers of devastating warheads, are conventional weapons upto a range of 20km, but beyond that range these are invariably regarded to be WMD that are required to be regulated by international law or code of conduct. The missiles for explosives delivery are understood to be capable of carrying nuclear warheads as well, though these are normally possessed by non-nuclear States with much dangerous non-nuclear explosives only but capable of causing indiscriminate mass deaths.

Carriers of WMD

Nuclear weapons require an effective delivery system to hit the targets. The use of big sub-sonic bombers for dropping nuclear bombs is now outdated, since efficient radar systems give sufficient time for intercepting the slow moving high attitude bombers. Now supersonic medium range warplanes, long-range missiles and cruise missiles are being preferred for carrying warheads for hitting the targets. Missiles are projectile rockets with body full of propellant fuel that, on ignition, pushes the missile opposite to the thrust of burst towards a target with great speed, like a bullet. The fuel is either liquid or solid. For war uses the missile has a high explosive filled nose, called warhead, and this may be conventional explosive or nuclear weapon. Missiles may be of short-range, few hundred metres, for destroying battle-tank, armored vehicle or bunkers, of medium range covering 50 to 1000 km, or of long-range covering several thousand kilometers. An unguided military projectile is generally called 'rocket' but a missile always has a guiding and control mechanisms for hitting a target as much accurately as possible. Accuracy of missiles is measured by 'circular error of probability' (CEP) that would take in 50 per cent of the impact points and by 'bias', that is, the deviation of the mean impact point from the actual aim point. An underwater missile is generally called a torpedo and does not carry nuclear warhead. Ballistic missiles are a brief rocket-fire propulsion weapons and are pushed forward by momentum in an arcial or parabolic trajectory like an artillery shell after launched into flight. These missiles may be guided or unguided, depending on the distance to be covered. The ballistic missiles might be of multistage built that fire boosters intermittently as desired. The ballistic missiles might be made for greater accuracy, but then such missiles carry low explosive power or yield; else larger missiles with higher yields hit with less accuracy or wider CEP. The strategic missiles are intermediate-range ballistic missiles (IRBM) that cover a range of about 600 to 3,500 miles and the intercontinental ballistic missiles (ICBM) having ranges exceeding 3,500 miles. Both of them are re-entry vehicles (RV), that is, these go out of atmosphere and re-enter back into the atmosphere just above the target so as to leave little time for interception. Land-fired 'strategic' missiles are generally of ICBM range, whereas the sea or submarine launched ballistic missile (SLBM) is of intermediate range. Air-to-surface and ship-to-land launched missiles are of shorter range as compared to IRBM and are called tactical or battle missiles. Now ballistic missiles are controlled to glide over the territory at a height less than two hundred feet in order to avoid detection by radar and are called 'cruise' missiles. They have lifting wings and fins for regulating their flight; and have jet-propulsion system for sustained flight. Extremely sophisticated guidance systems, radio, infrared sensor or video-image controlled, are required for flying cruise missiles on to the targets. The cruise missiles are being produced in various capabilities: The sea-launched cruise missile (SLCM) for navy and the ground-launched cruise missile (GLCM) require solid fuel boosters, while the air-launched cruise missile (ALCM) for air forces do not require rocket boosting. India, in collaboration with Russia, is developing BrahMos supersonic nuclear warhead capable cruise missile with a range of about 300 km. The U.S. cruise missiles are intermediate-range guided weapons that fly at an altitude of 100 feet to a range of 1,500 miles either with a high conventional explosive or up to a 200-kiloton nuclear warhead. The GLCM carry a low-yield nuclear warhead of 10 to 50 kilotons. Now the advanced cruise missile might have a range of over 1,800 miles and are capable to cover 50 per cent of the impact points. The missiles can deliver high-explosive cluster bomb-lets, an atomic warhead of 1 to 100 kilotons, or an "enhanced-radiation (neutron) thermonuclear warhead of about 1 kiloton". USA has adopted four categories for its ballistic missiles: The Intercontinental Ballistic Missiles (ICBM) having a range of over 5,500 km; the Intermediate Range Ballistic Missiles (IRBM) that cover a range of 3,000 to 5,500 km; the Medium Range Ballistic Missiles (MRBM) of 1000 to 3000 km range; and Short Range Ballistic Missiles (SRBM) of up to 1000 km striking range.

Terrorists for WMD

The United Nations has considered the dangers of weapons of mass destruction in the context of increasing dimensions of terrorism for the first time in the Conference on Disarmament during its 1994, 1995 and 1996 sessions. This aspect of WMD was not pressing in those years, though it was rightly taken to be pertinent particularly due to increase in the arms procurement capacity of terrorist groups operating in Central America or in the Middle East. State terrorism had also become disturbingly prominent. The terrorist attacks of 11 September 2001 in the United States of America, however, caused the international community to focus on the relativity of WMD with terrorism with a renewed intensity. Osama bin Laden had also threatened the use of 'dirty bomb'. It is a nuclear bomb of different kind of small intensity that releases lethal radioactivity from nuclear waste thrown out by the crude bomb on explosion in the targeted area. Terrorism is now a global threat with global effects and its consequences affect every aspect of the United Nations agenda, that is, from development to peace, thereafter to human rights and to the rule of law. A 'Policy Working Group' on the project 'United Nations and Terrorism' was established at the behest of the Secretary-General in October, 2001. Its purpose is to identify the longer-term implications and broad policy dimensions of terrorism for the United Nations and to formulate recommendations on the steps that the United Nations might take or ought to take in order to deal with the issue. The discussions in this Policy Working Group included the issues of the potential use of weapons of mass destruction (WMD) in terrorist acts and the appropriate role of the United Nations in international efforts against WMD assisted terrorism.

WMD WITH NUCLEAR WARHEADS

The Nuclear Menace

International community has been concerned with the nuclear menace as part of the agenda for United Nations Charter on "Disarmament" and had appointed the Disarmament Commission in 1946. Originally, it was essentially a platform for dialogue between the USA-UK coalition, the basic nuclear powers since 1945, and Soviet Russia that became nuclear in 1949. Both sides were reluctant to debate the matter with or alongwith other States. Upto the end of 1950s the USA coalition were of the diplomacy that expansion of Soviet Russian Stalinist communism was to be resisted and halted and the best course was to finish it with nuclear weapons at an opportune time, but this opportunity did not materialize or had remained elusive. Emphasis on disarmament adopted by USSR was that nuclear weapons should be banned first while the West emphasized that nuclear weapons possessed by each should be destroyed effectively first accompanied with a foolproof territorial inspection system to which USSR was not agreeable. Both sides had remained adamant. Next phase started when Soviet Russia was first to develop long-range missiles and intercontinental ballistic missiles (ICBM) systems along with an efficient radar system capable of shooting down intruding American bombers. This made obsolete the American diplomacy of encirclement of Soviet Russia with airfields, including those in Pakistan, from where giant American bombers could drop nuclear bombs on Russian industrial or military centres. The "balance of terror" had been accepted and this had come to stay for the two big power blocs after both sides became invincible by one another with the advent of 1960s. China, which wanted to make Formosa part of mainland, became fourth nuclear power only in 1964. It was not a member of UNO and did not accept this "balance of terror" *détente*.

Prevention of Production of Nuclear Weapons

The common effort of the two power blocs thereafter was to prevent the evolution of new nuclear States that might upset the "balance of terror". In 1963 by the joint effort of USA, UK and Soviet Russia the Nuclear Test Ban Treaty was floated. This Partial Test Ban Treaty of 5 August 1963 prohibits nuclear tests or explosions in the atmosphere, in outer space and under water, including territorial waters. For violation of the treaty,[7] it is essential that nuclear explosion should 'cause radioactive debris to be present outside the territorial limits of the State under whose jurisdiction or control such explosion is conducted'. India has acceded to this treaty. The treaty is salutary but it has failed to achieve the diplomatic angle of disarmament. The reason being that a State can join or resign its membership at will. For the latter, only three months' notice to other parties is required. Further, two other superpowers, France and China, did not join the treaty till they had conducted tests necessary for development of the nuclear weapons. The treaty did not prohibit underground nuclear tests; such tests were continued to be made by USA and Soviet Russia. In 1974 and 1998, India also made underground nuclear tests, while Pakistan conducted such test in 1998. Israel acquired nuclear expertise theoretically and is not known whether it has developed nuclear weapons or not. North Korea is believed to have conducted underground tests vicariously through Pakistan in 1998. In early 1990s, the Partial Test Ban Treaty of 1963 was sought to be revised and replaced by Comprehensive Nuclear Test Ban Treaty (CTBT or CNTBT). The Comprehensive Nuclear Test Ban Treaty is to ban all nuclear explosions, for military or civil purposes. After three years of negotiations in the Conference on Disarmament of the United Nations General Assembly, the CTBT, as a resolution of France, was adopted on 10 September 1996. The Treaty commended by the UN General Assembly was opened for signatures on 24 September 1996, but it has gone into hibernation[8] since 1998, when the USA, one of 44 essential State Parties for a consensus 'entry into force' of the Treaty by its Article VIII, for the present decided not to ratify the CTBT and this decision led to apparent deactivation of the CTBT. This Treaty has the purpose of attracting the adherence of all States to the objective of contributing effectively to the prevention of the proliferation of nuclear weapons in all aspects and thereby to lead to the process of nuclear disarmament. The Treaty regards that this shall enhance the international peace and security. Each State party would, under the Treaty, undertake not to carry out 'any' nuclear-weapon test explosion or any other nuclear explosion and to prohibit and prevent any such nuclear explosion at any place under its jurisdiction or control. More specifically, each party also undertook "to refrain from causing, encouraging, or in any way, participating in the carrying out of any nuclear-weapon test explosions or any other nuclear explosion".

Prevention of the 'Proliferation' of Nuclear Expertise and Weapons

The Treaty on the Non-Proliferation of Nuclear Weapons (NPT) of 1967 is a landmark multilateral treaty discussed, sponsored and launched by the United Nations General Assembly. The Treaty was opened for signature on 1 July 1968; it entered into force on 5 March 1970. A total of 188 States, excluding India, Pakistan and Israel, and including the five nuclear-weapon States have joined the Treaty till now. More States have ratified the NPT than any other arms limitation and disarmament treaty. The objective of the Treaty is to prevent the spread of nuclear weapons and weapons technology to non-nuclear States, to promote cooperation in the peaceful uses of nuclear energy and to further the goal of achieving general and complete nuclear disarmament. The Treaty also incorporates a correspondingly binding commitment by the nuclear weapon States at the multilateral level to pursue the goal of nuclear disarmament. In this direction, a collateral agreement has now been made by some States in the nature of guidelines or conditions that the members of the agreement, the 'Nuclear Suppliers Group' (NSG) States,[9] would follow when exporting nuclear material, equipment or technology to other States has taken place. These conditions include facilities or equipments for reprocessing nuclear fuel, enrichment of uranium and production of heavy water. The conditions of 'Suppliers Group' States, for example, are: a formal assurance from export recipient State that would exclude uses of material, resulting in nuclear explosive devices, effective physical protection by the importing country to prevent an unauthorized use or handling of the material, and the application of IAEA safeguards to the exported item,[10] among other conditions. The agreement was made in London in September 1977, and IAEA was made the enforcement and verification agency for this Agreement of NSG formally on 11 January 1978. Though NPT is discriminatory in favour of nuclear State Parties who can develop or improve their nuclear expertise as against non-nuclear States that are compelled not to go nuclear when faced in a conflict with a nuclear power, for example, China-Pakistan alliance and India or USA and North Korea,[11] yet its popularity is taken to be a testament of the Treaty's significance in international diplomacy. India indigenously and North Korea through purchase from Pakistan acquired nuclear technology in order to balance position in circumstances of a war. There is no doubt that the NPT is popular and necessary. It is another aspect, decadence of international diplomacy rather, which made certain specific States like India and Israel to avoid this Treaty. The reason is that the Treaty is deficient for not providing a nuclear umbrella to non-nuclear States when confronted by nuclear States with a war situation. That means that under international law, politics and diplomacy, a nuclear State must not, in any circumstance, use nuclear weapons against non-nuclear States of NPT. In a critical assessment, NPT gives a diplomatic one-up status to nuclear States over non-nuclear States who are party to the Treaty, such as, Germany, Poland, Japan or Australia.

OTHER WEAPONS OF MASS DESTRUCTION

Chemical Weapons

The Chemical Weapons Convention (CWC) was adopted by the Conference on Disarmament, a UN General Assembly appendage, in Geneva on 3 September 1992, after 12 years of negotiations. The CWC contains a 'compliance verifying mechanism' among its provisions and that is considered to be unprecedented both in scope and in the stringency. The General Assembly thereafter adopted the 'Convention on the Prohibition of the Development, Production, Stockpiling and Use of Chemical Weapons and on Their Destruction'.[12] The CWC opened for signature in Paris on 13 January 1993, and entered into force on 29 April 1997. This CWC is the first disarmament agreement negotiated within a multilateral framework that provides for the elimination of an entire category of chemical weapons of mass destruction under a universally applicable international control. More than one hundred sixty five States have signed it. The convention shows the determination of the United Nations to achieve the effective prohibition extending to the development, production, acquisition, transfer, stockpiling and the use of chemical weapons alongwith their destruction. All possessors of chemical weapons, chemical weapons production facilities or chemical weapons development facilities would be among the original parties to the convention and, in this context, it is significant to note that United States of America and the Russian Federation have declared possession of chemical weapons and both are among the original States parties to the convention.

Bacteriological (Biological) and Toxin Weapons

The 'Convention on the Prohibition of the Development, Production and Stockpiling of Bacteriological (Biological) and Toxin Weapons and on Their Destruction', popularly known as Biological Weapons Convention (BWC)) was adopted by the General Assembly[13] in 1971. The 'Geneva Protocol Prohibiting the Use in War of Asphyxiating, poisonous and other gases, and of Bacteriological Methods of Warfare' already prohibits the content of the convention since 1925. However, as a result of prolonged efforts by the international community to establish a new instrument that would supplement the erstwhile Geneva Protocol of 1925, the Biological Weapons Convention (BWC), was opened for signature on 10 April 1972. The BWC entered into force on 26 March 1975. This is the first multilateral disarmament treaty that bans the production and use of an entire range of biological weapons. However, the absence of any formal verification regime to monitor compliance has limited the effectiveness of the BWC. This shortcoming has been, in a general way, tackled by the WMD resolution of General Assembly in 1996.

Indiscriminately Destructive Conventional Weapons

The convention on Certain Conventional Weapons (CCW), 1980, also known as the 'United Nations Convention on Inhumane Weapons', is marked as the first attempt to restrict the use of landmines along with other similar weapons. Protocol II of the convention prohibits the indiscriminate use of mines, and their intentional use against civilians. It also requires that remotely delivered landmines must have effective self-destructing and self-deactivating mechanisms.[14] The landmines, because of their destructive nature and because these are left undiffused in the former battlefields after the war is over, have come into the category of obnoxious weapons of destruction that kill or injure innocent people who as and when tread upon them unknowingly. This deferred and after war is over effect of left-over live landmines on people is now regarded to be inhuman. The total numbers of causalties since 1960s run into several millions, territorially extending into Asia, Europe and Asia. By concerted efforts of States and the NGO's in early 1990s due to a growing public awareness of the human rights problems, 'The Anti-personnel Mine Ban Treaty' was devised. It opened for signature in Ottawa in December 1997, and it entered into force on 1 March 1999. As of 17 September 2001, there were 120 States Parties to the Treaty. "The States Parties to the Treaty agree:

> Never to use, develop, produce, stockpile or transfer antipersonnel landmines, or to assist any other party to conduct these activities;
>
> To destroy all stockpiled antipersonnel landmines within four years of the Treaty's entry into force;
>
> To clear all laid landmines within ten years of the Treaty's entry into force;
>
> When it is within their means to provide assistance to mine clearance, mine awareness, stockpile destruction, and victim assistance activities worldwide."[15]

Public awareness of the landmine problem was heightened significantly when the Nobel Peace Prize was awarded to the NGO, 'International Campaign to Ban Landmines' and to its coordinator, Jody Williams, in December 1997. Now, landmines, though an ordinary conventional weapon, are regarded to be on the borders of WMD concept. The explanatory situation is that the landmines are not banned, as illegal weapon of warfare but create international crime when left live after the war is over.

Cluster Bombs

So also is the emerging problem with the 'cluster bombs' used by the USA and NATO allies in Yugoslavia or Afghanistan. The unexploded components of a cluster bomb[16] are a potential danger to civilian humans. In Kosovo War, the NATO forces dropped 220,000 cluster bombs in one month of which more than 15,000 did not explode as intended, which are live or are just buried under dust. Despite a massive clearance program by military and non-governmental organizations, the unexploded cluster bombs or BLU have killed about 200 civilians since the close of Kosovo War on the same pattern as the landmines. However, the US-UK led use of such ferocious devices has since 1990s given a diplomatic edge to USA over other States, like Iran or North Korea, that might dare to incur the US displeasure.

Missile Technology and WMD

The development of missiles as carriers of warheads has had tremendous effect on diplomatic equations. The missiles escape early detection of their launch and the direction of their intended targets and have lately converted several conventional weapons into weapons of mass destruction. In earlier stages the Second World War had witnessed the Nazi attack on UK with unguided missiles called flying or V bombs which were fired from the coast of occupied France and which struck the coastal towns of southern England, a distance upto 30 km across the sea, causing indiscriminate damage to civilian property and causing substantial number of civil casualties. The war had ended in August 1945 with bombers aircraft used for dropping of nuclear bombs on Nagasaki and Hiroshima. At present, heavy bombers are conventional weapons, whereas nuclear bombs are in WMD category. Now the guided missiles combine both the V bombs and the heavy long distance bombers that penetrate deep into enemy territory with nuclear bomb as missile warhead. While missiles upto range of 20 km are considered to be normal weapon carriers, beyond this limit these come under dangerous category. The long range missiles of beyond 500 km range can be detected by radar, and admit warning of impending danger but the short range missiles, particularly the 'scud' or 'patriot' missiles, escape detection by radar. Medium range and long-range missiles can carry both nuclear and conventional warheads. The highly sophisticated intercontinental ballistic missiles (ICBM) enter outer space and re-enter atmosphere to strike at the target, covering long distances in a very short time. These are very costly items and are supposed always to carry and strike with nuclear warhead. Soviet Russia was first to develop ICBM in early 1960s and has been ahead of the USA in this missile weapon carrier system technology. As part of disarmament of WMD, the two States, USA and USSR had bilaterally discussed an anti ballistic missile (ABM) control system treaty but had subsequently shelved it on the advent of 'star war' race of mid-1980s.

Missiles as matter of International Concern

The USSR had made history when it had defensively used on 1 May 1960, a missile to shoot down a US spy-plane[17] U-2, flying at height of more than 70,000 ft over its territory. This was a high-tech accomplishment using both radar system and accurately hitting a small target in atmosphere by a missile. The international community has since 1960s been concerned by the accumulation, proliferation, technical refinement and diplomatic threat and the use of ballistic and other types of missiles in an international conflict. Since the year 2000, fears have also been expressed that missiles in the hands of fundamentalist terrorist outfits are a menace and more so when these outfits might acquire nuclear 'rogue' or 'dirty' warheads. Such a development is feared by USA and India, which are threatened by such outfits. In response, States have occasionally pursued various unilateral, bilateral and multilateral measures. Nonetheless, as yet there is no universally accepted norm or instrument specifically governing the development, testing, production, acquisition, transfer, deployment or use of missiles. Encouraged by the US and Russian concern on the issue, the General Assembly,[18] by a resolution entitled "Missiles", had requested the Secretary-General to prepare a report with the assistance of a Panel of Governmental Experts (missiles) for the consideration of the General Assembly at its 57th session (year 2002) on the issue of missiles in all its aspects. The Panel, after holding three sessions in 2001 and 2002, adopted a report[19] by consensus and submitted it to the General Assembly at its 57th session.[20] The Report was prepared by the Panel of Governmental Experts, established pursuant to the resolution of General Assembly plenary session,[21] to examine the issue of missiles in all its aspects. The General Assembly had, in this context, stressed the paramount importance of full and strict compliance by the parties with the 1972 Treaty on the Limitation of Anti-Ballistic Missile Control Systems (ABM Treaty) between USA and former USSR, had called for continued efforts to strengthen it and to preserve its integrity and validity, so that it remained a 'cornerstone' in maintaining a global strategic missile stability.[22] The Report considered by the General Assembly in 2002 provides an overview of the subject by providing the background and current situations in the field of missiles. It also describes a number of areas of concern. These concerns, among other issues, stressed upon in the Report, refer to the increasing number, range, technological sophistication and geographic spread of missiles; the capability of missiles of delivering weapons of mass destruction, in particular nuclear weapons, as well as conventional weapons; missile defenses and their strategic consequences; the potential use of space-launch vehicle technology for the development of missiles, and the role of missiles in military doctrines. The Panel concluded, among other things, that these and other issues are to be regarded as matters of serious concerns for international peace and security. It noted that there are multiple approaches currently undertaken to deal with the issue of missiles, both within and outside the United Nations. The Panel also stated that it is essential to continue efforts in this regard and noted the role of the United Nations in this context. Finally, it concluded that all approaches undertaken at the national, bilateral, regional and multilateral levels, including the initiatives described in the report, 'need to be further explored'[23] in order to limit any diplomatic misuse of possession of superior missile technology as international threat or coercion.

IRAQ WITH WMD, 2003-2004, DIPLOMATIC AND LEGAL CONFUSION

To recapitulate the developments discussed above, as part of the move for general disarmament in the world, the United Nations has firmly moved for "Prohibition of the Development and Manufacture of New Types of Weapons of Mass Destruction and New Systems of Such Weapons", the subject matter of this Chapter under discussion, on the report of the Conference on Disarmament. The 'prohibition' extends to radiological weapons, lethal chemical weapons and other emerging new types of Weapons of Mass Destruction (WMD), nuclear or conventional, that have characteristics comparable in destructive effect to those of weapons of mass destruction identified in the definition of weapons of mass destruction adopted by the United Nations in 1948. It has called upon all States, immediately to follow the recommendations of the Conference on Disarmament. It is interesting but alarming that a culmination of perhaps a negative use of international effort for prohibition of WMD, as instrument of international politics and diplomacy, took place at the hands of USA and UK in Iraq during 2003-2004. USA and United Kingdom had, with some allies, jointly but unilaterally without sanction of the United Nations took armed action in Iraq in 2003, in order to destroy WMD and chemical weapons supposedly possessed by Iraq. The State of Iraq was overrun, was badly devastated and the government of President Saddam Hussein was ousted and the President was arrested for trial for punishment for alleged murders, etc., but no WMDs were found on the territory of Iraq. The trial began only in October 2005. The credibility of UN as keeper of world order was badly affected and shaken since the happenings showed that rules made by it in good faith for peace and security in the world could be hijacked by bully States. Whatever personal satisfaction of the US President George Bush and of UK Prime

Minister Tony Blair may have derived out of their cavalier approach towards the international organization, the world public opinion regards that the armed action against Iraq was *ab initio* on wrong track. By the end of October, American forces have suffered 2000 deaths and about 15,000 casualties were 'brought home'. A pacifist NGO of US estimated[24] that "Washington has spent around $ 200 billion on the war". The details of the Iraqi nuclear and WMD destruction adventure-episode are examined in tenth chapter of this book.

ENDNOTES

1. While nuclear war was generally regarded to be immoral if not expressly illegal, the use of any conventional weapon was allowed unless a weapon system was expressly prohibited by a convention or treaty. Missiles that can be fitted with nuclear warheads are alsc used to carry conventional explosives of high yield for short-range attack.
2. It is regarded by customary international law that war effects should be confined to combatants only. The modern 'total war' concept does not care for this legal limitation on the conduct of war by a sovereign State. Also, the laws of neutrality require that belligerent activities should not injure neutral nationals living in their own State or another neutral State. The nuclear fallout of a nuclear explosion that would settle on neutral territories cannot be justified by any doctrine of sovereign rights of belligerent States to use nuclear bombs.
3. General Assembly Resolution 46/36 of 6 December 1991.
4. General Assembly Resolution 51/37 of 10 December 1996 on "Prohibition of the Development and Manufacture of New Types of Weapons of Mass Destruction and New Systems of such Weapons":

   The General Assembly,

   Recalling its previous resolutions on the prohibition of the development and manufacture of new types of weapons of mass destruction and new systems of such weapons,

   Taking note of paragraph 77 of the Final Document of the Tenth Special Session of the General Assembly,

   Determined to prevent the emergence of new types of weapons of mass destruction that have characteristics comparable in destructive effect to those of weapons of mass destruction identified in the definition of weapons of mass destruction adopted by the United Nations in 1948,

Noting that the item entitled "New types of weapons of mass destruction and new systems of such weapons: radiological weapons" was considered in the Conference on Disarmament during its 1994, 1995 and 1996 sessions, ...

(1) Reaffirms that effective measures should be taken to prevent the emergence of new types of weapons of mass destruction;

(2) ...

(3) Calls upon all States, immediately following any recommendations of the Conference on Disarmament, to give favourable consideration to those recommendations;

(4) Requests the Secretary-General to transmit to the Conference on Disarmament all documents relating to the consideration of this item by the General Assembly at its fifty-first session.

5. PTI report of the briefing from Washington, *The Times of India, Lucknow Ed.*, September 2005.
6. GA Resolution 46/36 of 6 December 1991.
7. Article 1 (b): of the Treaty.
8. China, France, India and United States of America have not signed or ratified this Treaty and so it is yet to come into existence. India regards this Treaty as based on inequality and is favorable to the existing nuclear powers. India is not yet recognized as a nuclear power, though it has legally developed nuclear technology by its own resources and researches without violating 1963 Test Ban Treaty, of which it is a member and the NPT of 1967, of which it is not a member.
9. The member States of this agreement are: Belgium, Canada, Czechoslovakia, France, Federal Republic of Germany, Holland, Italy, Japan, the Netherlands, Poland, Sweden, Switzerland, United Kingdom, the USA and the USSR.
10. Indirectly it means that nuclear exports to those States which are not members of Statute of IAEA, like India, are prohibited under the agreement. While India has developed nuclear reactors and nuclear weapons since 1970s on its own resources and researches, Pakistan relied on clandestine purchases of nuclear materials, etc., from nuclear black-market run by NPT member European States.
11. Pakistan, India and North Korea are non-nuclear States under NPT.
12. General Assembly Resolution 47/39 of 30 November 1992: Convention on the Prohibition of the Development, Production, Stockpiling and Use of Chemical Weapons and on Their Destruction, 30 November 1992:

The General Assembly,

Recalling the long-standing determination of the international community to achieve the effective prohibition of the development, production, stockpiling and use of chemical weapons, and their destruction, as well as the continuing support for measures to uphold the authority of the Protocol for the Prohibition of the Use in War of Asphyxiating, Poisonous or Other Gases, and of Bacteriological Methods of Warfare, signed at Geneva on 17 June 1925, as expressed by consensus in many previous resolutions,

Recalling in particular its resolution 46/35 C of 6 December 1991, in which the assembly strongly urged the Conference on Disarmament, as a matter of the highest priority, to resolve outstanding issues so as to achieve a final agreement on a convention on the prohibition of the development, production, stockpiling and use of chemical weapons and on their destruction during its 1992 session,

Bearing in mind the Final Declaration of the Conference of States Parties to the 1925 Geneva Protocol and Other Interested States, held in Paris from 7 to 11 January 1989, in which participating States stressed their determination to prevent any recourse to chemical weapons by completely eliminating them,

Determined to make progress towards general and complete disarmament under strict and effective international control, including the prohibition and elimination of all types of weapons of mass destruction,

Convinced, therefore, of the urgent necessity of a total ban on chemical weapons, so as to abolish an entire category of weapons of mass destruction and thus to eliminate the risk to mankind of renewed use of these inhumane weapons,

Welcoming the draft Convention on the Prohibition of the Development, Production, Stockpiling and Use of Chemical Weapons and on Their Destruction, adopted by the Conference on Disarmament and contained in its report, the result of many years of intensive negotiations, which constitutes an historic achievement in the field of arms control and disarmament,

Also convinced that the convention, particularly as adherence to it approaches universality, will contribute to the maintenance of international peace and improve the security of all States and that it therefore merits the strong support of the entire international community,

Further convinced that the implementation of the convention should promote expanded international trade, technological development and economic cooperation in the chemical sector, in order to enhance the economic and technological development of all States Parties,

Determined to ensure the efficient and cost-effective implementation of the convention,

Recalling the support for the prohibition of chemical weapons expressed in the declaration by representatives of the world's chemical industry at the Government-Industry Conference against Chemical Weapons, held at Canberra from 18 to 22 September 1989,

Bearing in mind the relevant references to the convention in the final documents of the Tenth Conference of Heads of State or Government of Non-Aligned Countries, held at Jakarta from 1 to 6 September 1992,

Welcoming the invitation of the President of the French Republic to participate in a ceremony to sign the convention in Paris on 13 January 1993,

(1) Commends the Convention on the Prohibition of the Development, Production, Stockpiling and Use of Chemical Weapons and on Their Destruction, as contained in the report of the Conference on Disarmament;

....

13. General Assembly Resolution 2826 (XXVI), dated: 16 December 1971.

14. Amended Protocol on Prohibitions or Restrictions on the Use of Mines, Booby-Traps and Other Devices (Amended Protocol II), Annexed to the 'Convention on Prohibitions or Restrictions on the Use of Certain Conventional Weapons which may be Deemed to be Excessively Injurious or to have Indiscriminate Effects'.

Article I—Scope of application

(1) This protocol relates to the use on land of the mines, booby-traps and other devices, defined herein, including mines laid to interdict beaches, waterway crossings or river crossings, but does not apply to the use of anti-ship mines at sea or in inland waterways.

(2) This protocol shall apply, in addition to situations referred to in Article I of this convention, to situations referred to in Article 3 common to the Geneva Conventions of 12 August 1949. This protocol shall not apply to situations of internal disturbances and tensions, such as riots, isolated and sporadic acts of violence and other acts of a similar nature, as not being armed conflicts.

(3) In case of armed conflicts not of an international character occurring in the territory of one of the High Contracting Parties, each party to the conflict shall be bound to apply the prohibitions and restrictions of this protocol.

(4) Nothing in this protocol shall be invoked for the purpose of affecting the sovereignty of a State or the responsibility of the Government, by all legitimate means, to maintain or re-establish law and order in the State or to defend the national unity and territorial integrity of the State.

(5) Nothing in this protocol shall be invoked as a justification for intervening, directly or indirectly, for any reason whatever, in the armed conflict or in the internal or external affairs of the High Contracting Party in the territory of which that conflict occurs.

(6) The application of the provisions of this protocol to parties to a conflict, which are not High Contracting Parties that have accepted this protocol, shall not change their legal status or the legal status of a disputed territory, either explicitly or implicitly.

Article 2—Definitions

For the purpose of this protocol:

(1) 'Mine' means munitions placed under, on or near the ground or other surface area and designed to be exploded by the presence, proximity or contact of a person or vehicle.

(2) 'Remotely-delivered mine' means a mine not directly emplaced but delivered by artillery, missile, rocket, mortar, or similar means, or dropped from an aircraft. Mines delivered from a land-based system from less than 500 metres are not considered to be remotely delivered, provided that they are used in accordance with Article 5 and other relevant Articles of this protocol.

(3) 'Anti-personnel mine' means a mine primarily designed to be exploded by the presence, proximity or contact of a person and that will incapacitate, injure or kill one or more persons.

(4) 'Booby-trap' means any device or material which is designed, constructed or adapted to kill or injure, and which functions unexpectedly when a person disturbs or approaches an apparently harmless object or performs an apparently safe act.

(5) 'Other devices' means manually-emplaced munitions and devices, including improvised explosive devices designed to kill, injure or damage and which are actuated manually, by remote control or automatically after a lapse of time.

15. See, U.N. Gupta, *The Human Rights: Conventions and Indian Law,* Chapter IX–"Humanized War and Warfare". Paragraph 9.13.
16. A cluster bomb is a 1,000 pound canister which, on explosion, fragments into 200 or more Bomb Live Units (BLU) of the size of a drink can. When the bomb explodes each BLU sends flying shrapnel in all directions at speeds which can pierce armor. It is used to destroy armored vehicles, kill people with shrapnel fragments and ignite fires in military targets such as ammunition dumps or oil depots. The BLU is effective upto a distance more than 100 meters in all directions from the place of detonation.
17. USA replaced U-2 by another more powerful SR-71 spy plane, now their work is done by artificial satellites.
18. GA Resolution 55/33 A of 20 November 2000.
19. GA Resolution, 57/229 (2002).
20. General Assembly has inconclusively but encouragingly discussed the matter every year, e.g., vide, GA resolution 58/37 (2003), 57/229 (2002), 56/24B (2001).
21. GA Resolution 55/33 A of 20 November 2000.
22. General Assembly Plenary-1b-Press Release GA/9829 69th Meeting (PM) 20 November 2000.
23. The UN Secretary-General in a Statement of 25 November 2002, made a strong recommendation for development of an International Code of Conduct against Ballistic Missiles Proliferation.
24. "Out there in Iraq: $ 200b, 2000 dead soldiers" Report on protests of "United For Peace and Justice" (UFPJ) from Washington: by Chidanand Rajghatta/TNN, *The Times of India, Lucknow Ed.,* 22 October 2005.

4

Prevention of Proliferation of Nuclear Weapons

The post Second World War period had begun with the efforts in background for prevention of world wars of future under a collective security system to be provided by the United Nations Organization. This was a joint diplomatic move of the USA, UK and USSR against the defeated Axis powers of Second World War. This move was also against repetition of situations that might lead to another similar war. Statesmen and diplomats of the time recognized that power is a heady phenomenon that corrupts balanced judgment and that possession of nuclear weapons might lead States to indulge in a war more for vengeance and less for its substance or worth. Soon or rather as concluding chapter of World War the USSR, the second big power after the USA, had showed its expansionist designs in favour of communist governments to be installed worldwide. At the same time USA mesmerized by being the singular nuclear power[1] it internally debated during 1945 to late 1950s as to what would be the right time to make pre-emptive nuclear attack on USSR to break it. It may be mentioned that till 1960s USSR did not have a countrywide radar system, while USA did not have long-range missiles to strike deep into USSR. The US heavy bombers from air bases in France, Italy, Greece, Turkey, Iran, Afghanistan, Pakistan, South Korea or Japan under various alliances, encircling USSR could conveniently reach its industrial and strategic areas. Accordingly, the US 'brink of war' diplomacy of the time had concentrated on making military alliances or pacts with all the peripheral States around USSR. Correspondingly, USSR worked hard to become a nuclear power, that it eventually became in 1949, to create or align with buffer States along its borders, like Afghanistan, China, etc., which were either neutral, non-aligned or Marxist. The USSR was also moved to develop long-range intercontinental missiles as additional alternative to heavy bombers that were capable of carrying nuclear warheads to cover Europe and the USA. In spite of conclusion of Second World War, there was widespread race for superior armaments and for forming military alliances, like NATO, SEATO or Warsaw Pact. A third World War that was to be a nuclear war was always on cards during 1950s.

TREATY ON THE NON-PROLIFERATION OF NUCLEAR WEAPONS (NPT)

Making of NPT

The whole situation of confrontation between erstwhile allied superpowers soon led to creation of a military balance between US endeavors against expansionist USSR and counter measures adopted by USSR. After the communist China became a nuclear power in 1964, there was a change in world diplomacy moves and the West as well as USSR found it to be in their interest[2] to prevent other States from becoming nuclear powers, since that would change the concept of superpowers as well and increase the chances of small or local wars escalating into nuclear world wars. Henceforth, USA, UK, and USSR, which were known as Big Three of the Second World War, with the support of UN, became interested in formulation of an international agreement on non-proliferation of nuclear weaponry. These jointly produced the Treaty on Non-Proliferation of Nuclear Weapons (NPT).[3] The NPT was signed on 1 July 1968 and it entered into force in 1970. The UN General Assembly by a resolution recommended it on 12 June 1969 by 98 votes in favour 5 against and 21 abstentions. France, the fourth nuclear power, did not sponsor the Treaty and abstained from voting but joined NPT later only in 1992. India also had abstained from voting.[4] Israel made reservations regarding signing of the treaty. Communist China, the fifth nuclear power, was not a member of UNO in 1968, it replaced Chiang Kai-Shek Government in the UN General Assembly on 15 November 1971 and in Security Council on 23 November

1971 but it joined the Non-Proliferation Treaty in 1992. The NPT was second of the Treaty on disarmament with USA, UK and USSR being the original parties. The first had been the partial Nuclear Test Ban Treaty of 1963, which professed to be more of humanitarian or environment protection nature by way of saving humanity, flora and fauna from evil effects of nuclear fallout after nuclear test in air, ocean or on ground; it did not prohibit underground nuclear tests. At the same time this argument was an act of diplomacy, since it made development of nuclear weapons by other States difficult because nuclear tests in air are deemed to be necessary in the development of accuracy in nuclear explosion technology.

NPT against Wars

The framers of NPT took serious note of the catastrophic 'devastation that would be visited upon all mankind by a nuclear war' and worked on the eventuality that 'the proliferation of nuclear weapons would seriously enhance the danger of nuclear war'. The NPT restated the resolve of the United Nations General Assembly on the prevention of wider dissemination of nuclear weapons through the application of International Atomic Energy Agency 'safeguards' on peaceful nuclear activities. At the same time while pursuing the diplomacy of preventing proliferation of nuclear weaponry to non-nuclear States, the Treaty affirmed in principle that the benefits of peaceful applications of nuclear technology, 'should be available for peaceful purposes to all Parties to the Treaty, whether nuclear-weapon[5] or non-nuclear-weapon States'. Of course, the acquisition of 'peaceful applications of nuclear technology' was to be commercial, that is, according to the purchasing capacity of individual non-nuclear State. Leaving aside non-parties, all parties to the Treaty on Non-Proliferation, including non-nuclear States, are in their interest entitled to indigenously further develop the applications of atomic energy for peaceful purposes.

Nuclear Arms Race

The NPT as a necessary corollary emphasized its intention to achieve at the earliest possible date the cessation of the 'nuclear arms race' and 'to undertake effective measures in the direction of nuclear disarmament' by the nuclear weapon States. At the same time the 'nuclear arms race' between nuclear States is not as such directly prohibited. The resolves and the obligations under the NPT, relating to the sale, acquisition or transfer of nuclear weapons technology also do not apply to non-parties, that is, the States that do not join the NPT. The signatories to the NPT have to join it by ratification process in order to become its full members. The parties to NPT can withdraw from membership at will.

NPT for Success of Disarmament

The NPT has sponsored the pursuit of disarmament, that is, the States should destroy their existing stock of harmful or banned weapons, by becoming part of the history of disarmament. Looking back, the League of Nations had failures on this score and it could not go beyond pious resolves. Disarmament under the Charter of UNO was by 1950s reduced to the real-politics of cold war era led by the USA and USSR: One asking for international law ban of nuclear weapons first followed by destruction of nuclear arsenals possessed or developed by States and the other insisting on destruction of existing weapons as the starting point. Ultimately in 1960s disarmament effort under the patronage of UNO was limited to bilateral negotiations and diplomacy between the two great rivals through the imperfect Strategic Arms Limitations Treaty (SALT). Following the end of cold war on the demise of the USSR in 1991, disarmament became a backbench matter of international politics and diplomacy. However, it is observed that the USA is in the new century unilaterally pursuing disarmament against the self-defined and so-called 'axis of evil' States. Now, the realities of the international community in the matter of disarmament in the first decade of twenty-first century are different. These attitudes have been aptly described in the commentary[6] entitled, "Non-Proliferation and Disarmament Go Hand in Hand" made and signed in 2004 by Foreign Ministers of seven States, namely, Brazil, Egypt, Ireland, Mexico, New Zealand, South Africa and Sweden, who flayed the 'nuclear powers for failing to heed international disarmament and non-proliferation agreements'. It is observed:[7]

> "The NPT cannot be complied with a *la carte*" ... "In 2000, the nuclear powers made an unequivocal undertaking to eliminate their nuclear arsenals" but "since then, however, very little progress has been made" ... "Instead of destroying their nuclear warheads, the United States and Russia store them, ... Instead of working toward the entry into force of nuclear test-ban treaty (CTBT), the United States, which was the first country to sign the treaty, has withdrawn its support, and China delays its ratification process year after year."
>
> "Some even entertain the notion that nuclear weapons may be used pre-emptively against non-nuclear weapon States". ... It (the Commentary) urged all nations to "comply with their commitments under the NPT" and that the NPT be made universal.[8]

Objectives of NPT

The Treaty on Non-Proliferation of Nuclear Weapons (NPT) is a singular multinational treaty, the objectives of which in the interest of mankind are (1) to prevent the proliferation of nuclear weapons and the related technology, (2) to promote cooperation in the peaceful uses of nuclear energy, and (3) to provide steps for achievement of the goal of nuclear disarmament alongwith general and complete disarmament. The Treaty contains a binding commitment to the goal of disarmament on the part of nuclear weapon States who are also permanent members of the UN Security Council towards disarmament. The Treaty reflects the diplomatic anarchy and instability in international politics developed and existing in the world in the cold war era of the then last ten years. The Cuban confrontation of 1962 between USA of President Kennedy and USSR of Khrushchev had invited a nuclear war, which Khrushchev had averted by withdrawal from Cuba. Again, confronted with a nuclear war with USA if communist China proceeded with attack on Formosa (Taiwan) for annexation, China had in the first instance postponed such action. Instead China had with the help of USSR and by spying success tested its first nuclear bomb in 1964 and had itself become a nuclear power capable of attacking South Korea or Japan if not USA. The Fifth Review Conference of the Parties extended for indefinite period the Treaty on Non-Proliferation of Nuclear Weapons (NPT) on 11 May 1995. A total of 188 States, including the five nuclear-weapon States, became parties to the Treaty by 2002.[9]

In order to achieve its goal of non-proliferation and for mutual confidence-building measure between States Parties, the Treaty has established a safeguards system, that is, the International Atomic Energy Agency (IAEA) which is a watchdog organization with a Board of Governors in attendance. The IAEA has powers to define and enforce 'Safeguards' and to verify compliance with the Treaty through inspections conducted by it of nuclear facilities of the parties. The NPT promotes cooperation in the field of peaceful nuclear technology, particularly the nuclear power generation and equal access to this technology for all States Parties, while it enforces safeguards to prevent the diversion of fissile material needed for the civil use reactors to military weapon systems. The NPT recognizes the human catastrophe that follows from a nuclear war and links itself to the determination to counter this by falling in unison with the concern expressed by the parties to the 1963 Treaty banning nuclear weapons tests in the atmosphere, in outer space and under water. The NPT reminds the parties that in accordance with the Charter of the United Nations, States are to refrain in their international relations from the threat or use of force against the territorial integrity or political independence of any State, or in any other manner inconsistent with the Purposes of the United Nations, and that the establishment and maintenance of international peace and security are paramount. As a special case, India, which has felt threatened by nuclear powers, China and Pakistan, holds the view that UN should provide automatic security, a nuclear umbrella, to its non-nuclear members against aggression by nuclear powers if the NPT is to be meaningful and non-discriminatory. It is notable with regret and concern that some nuclear powers have asserted their option to use their nuclear weapons in a war whether defensive or aggressive, and are not agreeable to fight a war limited to conventional weapons only while keeping nuclear weapons safe or resting in their armory. For example, the USA wages wars with the option to use nuclear weapons open except when pitted against another nuclear power. In India and Pakistan acrimony while India has unilaterally made a declaration of 'no first use' of nuclear weapons, Pakistan has declared that it will use nuclear weapons on India in any war for whatever reasons it takes place. When a State does not accept the hegemony of nuclear States Parties to the Treaty or is threatened by a nuclear State Party, the vice of diplomatic incongruity is inherent in the provisions of NPT in absence of internationally operated nuclear umbrella. Also, the NPT reflects the nuclear capabilities if States in and around 1967. It does not accommodate or fails to take cognizance of the changes in international polity and power balance structure of the present century, particularly when the proposed CTBT has gone into oblivion.

THE IMPLICATIONS OF NPT

NPT on Acquisition of Nuclear Technology

The Treaty on Non-Proliferation of Nuclear Weapons (NPT) is highly diplomatic in action. It basically is one-sided, since it prevents acquisition of such nuclear technology by its non-nuclear States Parties, which may be used for war purposes. There is no doubt that proliferation of nuclear weaponry is dangerous to the future of mankind. The proliferation of nuclear weapons technology places the future of mankind at stake at all times and at any place on the globe. Around 1968 only USA, UK and USSR were full-fledged nuclear powers and these were the original members of the Treaty. China and France were nuclear States but lacked full technology for full and effective use of nuclear weapons. Moreover, France did not have enemies worth using nuclear weapons, and communist government of China was not representing China of UNO and had in USA its arch-enemy which was far superior nuclear power. After communist China[10] had become a nuclear power in 1964, USSR had ceased to have further doctrinaire interest in increase in the number of nuclear weapon States and had no hesitation in sponsoring NPT that fully protected its future interest as an existing nuclear powers under the NPT; significantly 1970 is the cut-off year for acquisition of the status of nuclear State Party of this NPT.

Implementation of Objectives

The approaches of the NPT for achievements of its purposes in this direction are threefold: (1) Obligation on nuclear States not to transfer nuclear technology to non-nuclear States. (2) Obligations on non-nuclear States not to acquire or develop nuclear technology that may evolve nuclear weapons. (3) Establishment of a watchdog, the International Atomic Energy Agency (IAEA), to keep the activities of non-nuclear States under observation and control with a system of safeguards.

NPT: Obligation of Nuclear States Parties

The Treaty made a distinction between nuclear States Parties and *de facto* nuclear States possessing nuclear technology and nuclear weapons by 1970. The *de facto* nuclear States are either covered under the term 'non-nuclear States Parties' or have not become Parties to the Treaty, as are the cases with India and Pakistan. Article 1 of the Treaty defines both the obligations and freedoms of nuclear States Parties.[11] As of 2004 there are only five nuclear States Parties, viz., United Kingdom (27 November 1968), United States (5 March 1970), Russian Federation (5 March 1970), China (9 March 1992) and France (2 August 1992). India, North Korea and Pakistan, probably Israel also, are *de facto* nuclear States. The obligations cover all kinds of States that is to 'any recipient whatsoever' and not only to the non-nuclear States Parties under the Treaty. Obligations are 'not to transfer' their nuclear technology, skills, nuclear weapons, etc. and not to 'assist, encourage, or induce any non-nuclear-weapon State' to 'acquire nuclear weapons or other nuclear explosive devices, or control over such weapons or explosive devices'. This has meant that India cannot purchase or barter nuclear technology, equipments or parts from the members of NPT. The nuclear reactors for power generation are not covered by this provision but some processes involving production of nuclear fuel for nuclear reactors have generated international debate, since these processes are common with manufacture of nuclear weapon. As for freedoms of nuclear States Parties, the provision does not create any corresponding obligation for them to freeze their nuclear programmes. The nuclear States Parties, USA, Russia, China, have been regularly making innovations in their nuclear weaponry, making these more and more sophisticated, ferocious and making the stockpile of nuclear weapons bigger and larger. It is generally accepted that nuclear States Parties proliferate directly or indirectly their nuclear technology to other States selectively and secretly; 'sting operations' have been many that involved secret transactions and are discussed elsewhere. It may be remembered that France is understood to have bargained and supplied nuclear technology to Israel, and China to Pakistan but this took place before France and China became nuclear States Parties of the NPT.

Obligations of Non-Nuclear States Parties

The NPT is devoted and committed to prevent proliferation of nuclear arms and related technology by gift, exchange, sale or otherwise from nuclear States Parties to non-nuclear States Parties.[12] To this is added the obligations to accept the safeguards to that end as laid own by the treaty. Prohibition is indirectly worded in that a non-nuclear State Party 'undertakes not to receive the transfer from any transferor whatsoever' the prohibited transfers. Not to receive includes not acquiring, but it does not include indigenous research and development by a non-nuclear State Party that is not assisted by other nuclear technology possessing States. The researches by non-nuclear States Parties must stop at the point at which the process for manufacturing of nuclear weapon starts. Japan is understood to be a State of this category. As for non-members of NPT, from 1974 to 1995 India had capability to manufacture nuclear bombs but had not manufactured these. Pakistan, also a non-member, was from early 1980s trading nuclear weapon technology but probably by 1990 it had started making nuclear weapons and was desperately searching for missile system or acquiring US F-16 warplanes[13] for dropping these on Indian targets. Ultimately, Pakistan under a barter agreement successfully obtained sophisticated missile system from North Korea in exchange for nuclear bomb technology. Israel, India and Pakistan have not become members of NPT.

Iran and NPT

Again the prohibitions of Article II apply to 'nuclear weapons or other nuclear explosive devices'. These do not apply to acquiring of nuclear reactors for generation of electricity and the manufacture of fuel for such reactors by enrichment of uranium. But, the problem is that this is a process common to manufacture of Uranium–235 for nuclear bomb also. In the matter[14] of Iran of 2004 while USA insisted that the uranium enrichment plant attached to its nuclear research facility was for military purposes banned by NPT of which Iran was a non-nuclear State Party, Iran insisted that it had no intention or plans to manufacture nuclear weapons and the plant was for legitimate peaceful purposes only, that is, production of energy for civil use. The USA supplemented the charge with the argument that the plant was situated close to a military airfield, which Iran regarded to be an irrelevant fact. Iran rejected European demands in mid-2004 to abandon its sensitive nuclear activities involving working on, mastering or developing of nuclear fuel cycle that can be used to make a nuclear bomb while reiterating its readiness to provide assurances that its nuclear ambitions are peaceful.[15] This stand-off continues and President Bush has in January 2005, clarified that if Iran "continues to stonewall the international community about its nuclear weapon programme" then he will "never take any option off the table". This is taken to mean that US strikes against Iran are not ruled out.[16] Iran did not react to this in a cowed down manner. Further, under Article III (2) each State Party to the Treaty, including non-nuclear State Party, undertakes not to provide: (a) source or special fissionable material, or (b) equipment or material especially designed or prepared for the processing, use or production of special fissionable material, to any 'non-nuclear-weapon State' under NPT even for peaceful purposes, unless the source or special fissionable material is made subject to the safeguards required by Articles III and IV of the NP Treaty.

Sanction for NPT

The International Atomic Energy Agency has come out to be important instrument in selective diplomatic enforcement of the provisions of NPT on non-nuclear States Parties, of course, when it is viewed from Indian standpoint. The IAEA is nuclear watchdog or inspectorate of the NPT, functions under its Statute alongwith the powers and duties entrusted to it by the NPT. The non-nuclear State Party members of NPT are obliged by Article III (1) of the Treaty to accept 'safeguards', and those are for the IAEA to set forth. For this, an agreement is to be negotiated and concluded by non-nuclear States Parties with the International Atomic Energy Agency in accordance with the Statute of the International Atomic Energy Agency and the Agency's safeguards system with reference to the existing nuclear facilities in their respective territories.[17] Currently, the IAEA inspects nuclear and related facilities under safeguards agreements with more than 140 non-nuclear State Party States. The objective of the safeguards agreements being that there is no diversion of nuclear energy by non-nuclear State Party from its peaceful uses to nuclear weapons or other nuclear explosive devices. The safeguards system provided by the IAEA under Article III is to apply with respect to special fissionable material whether it is being produced, processed or used, in all peaceful nuclear activities of the State, within any of its principal nuclear facility or outside any such facility. The installation or the use of such materials or nuclear facilities may be within the territory of such State, a territory under its jurisdiction, belligerent occupation or under its control anywhere. That is to say, artificial islands, territories under lease, etc. The safeguards are also applied on all sources of special fissionable material, such as uranium ore, located as above. However, the safeguards required by Article III of the NPT are to be implemented in a manner designed to comply also with Article IV of this Treaty, that is, to avoid hampering of the economic or technological development of the parties or international cooperation in the field of peaceful nuclear activities, including the international exchanges of nuclear material and equipment for peaceful purposes in accordance with the provisions of Article III and the principles of safeguards relating to the processing, use or production of nuclear material that are set forth in the Preamble of the Non-Proliferation Treaty.

Limitations on NPT Safeguard System

Article IV of NPT does not provide plenary or sovereign powers to IAEA in defining and imposing 'safeguards' on non-nuclear States Parties but these are made subject to some natural attributes of all sovereign States. These extend to:

(1) The inalienable right of all the Parties to the Treaty to develop research, production and use of nuclear energy for peaceful purposes without discrimination and in conformity with Articles I and II of this Treaty;

(2) The right of States to mutually cooperate, facilitate, participate and exchange equipment, materials and scientific and technological information, for the peaceful development, applications and uses of nuclear energy, with due considerations of the needs of the developing areas of the world, which contain most of the non-nuclear States Parties.

However, as discussed elsewhere, Articles III and IV of NPT while applied in cases of North Korea and Iran in 2002-2004 could not be harmonized and this has rather led to diplomatic frustration of nuclear States Parties.

India and NPT

India, a *de facto* nuclear state has felt that the NPT is 'flawed very seriously' and it does not really aim to bring about non-proliferation of nuclear technology or curtailing the sophistication of such weapons. At the third NPT Conference, 15 years after the coming into force of the Treaty, India[18] made the following points:

"(1) The Treaty did not ensure the non-proliferation of nuclear weapons but only stopped the dissemination of weapons to non-nuclear weapon States without imposing any curbs on the continued manufacture, stockpiling and sophistication of nuclear weapons by the existing nuclear weapon States.

(2) The Treaty did not do away with the special status of superiority conferred on those powers, which possessed nuclear weapons.

(3) The Treaty did not provide for a balance of obligations and responsibilities between nuclear weapon States and non-nuclear weapon States. While all the obligations were imposed on non-nuclear weapon States, the nuclear weapon States had not accepted any.

(4) The Treaty did not constitute a step by step approach towards nuclear disarmament.

(5) The Treaty did not prohibit one nuclear weapon State from assisting another nuclear weapon State by providing technical aid.

(6) ....

(7) Article VI of the Treaty did not create a judicial obligation in regard to the cessation of the nuclear arms race at an early date.

(8) The Treaty imparted a false sense of security to the world.

(9) It was discriminatory in regard to peaceful benefits of nuclear explosions.

(10) It was discriminatory in regard to the safeguards and controls, which were all imposed on the non-nuclear weapon States while none whatsoever, were imposed on the nuclear weapon States.

(11) The security assurances to non-nuclear weapon States could not be a *quid pro quo* for the acceptance of the Treaty. This must be obligatory for the nuclear weapon States."

Making official clarification of Indian nuclear policy, President of India, A.P.J. Abdul Kalam, told the senior members of Duma, the Russian Parliament that India would never be a proliferator of weapons of mass destruction. "When we are surrounded by nuclear armed counties, we did not have any other alternative but to become a nuclear weapon State" ourselves.[19]

Peaceful Applications of Nuclear Explosions, Article V

While nuclear explosions for war and weapon purposes are preferred, rights of nuclear weapon States Parties, potential benefits from any 'peaceful applications of nuclear explosions' are to be made available to non-nuclear-weapon State Party to the Treaty also on a non-discriminatory basis on payment of lowest possible charges to nuclear parties for covering the cost of devices used for the nuclear explosions. The parties can have joint agreements to this effect. The non-nuclear-weapon State Party to the Treaty may also obtain such benefits pursuant to bilateral agreements if they so desire. All these are, however, to take place under appropriate international observation and through appropriate international procedures but by bringing in the IAEA.

Obligations for Nuclear Weapon States

Article VI of the NPT provides that each of the parties to the Treaty undertakes to pursue negotiations in good faith on effective measures relating to 'cessation of the nuclear arms race' at an early date and to 'nuclear disarmament', and on a 'treaty on general and complete disarmament' under strict and effective international control. The obligation thus is limited to making of negotiations only. In practice, it is limited to the danger perception of war between two or more nuclear powers, viz. the USA and USSR following the Cuba standoff of 1961 till late 1990s. The much-prolonged negotiations between these two superpowers failed at the take-off stage. Since 2001 USA and North Korea have also negotiated nuclear restraint in view of US pre-emptive nuclear strike on States of the 'axis of evil' and the counter declaration of North Korea to accurately drop at least six nuclear bombs on USA; North Korea already has had mastery over long-range missile technology. Again, the NPT also provides for nuclear weapons free zones on regional basis comprising of the territories of the States forming the region.[20] However, the nuclear States Parties have reservations favourable to them even here and therefore this has become a meaningless proposition. At the most this involves commitment only on the part of some States not to go for indigenous research for producing nuclear weapons, even in so far as it might be valid or legal within the framework of NPT.

Assessment of NPT

The NPT has attempted to delay or to dissuade the States from developing or acquiring nuclear weapons, since it does not have a perennial or permanent nature and the character of a self-executing law. Joining and withdrawal from the NPT are easy and unrestricted. Article IX provides: "1. This Treaty shall be open to all States for signature. Any State which does not sign the Treaty before its entry into force in accordance with paragraph 3 of this Article may accede to it at any time." At the same time Article X significantly lays down: "1. Each Party shall, in exercising its national sovereignty, have the right to withdraw from the Treaty if it decides that extraordinary events, related to the subject matter of this Treaty, have jeopardized the supreme interests of its country. It shall give notice of such withdrawal to all other Parties to the Treaty and to the United Nations Security Council three months in advance. Such notice shall include a statement of the extraordinary events it regards as having jeopardized its supreme interests." The requirement of three months' advance notice is conclusive for withdrawal. North Korea has exercised the right of withdrawal once, the reason being a threatened pre-emptive nuclear attack by USA in 2002 and Iran had threatened to do so in 2004. There is no standing forum, council or secretariat to work out the NPT. There do take place quinquennial Conferences of the members of NPT to review where the NPT stands but with growing disillusionment on disarmament part of it. At other times, the Treaty States Parties accuse others or defend themselves through international media, State statements or at conferences for compliance or non-compliances of NPT. In this process the IAEA may get a jurisdiction as fact-finding instrumentality under NPT when agreed. The errant situation arising from non-compliance of the NPT may be referred to or be taken up by an international conference impromptu or can be called to make a review of the errant problem. Since, there is no pre-laid procedure for convening such conferences, these may also take place under a resolution of UN General Assembly.

THE INTERNATIONAL ATOMIC ENERGY AGENCY (IAEA)

In 1950s the international community was moved to establish of the IAEA by the desire to work upon, improve and achieve the idea of disarmament for a lasting peace among nations. Pending this achievement, need was felt for restrictively regulating the war use and a wild, uncontrolled proliferation of destructive nuclear technology and to advise the UN on the fine points. The best status for IAEA came when after the conclusion of the Non Proliferation Treaty the Agency (IAEA) was made its integral standing body. The IAEA is not a deliberative forum for the NPT, but as already observed, it functions as the watchdog for the NPT.[21] In the field of international diplomacy, it does not restrict the freedom of action of the nuclear States Parties of the NPT but prevents other parties from developing nuclear weapon technology. In its earlier development history, the Statute of the International Atomic Energy Agency was approved and adopted on 23 October 1956, by a special International Conference on the Statute. This International Conference was held under the patronage of the United Nations[22] at its Headquarters. The Statute[23] of the International Atomic Energy Agency was set into operation by a Preparatory Commission[24] set up by the said International Conference of IAEA. The Statute came into force on 29 July 1957, upon the fulfillment of the relevant provisions of paragraph E of its Article XXI. Till 2004, more than 140 States have become parties to it and these form its General Conference. The Statute of the International Atomic Energy Agency has been amended three times, by application of the procedure laid down in paragraphs A and C of Article XVIII. On 31 January 1963 some amendments to the first sentence of the then paragraph A.3 of Article VI dealing with the Board of Governors came into force. The Statute was further amended on 1 June 1973 by a number of amendments made to paragraphs A to D of the same Article VI and on 28 December 1989 an amendment in the paragraph A.l came into force.[25] The General Conference made amendment to Article VI of the Statute on 1 October 1999.[26] All these amendments have been incorporated in the text of the Statute and which have superseded all the earlier editions of the Statute of IAEA.

IAEA and NPT

The Treaty on Non-Proliferation of Nuclear Weapons (NPT) has established a standing safeguards system under the responsibility of the IAEA in order to further the goal of non-proliferation and also as a confidence-building measure between its States Parties in the matters related both to NPT and general nuclear disarmament.[27] Safeguards are used to verify compliance by non-nuclear States Parties with the Treaty through inspections conducted by the IAEA. The IAEA and the NPT promote foster and ensure among its members mutual cooperation in the field of peaceful nuclear technology and equal access to this technology for all States Parties, while the safeguards enforced by IAEA prevent the diversion of special fissile material[28] for weapons use, and thus there is a lot of common ground between these two. The Statute of International Atomic Energy Agency expresses full support for research, development and other efforts by the States to further the civil or peaceful application of nuclear technology and to effect the flow of nuclear resource and of special fissionable materials within the framework of its safeguards system. It safeguards the use of instruments and techniques required for application at various strategic stages in making peaceful use of atomic energy. Erstwhile this was a sovereign right that now is a permitted right for the NPT States Parties only; in other words, the proliferation of nuclear technology, science and research for peaceful purposes cannot be subject of international diplomacy or blackmail.

Objectives and Functions of IAEA

The Agency is to seek the acceleration and enlargement of the contribution of 'atomic energy' to peace, health and prosperity throughout the world. It is also to ensure under its capacity and capability that assistance provided by it or at its request or under its supervision or control to a State is not used in such a way as to further any 'military purpose'. For example, in the matter of Iran (2004) while Iran has claimed that its nuclear enrichment programmes are intended only to produce electricity and the facility would not be used to make highly enriched fuel for bombs, the USA, France, Britain and Germany have not believed the assertions of Iran and have called upon the IAEA to take steps to halt and freeze the uranium enrichment programme of Iran.[29]

To this end, Article III of its Statute grants legislative and guidlines making functions to the Agency when it authorizes the Agency:

(a) That it can make provisions for supply and availability of materials, services, equipment, and facilities required to meet the needs of States for research on and development and practical application of atomic energy for peaceful purposes, including the production of electric power with due consideration for the needs of the underdeveloped areas of the world.

(b) That it can establish and administer a system of safeguards designed to ensure that special fissionable and other radioactive[30] materials, services, equipment, facilities, and information that are made available by the Agency or at its request or under its supervision or control are 'not used in such a way as to further any military purpose'; and to apply such safeguards, at the request of the parties, to any bilateral or multilateral arrangement, or at the request of a State, to any of that State's activities in the field of atomic energy.

(c) To establish or adopt, in consultation and, where appropriate, in collaboration with the competent organs of the United Nations and with the specialized agencies concerned, the 'standards of safety for protection of health and minimization of danger to life and property' (including such standards for labour conditions).

(d) To ensure that special fissionable materials supplied by it or through it to the States shall be safeguarded against hazards of the weather, unauthorized removal or diversion, damage or destruction, including sabotage, and forcible seizure. When storing special fissionable materials in its possession, the Agency shall ensure that adequate safeguards are applied and the storage is not done at one place but is geographically distributed to avoid damage or destruction, including sabotage, and forcible seizure of the special fissionable materials.[31]

(e) To provide for the application of the safeguard standards.

(f) To verify as an authority that the States which have internationally committed themselves by agreements not to possess special fissionable radioactive materials or nuclear weapons,[32] concluded pursuant to the global Treaty on the Non-Proliferation of Nuclear Weapons (NPT) also, have adhered to their commitments.[33]

Decision-Making Process of IAEA

The decisions of IAEA are termed as decisions of the 'Agency' and are coordinated decisions of the General Conference, Board of Governors, expert committees and inspectors, each functioning under the Statute.

(1) *The General Conference*. It is composed of all members[34] of the Agency on the basis of equality. It has the authority particularly:

(a) To discuss any questions or any matters within the scope of this Statute or relating to the powers and functions of any organs provided for in this Statute, and may make recommendations to the membership of the Agency or to the Board of Governors or to both on any such questions or matters;

(b) To take decisions on any matter specifically referred to the General Conference for this purpose by the Board of Governors;

(c) To propose matters for consideration by the Board of Governors and on request from the Board report on any matter relating to the functions of the Agency;

(d) To approve reports to be submitted to the United Nations as required by the relationship agreement between the Agency and the United Nations, except reports referred to in paragraph C of Article XII, or return them to the Board with its recommendations;

(e) To approve any agreement or agreements between the Agency and the United Nations and other organizations as provided in Article XVI or return such agreements with its recommendations to the Board, for resubmission to the General Conference.

(2) *The Board of Governors.* It is composed of members of both nominated and elected nature fluctuating in number around 45 on the basis of the determining principle provided under Article VI of the Statute; presently in 2004 it has 35 members. Each member of the Board of Governors has one vote. Two-third of all members of the Board shall constitute a quorum.

(a) Decisions on the amount of the Agency's budget are to be made by a two-third majority of those present and voting, as provided in paragraph H of Article XIV.

(b) Decisions on other questions are to be made by a majority of those present and voting, except those additional questions or categories of questions which the Board of Governors by a two-third majority determines to be decided by a two-third majority. However, the Board of Governors of IAEA prefers to adopt all decisions unanimously by consensus rather than by a formal vote taken. The Board of Governors may establish such committees, as it deems advisable to deal with the issues before it. The Board may also appoint persons to represent it in its relations with other organizations.

IAEA - VERIFICATION IN NORTH KOREA, IRAN AND IRAQ

Under the resolutions of UN Security Council, the IAEA is the appointed agency for nuclear-related monitoring and verification in North Korea, Iran and Iraq.[35] The IAEA Department of Safeguards is the organizational hub for its safeguards-related work. In Iraq, activities are carried out through the Iraq Nuclear Verification Office (INVO) of IAEA. The IAEA maintains a close relationship with the UN Security Council, with periodic reports on verification of matters related to the contention of Iran that its nuclear programme is confined to production of electricity and contrary contention of USA and some European States that Iran is actually engaged in uranium enrichment activity for manufacturing nuclear weapons. The verification task of IAEA in the Democratic People's Republic of Korea (DPRK) is different. There the IAEA is the verification authority pursuant to a bilateral 'Framework Agreement' of 1994 between USA and DPRK. This agreement is now an international matter as it is endorsed by a resolution of UN Security Council.[36] In Iran, it has had fluctuating status, depending on the decisions of the government of Iran, referred to earlier in the chapter also. In India it might have a role if and when India-US Accord of 2006 materalises. This role is as yet not peremptory and is examined in other chapters.

ENDNOTES

1. USA and UK had initially developed atom bombs as joint venture and since 1945, UK has coordinated and accepted the US decisions and policies related to Cold War, use of nuclear weapons and the oil diplomacy in the Middle East.

2. After the death of Stalin, there were differences as to which of the two was better communist: while China continued to be fundamentalist or Stalinist, USSR had become moderate or revisionist with regard to new emerging States being created out of empires under the principle of self-determination. There were acrimonious boundary disputes also between the two States.
3. Communist government on the mainland of China replaced Formosa based *de jure* KMT Nationalist government as representative of China State in UNO later in 1971 and joined NPT in 1992.
4. India has not joined the Treaty to date on the ground that it is biased in favour of nuclear States and it does not provide for automatic security of all non-nuclear States in case of aggression by nuclear States.
5. NPT Nuclear-Weapon State Parties are: United Kingdom (27 November, 1968), United States (5 March 1970), the USSR and its successor Russian Federation (5 March 1970), China (9 March 1992) and France (2 August 1992).
6. Part of the proceedings of Sixth Review Conference of Treaty on Non-Proliferation held in 2005, at which non-nuclear State members had expressed their dissatisfaction over the no-progress status in disarmament matter by nuclear parties of NPT.
7. Published in International Herald Tribune: See "Seven Nations Flay Nuclear Powers". APP news from Paris in *The Times of India,* Lucknow. Ed., 23 Sept 2004.
8. This is a quote of the substance of the Commentary.
9. North Korea and Iran might or might not be Parties to the Treaty at a particular time of inquiry.
10. China had two governments till 1969: unrecognized communist government on mainland and the *de jure* KMT government functioning in Taiwan (Formosa). The communist government was recognized as *de jure* government by USA in 1969. Till 1971, the KMT government represented China in UNO, including its Security Council as permanent member.
11. Article I of NPT:

    "Each nuclear-weapon State Party to the Treaty undertakes not to transfer to any recipient whatsoever nuclear weapons or other nuclear explosive devices or control over such weapons or explosive devices directly, or indirectly; and not in any way to assist, encourage, or induce any non-nuclear-weapon State to manufacture or otherwise acquire nuclear weapons or other nuclear explosive devices, or control over such weapons or explosive devices."

12. Article II of NPT
"Each non-nuclear-weapon State Party to the Treaty undertakes not to receive the transfer from any transferor whatsoever of nuclear weapons or other nuclear explosive devices or of control over such weapons or explosive devices directly, or indirectly; not to manufacture or otherwise acquire nuclear weapons or other nuclear explosive devices; and not to seek or receive any assistance in the manufacture of nuclear weapons or other nuclear explosive devices."

13. US President Bush (Sr.) had stopped supply of these planes to Pakistan in 1990 for the reason of vigorously pursuing of a nuclear weapon development programme by the latter.

14. For more details, Chapter on Iran, below.

15. "No Rethink on N-Tech: Iran" Reuters news from Tehran: *The Times of India,* Lucknow Ed. 13 Sept. 2004: "If the issue is that we cannot master nuclear technology for peaceful purposes that is out of question because we have already reached that point", it was observed.

16. "Strikes against Iran not ruled out, says Bush". TNN report from Washington of interview of President Bush by NBC News on 17 January, 2005, The *Times of India,* Lucknow. Ed., Dated 19 Jan. 2005.

17. Article III of NPT:

"(1) Each non-nuclear-weapon State Party to the Treaty undertakes to accept safeguards, as set forth in an agreement to be negotiated and concluded with the International Atomic Energy Agency in accordance with the Statute of the International Atomic Energy Agency and the Agency's safeguards system, for the exclusive purpose of verification of the fulfillment of its obligations assumed under this Treaty with a view to preventing diversion of nuclear energy from peaceful uses to nuclear weapons or other nuclear explosive devices. Procedures for the safeguards required by this Article shall be followed with respect to source or special fissionable material whether it is being produced, processed or used in any principal nuclear facility or is outside any such facility. The safeguards required by this Article shall be applied on all source or special fissionable material in all peaceful nuclear activities within the territory of such State, under its jurisdiction, or carried out under its control anywhere.

(2) Each State Party to the Treaty undertakes not to provide: (a) source or special fissionable material, or (b) equipment or material especially designed or prepared for the processing, use

or production of special fissionable material, to any non-nuclear-weapon State for peaceful purposes, unless the source or special fissionable material shall be subject to the safeguards required by this Article.

(3) The safeguards required by this Article shall be implemented in a manner designed to comply with Article IV of this treaty, and to avoid hampering the economic or technological development of the parties or international co-operation in the field of peaceful nuclear activities, including the international exchange of nuclear material and equipment for the processing, use or production of nuclear material for peaceful purposes in accordance with the provisions of this Article and the principle of safeguarding set forth in the Preamble of the Treaty.

(4) Non-nuclear-weapon States Party to the Treaty shall conclude agreements with the International Atomic Energy Agency to meet the requirements of this Article either individually or together with other States in accordance with the Statute of the International Atomic Energy Agency. Negotiation of such agreements shall commence within 180 days from the original entry into force of this Treaty. For States depositing their instruments of ratification or accession after the 180-day period, negotiation of such agreements shall commence not later than the date of such deposit. Such agreements shall enter into force not later than eighteen months after the date of initiation of negotiations."

18. K. Subramanian, "Nuclear Colonialism" reporting in media in August, 1985.
19. PTI news from Moscow, "India will never be a proliferator, says Kalam", *The Times of India,* Lucknow Ed., 24 May 2005.
20. Article VII of NPT.
21. "Additionally, the IAEA assists the international community in nuclear disarmament efforts. For example, under a Trilateral Initiative with the Russian Federation and United States, the IAEA is supporting steps to verify weapon-origin and other fissile materials that these two countries have released from their defense programmes".
22. The resolutions of the United Nations General Assembly had made calls for the conclusion of an agreement on the prevention of wider dissemination of nuclear weapons.
23. CONTENTS of Statute of IAEA
    ARTICLE I *Establishment of the Agency;* ARTICLE II *Objectives;* ARTICLE III *Functions;* ARTICLE IV *Membership;* ARTICLE V *General Conference;* ARTICLE VI Board *of Governors;* ARTICLE

VII *Staff;* ARTICLE VIII *Exchange of information*; ARTICLE IX *Supplying of materials;* ARTICLE X *Services, equipment, and facilities;* ARTICLE XI Agency *projects;* ARTICLE XII *Agency safeguards;* ARTICLE XIII *Reimbursement of members;* ARTICLE XIV *Finance;* ARTICLE XV *Privileges and immunities;* ARTICLE XVI *Relationship with other organizations;* ARTICLE XVII *Settlement of disputes;* ARTICLE XVIII *Amendments and withdrawals;* ARTICLE XIX *Suspension of privilege;* ARTICLE XX *Definitions*

24. From a UN Document: "A Preparatory Commission shall come into existence on the first day this Statute is open for signature. It shall be composed of one representative each of Australia, Belgium, Brazil, Canada, Czechoslovakia, France, India, Portugal, Union of South Africa, Union of Soviet Socialist Republics, United Kingdom of Great Britain and Northern Ireland, and United States of America, and one representative each of six other States to be chosen by the International Conference on the Statute of the International Atomic Energy Agency. The Preparatory Commission shall remain in existence until this Statute comes into force and thereafter until the General Conference has convened and a Board of Governors has been selected in accordance with article VI."

25. GC(43)/RS/19; GC(43)/RS/19/Corr. 1; GC(43)/DEC/12.

26. GC(43)/RS/8.

27. From a UN document : "Under a trilateral initiative with the Russian Federation and United States, the IAEA is supporting steps to verify weapon-origin and other fissile materials that these two countries have released from their defense programmes"; Under UN Security Council resolutions, the IAEA is or has been the inspectorate for nuclear-related monitoring and verifications in Iraq and North Korea (2003).

28. ARTICLE XX: *Definitions* as used in this Statute:

"(1) The term "special fissionable material" means plutonium-239; uranium-233; uranium enriched in the isotopes 235 or 233; any material containing one or more of the foregoing; and such other fissionable material as the Board of Governors shall from time to time deter mine; but the term "special fissionable material" does not include source material.

(2) The term "uranium enriched in the isotopes 235 or 233" means uranium containing the isotopes 235 or 233 or both in an amount such that the abundance ratio of the sum of these isotopes to the isotope 238 is greater than the ratio of the isotope 235 to the isotope 238 occurring in nature.

(3) The term "source material" means uranium containing the mixture of isotopes occurring in nature; uranium depleted in the isotope 235; thorium; any of the foregoing in the form of metal, alloy, chemical compound, or concentrate; any other material containing one or more of the foregoing in such concentration as the Board of Governors shall, from time to time, determine; and such other material as the Board of Governors shall from time to time determine."

29. "US accuses Iran of Bomb Plans": 'Agencies' report from Vienna, *Sunday Times of India,* Lucknow Ed, 19 Sept. 2004.
30. "radioactive material" means material that contains radio-nuclides above the clearance or exemption levels recommended by the International Atomic Energy Agency (IAEA)
31. Article XII of the Statute of IAEA.
32. "Nuclear weapon" means any explosive device capable of releasing nuclear energy in an uncontrolled manner but does not include the means of transport or delivery of such device if separable from and not an indivisible part thereof.
33. "With respect to any Agency project, or other arrangement where the Agency is requested by the parties concerned to apply safeguards, the Agency shall have the responsibilities to the extent relevant to the project or arrangement:
    It shall examine the design of specialized equipment and facilities, including nuclear reactors, and to approve it only from the view-point of assuring that it will not further any military purpose, that it complies with applicable health and safety standards, and that it will permit effective application of the safeguards provided for" in article XII A.
34. Specialized Agencies of UN can also be members of IAEA alongwith States which may or may not be members of UN.
35. Basically "the IAEA assists the international community in nuclear disarmament efforts. Under a Trilateral Initiative with the Russian Federation and United States, the IAEA is supporting steps to verify weapon-origin and other fissile materials that these two countries have released from their defense programmes".
36. Security Council Resolution 825 (1993) and the Statement of the President of Security Council of 30 May 1994.

5

Comprehensive Nuclear Test Ban Treaty

Nuclear weapons have been retrogressive development in international community from the wider point of view of progress of human civilization. The making, possession and use of nuclear weapons is linked with increase in the ferocity of modern wars and the consequent unnecessary sufferings of common people. The curtailment of the right to wage a war and preventing States from developing or acquiring dangerous weapons are the efforts of the United Nations in order to bring about order, reasonableness and sanity in international relations. Disarmament of States has been the quest of pacifists who hate war for atrocious suffering of people on massive scale since the First World War ended in 1919. Disarmament again attracted the attention both after witnessing the repeated sufferings of people of Europe and nuclear bombings of Hiroshima and Nagasaki during Second World War. The quest for disarmament is both in the form of reduction and destruction of existing nuclear and other weapons causing inhuman misery both on civilians and non-combatants, alongwith prevention of States from going for such weapons. Such weapons are now collectively termed as 'weapons of mass destruction'. The Charter of the United Nations advocates for disarmament on a priority basis. However, the history of nuclear disarmament is evasive and discouraging, though significant bilateral and multilateral efforts have taken place in this direction since 1945. The 1963 Treaty Banning Nuclear Weapon Tests in the Atmosphere, in Outer Space and Under Water[1] was the first concrete step and is the background for the sterile or failed step, Comprehensive Nuclear Test Ban Treaty (CTBT[2] or CNTBT) of 1996, for the achievement of nuclear disarmament.

NUCLEAR TEST BAN TREATY OF 1963

The Basics

The USA, UK and USSR were original sponsoring parties to this Nuclear Test Ban Treaty of 1963 signed in Moscow and which came into force on 10 October 1963. In retrospect assessment, the three States through this Treaty had worked to maintain their hegemony in international politics by possession of nuclear weapons that other States[3] did not have. They formulated that the basic aim behind the Treaty was a speedy achievement of an agreement on general and complete disarmament under a strict international control in accordance with the objectives set in the Charter of UNO. This entailed putting an end to obnoxious armaments race and, along with this, elimination of the incentive or desire of the nations to the production of nuclear weapons that follows nuclear explosive device testing in air, a few hundred metres above the land or sea. With this objective, the Treaty marked as its purpose the discontinuance of all nuclear test explosions of nuclear devices in all future times to come. The contamination of the environment by radioactive fallout after a nuclear explosion, which causes much extended human misery, was also taken to be a matter of common concern and that led to their justification for ban on testing of nuclear devices in ways that may lead to a radioactive fallout.

The Test Ban Treaty of 1963 has been framed with a sense of perpetuity. It is at all times open for signature by any State, new or existing, subject to its subsequent constitutional ratification. Membership of UNO was not considered to be necessary for participation in it. Even East Germany, while it was not a sovereign, State could join the Treaty through USSR. As of 31 January 1991, a total of 114 States had joined it. Though the Treaty is of unlimited duration its membership need not be permanent after joining it. Each party has a 'right to withdraw from the Treaty, if it decides that extraordinary events, related to the subject matter of the Treaty, have jeopardized the supreme interest of the country. It shall give notice of such withdrawal to all other parties to the Treaty three months in advance'.[4] In this process, the member-party is the sole judge of the supreme interest of the country for ceasing to be a member of the Treaty by withdrawal.

While achievement of a complete and permanent ban on all nuclear test explosions remains pending each of the Parties to the 1963 Treaty banning nuclear weapon tests has[5] undertaken "to prohibit, to prevent, not to carry out any nuclear test explosion or any other nuclear explosion, at any place under its jurisdiction or control". The term 'any place' extends to (1) the atmosphere and beyond its limits, including the outer space, or under water, including territorial waters and high seas, or, (2) any other environment when 'such explosion causes radioactive debris to be present outside the territorial limits of the State under whose jurisdiction or control such explosion is conducted'. The obligations extend 'to refraining from causing, encouraging, or in any way participating in the carrying out of any nuclear weapon test explosion, or any other explosion anywhere which would take place in any environment as described' above. It is to be kept in mind that causing or falling of radioactive debris is at the root of the prohibition of nuclear tests in the atmosphere. The Treaty is subject to amending process[6] in which the depository States, viz., the USA, UK and Russia have the final say or in other words the three States have 'veto power' in the matter of acceptance of the proposed amendment.

While meaning good at the hard core of its objective, the Treaty of 1963 at the same time was designed to maintain technological superiority and political hegemony of the then three nuclear States in the nuclear weaponry over other signatory States. From this perspective, the Treaty is looked upon as a long-term diplomatic surveillance by the three States on the score of future development of nuclear technology by the 'have-nots'.

The Legal Fallout of the Treaty

In application, the Nuclear Test Ban Treaty of 1963 is limited to the States that sign and ratify it. It is also possible to easily withdraw from the Treaty. In effect, the Treaty did not prohibit underground nuclear tests or researches by the States on nuclear weapons development projects. In mid-1960s it was technically believed that underground tests presumed the already acquisition or possession of nuclear technology by a State of a magnitude that can be acquired only after conducting atmospheric nuclear explosion tests. The underground nuclear explosions are to be needed only for perfecting nuclear devices for different ranges. A question arose whether the Nuclear Test Ban Treaty had laid down a general law in favour of humanity and protection of environment applicable to all members of international community. Two important States, France and China that were not members of the Treaty continued with their nuclear tests in atmosphere unmindful of adverse UN resolutions and the world opinion. When France proceeded with atmospheric nuclear tests scheduled in May 1973, on Mururoa Atoll in the South Pacific Ocean, Australia and New Zealand moved the International Court of Justice[7] to halt the tests on the ground that the nuclear tests on Mururoa Atoll would contravene international law, including the Charter of the United Nations. The ICJ on 22 June 1973, passed an interim order calling upon France to refrain from nuclear tests in the South Pacific Ocean pending its decision on the wider question, that is, whether the French nuclear tests would violate international law. France denied that ICJ had jurisdiction in the case and asserted that the tests were meant to develop nuclear deterrence and that USA and USSR had conducted 241 and 107 tests respectively since the signing of the Treaty in 1963 for further development and improvement of their nuclear arsenal. France conducted 4 or 5 nuclear tests. However, after these tests France declared that it would not conduct such tests in the South Pacific Ocean Atoll any further and the ICJ on 20 December 1974, dropped the case. China conducted its last atmospheric test in 1980.

The Underground Nuclear Tests

The 1963 Nuclear Test Ban Treaty did not ban 'underground nuclear tests and nuclear explosions'. The nuclear powers continued their underground nuclear explosion for assessing explosive power or range of nuclear devices. Such tests are marked for absence of nuclear debris, and in so far as there is no nuclear debris fallout these tests do not come within the purview of 1963 Treaty. Atmospheric explosions are done in order to determine the devastating range of nuclear weapons as well as to fix the relative height at which explosion is to be triggered by the detonator for most devastating effect of the nuclear device on the target. As such, the treaty was to be an obstruction to the new entrants in the nuclear club. India has joined the Treaty, did not conduct any nuclear test in atmosphere but it did its first underground Pokharan nuclear test on 18 May 1974 and second in 1998. Pakistan did its underground nuclear test in 1998 also. As was revealed, USA and USSR had conducted 241 and 107 underground nuclear tests between 1963 and 1974 respectively. By 1970s, it was being realized by nuclear powers that the diplomacy required that the underground nuclear tests were also to be curbed for prevention of proliferation of nuclear weapon technology. Technically simulated laboratory tests on computers equalizing atmospheric tests had become possible; this had made bypassing of atmospheric tests possible. Hence need for a new treaty was felt.

At the Moscow Summit meeting between US President and the Soviet Chief on 3 July 1974, an agreement was signed. It was agreed among other points that underground nuclear test for devices upto 150 kiloton (KT) yield were to be regarded as peaceful in nature but of explosive power above 150 KT yield, these would be taken to be of military armament character. They gave up their option for underground testing of devices of beyond 150 KT yield. This partial underground nuclear test agreement was to be effective from 31 March 1976. Following the mood set by this bilateral agreement, the General Assembly (XXXIII) on 14 December 1978 approved a resolution that recommended steps to be taken for ban on underground nuclear tests, a comprehensive nuclear test ban, and pending such a treaty, a moratorium on all kinds of nuclear tests. It also requested the Geneva Disarmament Committee to devise agreement for strengthening the security of non-nuclear States and for effectively curtailing the use of weapons of mass destruction. Again in 1990, proposal was mooted by the State Parties for holding a conference for amending the 1963 Treaty for converting it into an all comprehensive test ban treaty. This conference was held in January 1991, in New York. It was proposed that two protocols be added to the Treaty; the first protocol would commit the State Parties to prohibit, prevent and not to carry out any nuclear test explosion at any place under their jurisdiction, while the second protocol would provide verification procedures in detail. No unanimous conclusion was reached and the conference decided that further negotiations on the matter should be continued. The matter was also taken up by the United Nations that resulted in the resolutions of General Assembly on prohibition of Weapons of Mass Destruction (WMD) and the formulation of the Comprehensive Test Ban Treaty (CTBT) by 1996.

It should be remembered that the UN General Assembly has always been deeply interested in preventing arms race and arms control, in reduction of nuclear arms possessed by States, in giving incentive to bilateral and multinational endeavors to this end to disarmament, but in ultimate analysis it cannot disarm the States. The General Assembly represents the conscience of nations, which might at times be contrary or indifferent to the diplomacy and politics of 'Big Powers'. The world public opinion has often emphasized that arms race, including production of nuclear weapons and technology must be controlled, rather stopped, since it leads to 'immediate perils' for people of all nations and it creates more and more intractable problems affecting economic growth, economic equality, social development and environmental degradation. The United Nations had successfully launched the Nuclear Non-Proliferation Treaty of 1967, discussed in detail in another chapter. This Treaty was taken to be an incentive for further action on the matters of nuclear proliferation.

COMPREHENSIVE TEST BAN TREATY (CTBT)

The Disarmament Commission,[8] the existing Agency of the United Nations since 1952, did the work of preparing formulations for the achievement of the goal of disarmament.

The Conference on Disarmament, the Disarmament Commission meeting in a general conference,[9] began its substantive negotiations on a comprehensive nuclear test ban treaty in January 1994 within the framework of an *Ad Hoc* Committee established for that purpose. The Disarmament Commission had long been involved with the issue of nuclear test ban. In 1982 it had established a subsidiary body to pursue the matter. Disagreement over a mandate for that body blocked tangible progress in any constructive achievements by it for years. In 1988, taking into account the scramble among States for obtaining nuclear technology and nuclear weapons on a commercial basis also, it was realized by non-nuclear States that the time for revising of 1963 Nuclear Test Ban Treaty had come.[10] The underground nuclear tests, exception to the 1963 Test Ban Treaty, had malfunctioned according to several States. After intensive negotiations, the Chairman of the *Ad Hoc* Committee of the Conference on Disarmament, Ambassador Jaap Ramaker of the Netherlands, presented a final draft treaty to the Conference on Disarmament in June 1996. A big majority of Member States of the Conference expressed their readiness to support the draft treaty. India was the lone dissenter to the proposed draft of the Treaty. India stated that it could not go along with the consensus on the draft text and its transmission to the United Nations General Assembly. The main reasons for such a decision that India pointed out, were related to its strong misgivings about the provision of Article XIV of the Draft relating to the entry-into-force of the treaty,[11] which India considered it to be without precedent in multilateral practices and as running contrary to customary international law. India emphasized that the draft has failed to include a commitment by the nuclear weapon States to eliminate nuclear weapons within a time-bound framework. As a result of the attitude of India, the Draft was stalled. Australia, on 22 August 1996, requested the General Assembly to resume the consideration of standing agenda item 65 before it, entitled "Comprehensive Test Ban Treaty" (CTBT), vide, the earlier General Assembly resolution (50/65) of 12 December 1995. For that purpose Australia also submitted to the General Assembly for adoption a draft Comprehensive Nuclear Test Ban Treaty (CNTBT), identical to that negotiated in the Conference on Disarmament in June 1996. This became a part of the French resolution already on the agenda and which the General Assembly eventually adopted.

The GA resolution CNTBT[12] of 1996 has had the twin objectives of nuclear disarmament, including reductions in arsenals of nuclear weapons, as well as the prevention of proliferations of nuclear technology and nuclear weapons in all of their aspects. It is to strive for systematic and progressive efforts for reducing nuclear weapons, with the ultimate goal of eliminating those weapons globally, with a view to achieving a general and complete disarmament under strict and effective international control. The CNTBT recognized the obnoxious nature of nuclear weapon test explosions and all other nuclear explosions done in the development and qualitative improvement of nuclear weapons. There was need for effective measure of constraint for non-proliferation and nuclear disarmament. The CNTBT regarded that the most effective way to achieve the end to nuclear testing is through the conclusion of a universal and internationally effective verifiable system under it. In this process, the CNTBT noted that 1963 'Treaty Banning Nuclear Weapon Tests in the Atmosphere, in Outer Space and Under Water', which sought to achieve the discontinuance of all test explosions of nuclear weapons for all time, had contributed to the reduction of nuclear testing and the protection of the environment also from nuclear debris fallout.

Format of CNTBT

The Comprehensive Nuclear Test Ban Treaty is, as mentioned, in the form of a resolution of the General Assembly. The resolution has proposed a treaty that must be signed and ratified by the member States particularly by 44 States mentioned in its Article XIV. In this sequence, the Treaty has for the near future reached a 'dead end' as the USA, which was one of the initial signatories of the treaty, has failed or rather refused for the present to ratify the Treaty.[13] India and Pakistan, among the Article XIV States, had also reservations and would not have recognized or ratified the Treaty leading to the same consequence. Indian diplomacy requires that it should have either veto power in the Security Council of United Nations for sustaining its national interests in future or it should be at least recognized as an existing nuclear power as in the provisions of CNTBT. India feels uneasy in hostile nuclear armed States, with Pakistan being a *de facto* nuclear power while China is a *de jure* nuclear power. Pakistan is overtly hostile to India and China is trustworthy ally of Pakistan possessing veto power in Security Council of United Nations. Both Pakistan and China claim and have in occupation Indian territories and have attacked India in the past.

Functional Aspects of CNTBT

The Treaty bans all nuclear explosions, for military or civil purposes, 'at any place under its jurisdiction or control'[14] and this obligation is to operate under an international verification system. To oversee the verification system and the compliance by States of their obligations, a Comprehensive Nuclear Test Ban Treaty Organization is to be established by the Treaty alongwith necessary Technical Secretariat, which shall include the International Data Centre,[15] all functioning under this Treaty. The verification system of the Treaty is "to ensure the implementation of its provisions, including those for international verification of compliance with it, and to provide a forum for consultation and cooperation among States Parties". The verification activities shall be based on objective information, shall be limited to the subject matter of this Treaty, and shall be carried out on the basis of full respect for the sovereignty of States Parties and in a manner that is least possible intrusive and is consistent with the effective and timely accomplishment of the objectives of CNTBT. Correspondingly, each State Party shall refrain from any abuse of the right of verification. Further, each State Party is to establish a National Authority pursuant to Article III, paragraph 4, and this National Authority is to cooperate with the organization and with other States Parties in the verification of compliances with the obligations of the Treaty. The organization shall request from parties only such information and data as might be necessary to fulfill its responsibilities under this Treaty.

The CNTBT Organization

All States Parties are to be members of the organization with one State-one vote formula. It implies that the permanent members of the UNO or the nuclear powers of the world shall not have any special rights in the management of the activities of the CNTBT Organization after signing and ratifying the Treaty. The big nuclear powers would only have the option of withdrawing from the Treaty if adverse decisions were taken under one State-one vote quality formula. As compared to the NPT, this is a variation of significance. Those parties that disagree with majority decisions can only withdraw from the Treaty. This involved implication was regarded to adversely impinge on the national sovereignty of USA and on this ground the Senate of US Congress refused to ratify the Treaty. Further, the "organization, as an independent body, shall seek to utilize existing expertise and facilities, as appropriate, and to maximize cost efficiencies, through cooperative arrangements with other international organizations such as the International Atomic Energy Agency."[16] The organization shall enjoy on the territory and in any other place under the jurisdiction or control of a State Party such legal capacity and such privileges and immunities as may be necessary for the exercise of its functions. The established organs of the organization will be (1) the Conference of the States Parties, (2) the Executive Council and (3) the Technical Secretariat.

The 'Conference' of the States Parties

It[17] is to be composed of all States Parties. Each State Party shall have one representative in the conference, who may be accompanied by alternates and advisers. The Conference shall meet in regular sessions, which shall be held annually, unless it decides otherwise. A special session of the Conference can be convened: *(a)* When decided by the Conference; *(b)* When requested by the Executive Council; or *(c)* When requested by any State Party and supported by a majority of the States Parties. For the meetings of the Conference of the States Parties a majority of the States Parties shall constitute a quorum and each State Party shall have one vote. Within the organization, the Conference shall be its principal organ. It may consider any questions, matters or issues within the scope of this Treaty, including those relating to the powers and functions of the Executive Council and the Technical Secretariat, in accordance with this Treaty. It may make recommendations and take decisions on any questions, matters or issues within the scope of this Treaty when raised by a State Party or brought to its attention by the Executive Council. Apart from this, the Conference shall oversee the implementation of, review compliance with this Treaty and act in order to promote its object and purpose. It shall also oversee the activities of the Executive Council and the Technical Secretariat and may issue guidelines to either of them for the exercise of their functions. The Conference shall elect the members of the Executive Council and consider and approve the rules of procedure of the Executive Council submitted by the latter. Importantly, the conference shall consider and review scientific and technological developments in the States that could affect the operation of this Treaty.

The Executive Council

The Executive Council is to consist of 51 members formed by taking into account the need for equitable geographical distribution. The members of the Executive Council shall be elected by the conference and each member of the Executive Council shall have one representative on the Executive Council, who may be accompanied by alternates and advisers. The Executive Council shall itself elaborate its rules of procedure and submit them to the conference for approval. It shall elect its Chairman from among its members. The Executive Council shall meet in regular sessions and in taking decisions each member of the Executive Council shall have one vote. The Executive Council shall take decisions on matters of procedure by a majority of all its members while it shall take decisions on matters of substance by a two-thirds majority of all its members unless specified otherwise in the Treaty. When an issue arises as to whether the question is one of substance or not, that question shall be treated as a matter of substance unless otherwise decided by the majority required for decisions on matters of substance. In status, the Executive Council is to be the executive organ of the organization and shall be responsible to the conference. The Executive Council shall consider any concern raised by a State Party about possible non-compliance with this Treaty and abuse of the rights established by this Treaty and in so doing, the Executive Council would consult the States Parties involved and, where it considers as appropriate, request a State Party to take measures to redress the situation within a specified time.

The Technical Secretariat

The Technical Secretariat[18] is to assist States Parties in the implementation of this Treaty. The Technical Secretariat shall also assist the Conference and the Executive Council in the performance of their functions. As for its function in relation to the States Parties, it shall carry out the verification of the compliance by States of their treaty obligations and other such functions as might be entrusted to it by this Treaty. In addition, it will perform those functions as may be delegated to it by the conference or the Executive Council in accordance with this Treaty. The Technical Secretariat shall include International Data Centre, as its integral part.

The functions of the Technical Secretariat with regard to verification of compliance with the Treaty shall be in accordance with Article IV and the Protocol. It shall be responsible for operating, supervising and coordinating (a) the International Monitoring System; and (b) the International Data Centre. The Technical Secretariat is to develop and maintain, subject to approval by the Executive Council, operational manuals to guide the operation of the various components of the verification regime, in accordance with Article IV and the Protocol. The Technical Secretariat shall promptly inform the Executive Council of any problems that have arisen with regard to the discharge of its functions or that have come to its notice in the performance of its activities; and that it has been unable to resolve those problems through consultations with the State Party concerned. Each State Party is enjoined to respect the exclusively international character of the responsibilities of the Director-General of the Technical Secretariat, the inspectors, the inspection assistants and the members of the staff and shall not seek to influence them in the discharge of their responsibilities.

The Director-General of the Technical Secretariat

The Technical Secretariat is to comprise of a Director-General, referred to as "the Director-General", who shall be its head and chief administrative officer and other supporting staff. The Director-General shall be appointed by the Conference upon the recommendation of the Executive Council for a term of four years, renewable for one further term, but not thereafter. The first Director-General shall be appointed by the Conference at its initial session upon the recommendation of the Preparatory Commission. The Director-General shall be responsible to the Conference and the Executive Council for the appointment of the staff and for the organization and functioning of the Technical Secretariat. The Director-General may, as appropriate, after consultation with the Executive Council, establish temporary working groups of scientific experts to provide recommendations on specific issues. "In the performance of their duties, the Director-General, the inspectors, the inspection assistants and the members of the staff shall not seek or receive instructions from any government or from any other source external to the organization." Accordingly, they shall refrain from any action that might reflect adversely on their positions as international officers responsible only to the organization. The Director-General shall assume responsibility for the activities of an inspection team. In turn, each State Party shall respect the exclusively international character of the responsibilities of the Director-General, the inspectors, the inspection assistants and the members of the staff and shall not seek to influence them to their favour in the discharge of their responsibilities.

Implementation of Obligations by States Parties

The States Parties shall take necessary measures to implement its obligations[19] under this Treaty in accordance with their constitutional processes. In particular, the obligations are:

(a) To prohibit natural and legal persons, nationals or otherwise, anywhere on its territory or in any other place under its jurisdiction or under its control as recognized by international law from undertaking any activity prohibited to a State Party under this Treaty.

(b) To cooperate with other States Parties and afford the appropriate form of legal assistance to facilitate the implementation of the obligations under the Treaty; and to inform the organization of the measures taken pursuant to this Article.

(c) To designate or set up a National Authority that shall serve as the national focal point for liaison with the organization and with other States Parties.

(d) To accord to the organization such legal capacity and such privileges and immunities as are necessary for the exercise of its functions, on the territory and in any other place under the jurisdiction or control of the States Parties.

(e) To accord to the delegates of States Parties, together with their alternates and advisers, representatives of members elected to the Executive Council, together with their alternates and advisers, the Director-General, the inspectors, the inspection assistants and the members of the staff of the Organization such privileges and immunities as may be necessary in the independent exercise of their functions in connection with the organization.

EPILOGUE

Is Present the Future of the CNTBT?

As mentioned the Comprehensive Nuclear Test Ban Treaty, promoted by the UN General Assembly by a resolution in 1996 is now in hibernation or has suffered a virtual demise and may well be treated as a failed part of the history of disarmament in view of the rejection of it by the Senate of the US Congress. The USA is a necessary State for national ratifications for entry into force of the CNTBT. The fact remains that international legal order is neither fully autocratic nor fully democratic. It still functions on the concept of sovereign status of the members of international community. The whole effort for CNTBT is to be assessed by taking into view two emerging factors. First, there is no legal ban on the use of nuclear weapons by States that possess them already; the Treaty would only prohibit testing of nuclear devices for development of nuclear weapons by non-nuclear States. In this context, the CNTBT is to be read alongwith the NPT. Those States, which would have tried to develop nuclear weapons, would have attracted international sanctions after entry into force of the Treaty. Secondly, the CNTBT prohibited any further nuclear tests involving nuclear explosions of 'critical radioactive mass'. The nuclear powers, including India, are capable of conducting 'simulated' nuclear tests without explosions. As such the CNTBT did not in effect prevent the five nuclear powers from further improvement of their nuclear weapons. That is, the Treaty would have been a mirage in the achievement of desired form of disarmament. However, what failed the CNTBT was the end of cold war nuclear diplomacy by 1995 following the demise of the USSR. The peace encircling USA is no longer 'balance of terror'. Instead USA has become compelled to fight battle against invisible terrorists belonging to Islamic fundamentalists. The terrorists who threaten USA gravely now do not have one nationality and are working against entire USA-UK oil diplomacy involving several Middle East petroleum rich Islamic States. Similar problem from Islamic fundamentalist terrorism for different reasons is faced by Russian Federation, China and India also. Further, as India had pointed out, the CNTBT, apart from long-term inequality among States, contained a method for its entry into force that was unknown so far in international law and it failed at the hands of its promoters, thus, not bringing a surprise or bad name to India.

ENDNOTES

1. 5 August 1963: 480 UNIS, 43.
2. Comprehensive Test Ban Treaty (CTBT) was popular draft proposal that was renamed as Comprehensive Nuclear Test Ban Treaty (CNTBT) in the French Resolution placed before UN General Assembly.
3. France and China, two of the present superpowers, had not fully developed nuclear weapons in 1963.
4. Articles III and IV of the Nuclear Test Ban Treaty, 1963.
5. Article I of the Nuclear Test Ban Treaty, 1963.
6. Article II of the Nuclear Test Ban Treaty, 1963.
7. Nuclear Test Case (Australia v. France), (1974) ICJ Reports, 253, 457.
8. Disarmament Commission was established originally in 1952 by the UN GA (VI/502) to consolidate the UN Atomic Energy Commission and the UN Commission for Conventional Armaments. It became an Agency of the UN. It was a 24-member Commission that considered the problems related to disarmament and made recommendations to the General Assembly. It also worked in unison with non-UN organizations on disarmament negotiations such as the Eighteen Nation Disarmament Committee (ENDC). In 1978, all members of General Assembly became members of Disarmament Commission, as a deliberative and recommendatory body for the GA.
9. UN machinery under General Assembly for disarmament negotiations, vide, its consensus resolution of 30 June 1978.
10. See, UN General Assembly resolution, 50/65 of 12 December 1995.
11. In accordance with Article XIV of the Treaty, it will enter into force only after all the following 44 States listed in Annex 2 to the Treaty have ratified it: Algeria, Argentina, Australia, Austria, Bangladesh, Belgium, Brazil, Bulgaria, Canada, Chile, China, Colombia, Democratic People's Republic of Korea, Democratic Republic of the Congo, Egypt, Finland, France, Germany, Hungary, India, Indonesia, Iran (Islamic Republic of), Israel, Italy, Japan, Mexico, Netherlands, Norway, Pakistan, Peru, Poland, Romania, Republic of Korea,

Russian Federation, Slovakia, South Africa, Spain, Sweden, Switzerland, Turkey, Ukraine, United Kingdom of Great Britain and Northern Ireland, United States of America, Vietnam.

12. CNTBT is still popularly known as CTBT, since the contents of the two are identical.
13. Though the Senate of the US Congress might decide to ratify the Treaty at a future date.
14. "*Article I* : Basic obligations

    (1) Each State Party undertakes not to carry out any nuclear weapon test explosion or any other nuclear explosion, and to prohibit and prevent any such nuclear explosion at any place under its jurisdiction or control.

    (2) Each State Party undertakes, furthermore, to refrain from causing, encouraging, or in any way participating in the carrying out of any nuclear weapon test explosion or any other nuclear explosion."
15. Article II A 1 of the Treaty.
16. Article II A 8 of the Treaty.
17. Article II B of the Treaty.
18. Article II C of the Treaty.
19. Article III of the Treaty.

6

Nuclear North Korea

North Korea has sprung surprise in the world of active international diplomacy since 1990s by emerging as a hardened, militarily powerful, self-reliant and unbending State. North Korea is since 1990s lone Stalinist hardcore autocratic communist State[1] of the modern world, outside global free trade era. It regards its survival against poverty, energy shortage and its political ambitions to unite South Korea superior to international law procedures. North Korea and South Korea were parts of old times Korean kingdom.[2] South Korea, a highly industrialized democratic State under military protection of USA, also has been keen since mid-1990s to re-establish and renew cultural, social and trade ties with it. North Korea challenged nuclear USA with a nuclear retaliatory war in 2002 and has taken uncompromising attitudes against Russia and China also at negotiating conferences. Its claimed military capabilities include latest deadly conventional arms, WMD, nuclear bombs and long-range missiles capable of hitting any target accurately in the North America, particularly in USA. Now, the superpower USA feels presence of North Korea in the world as a power to be reckoned for whatever is its ferocious worth and that it has to be tackled cautiously. Pakistan has traded or bartered nuclear technology with North Korea in return for high missile technology capable of delivering nuclear warheads. With this commerce in between them, both North Korea and Pakistan are complete or full nuclear powers. North Korea is a military technology partner of autocratic Pakistan and both Pakistan and North Korea in turn are dependant on strength of communist China to varying degrees in international politics or military alliance. This diplomatic triangle has hurt India by making it to hasten upgrading its non-conventional military arsenal.

POLITICAL NORTH KOREAN STATE

Political Heritage and the Presence of North Korea

North Korea is a post Second World War *de facto* State which has put on the political personality of its first totalitarian President, Kim Song Ju,[3] who ruled with one title or other since 1948, when the State of North Korea was created till his death in July 1994. He was premier from 1948 to 1972, Chairman of the dominant Korean Workers (Communist) Party from 1949 and President and Head of North Korea from 1972 onwards till his death. He had a patriotic past; he was son of a peasant who had fled to Manchuria in 1925 to escape from the Japanese annexation of Korea. He had joined the Korean guerrilla resistance against the Japanese occupation in the 1930s. Later, Kim was noticed and patronized for being a good communist by the Soviet military authorities and he was sent to the Soviet Union for military and political training. During World War II, Kim rose to be a major of Korean contingent of the Soviet Red Army. After the Japanese surrender in 1945, northern part of Korea was under international occupation by Soviet Russia. Kim led the Korean Brigade of Soviet army and the Brigade came over to the Soviet occupied part of Korea, which later became North Korea. Kim Song Ju became the first premier of the Democratic People's Republic of Korea (DPRK) formed in 1948. The division of Korea between North and South entities has not been acceptable to Koreans. Kim attempted to reunify Korea under his rule by launching a surprise invasion of South Korea in 1950; this resulted in the Korean War and UN forces led by USA came to the aid of South Korea. The UN forces repulsed the attack and entered North Korea but massive Chinese support came to the aid of North Korea and Kim could repel and contain the action led by UN forces. After the Korean War ended with armistice in 1953 on equal note, North Korea had a standing in world polity. On domestic front Kim II-Sung crushed political opposition and eliminated his rivals and became life-long sole power within North Korea's Communist Party. Kim adopted the policy of self-reliance in economic and military affairs free from any non-communist external help, remaining part of cold war. In this process when after 1956 the Sino-Soviet mutual conflict and differences arose, North Korea had to often change its pro-Soviet to pro-Chinese tracks and from these to neutral stances. But in the meantime, Soviet Russia had fully modernized North Korean army, militia and air force alongwith with construction of large airfields and underground aircraft hangars as part of the cold war. Soviet Union, China and States of Eastern Europe had also helped North Korea to establish an economic development infrastructure on Marxist lines. Kim developed North Korea into a highly regimented and repressive society and maintained the goal of the reunification of the Korean Peninsula under North Korean rule. The neutral stance between Soviet Union and Chinese pattern of communism increased since 1960s, this correspondingly reduced economic aid from Russia and China and this resulted in economic stagnation and isolation of North Korea in world politics. The end of cold war alongwith China and US becoming friends made it a State under starvation. By and during 1990s, North Korea suffered from severe energy crisis and acute food shortages.

The US Initiatives on North Korea

After the demise of the State of Soviet Union, by 1992 the 'Iron Curtain' had been lifted and all such States had embraced multiparty democracy, human rights for people and free economy. Only, North Korea with Stalinist political thinking remained isolated national entity. China had also adopted mutual or global trade contacts and industrial partnerships with countries of the West. China had found market outlets for earning foreign exchange. On ideological front the USA saw in North Korea "an end-game of the Cold War."[4] President Clinton started[5] the wise diplomacy of softening North Korean rigidity in international relations. Accordingly, USA negotiating matters for the solution of acute food shortages and energy starvation problems facing North Korea since the mid-1980s. The per capita income of North Koreans was very low. The US interest and strategy in return was to prevent the North Korea from crossing the so-called "red line",[6] which meant preventing its capability of making and using nuclear weapons. This diplomacy was also supported by South Korea, Japan, Russia and China, which wanted that Korean Peninsula should be a nuclear weapon free zone. Accordingly, President Clinton Administration made a long-term bilateral deal 'Agreed Framework' (AF), 1994, with North Korea. The AF of 1994 was a bilateral accord that committed:[7]

(1) North Korea to a policy of nuclear non-proliferation.
(2) North Korea to "shut down" the 5-MW research Yongbyon atomic reactor; that, apart from supplying electricity, could alongwith yield "weapons-grade" plutonium; and accordingly, surveillance cameras and the "seals" were installed on the reactor by the International Atomic Energy Agency (IAEA) at the behest of USA.[8]
(3) In exchange, (a) the Korean Peninsula Energy Development Organization (KEDO), a Washington-sponsored consortium,[9] was to be established which was to construct on turn-key basis two 50 MW and 200 MW civilian nuclear reactors that would provide electricity to North Korea; the deadline laid down for the completion of the first plant was 2003. (b) USA was to make an annual supply of 5,00,000 (Five Lakh) tonnes of heavy oil for production of electricity by North Korean power plants till the reactors were installed.

Moving further ahead in the direction of implementing the FA of 1994, US Defense Secretary, William Perry, in charge of American diplomacy under Clinton Administration, negotiated a North Korean missile test moratorium in September 1998 with North Korea. This was to take place in exchange for the partial lifting of economic sanctions. Further, at the fag end of the Clinton presidency in 2001, North Korea also tacitly agreed to end all missile-related exports and stop missile production while in return, the North Korean negotiators agreed to accept non-monetary compensation, such as satellite launches and food aid.

Military Capabilities of North Korea

As the cold war era ended around 1992, the Soviet Russia was transformed into a multiparty democracy and it broke into Russian Federation and more than nine other independent States. Yugoslavia and other east European States of the 'Iron Curtain' also became multiparty democracies with recognition of private property and human rights. The successor to Soviet Russia, the Russian Federation, left the Russian military arsenals, including nukes installations in some of its secret bases all around in their locations that had become part of new States. North Korea also benefited with this desertion and had Soviet hi-tech military establishments, large underground aircraft hangars with missiles, nuke launching bases conceivably without nuclear warheads, etc., on its territory, all of which it became possessor and user. North Korea had also developed or possessed, it is believed, ballistic missiles and infrastructure capable of launching satellites into space. North Korea had adopted the policy of uniting South Korea under the government of North Korea while South Korea, Japan and the USA resisted any military move for this purpose and both successors Russia and China adopted the policy that Korean peninsula should not be allowed to become a theatre of a major post-Cold War brinkmanship, particularly a military one involving either the USA or the North Korea or both. In active diplomacy on this score, China had acquired a strategic relevance for USA since it was taken to be an undeclared but duly accepted interpreter of the North Korean foreign policy moves that might involve nuclear questions in the peninsula. On the whole, North Korea was in 2002 and is now rated as a military power in the area not to be treated lightly and not to be forced into a war.

North Korea and NPT

Soviet Russia was active adherent of the NPT of 1967. It was logically to its advantage that the countries to which Soviet Russia had given nuclear and missile technology for the purposes connected with ongoing cold war with USA should not trade it with other States. The NPT was a sort of patent law situation between Soviet Russia and recipients from it of nuclear technology whereby to varying degrees it could control the nuclear expertise and materials transferred by it to the recipient States. Under the pressures or persuasions of Soviet Russia the Democratic People's Republic of Korea (DPRK) had joined the NPT in December 1985. Interestingly, when Soviet Russia got liquidated, North Korea promptly pulled out of the NP Treaty in March 1993. The reason was obvious, that is, escaping from economic stagnation. North Korea had missiles and modern military hardware arms, like AK-47 rifles, alongwith production technology as the only exportable items. Here the terrorist groups or States like Pakistan or north African States fitted in. However, for economic aid reasons under the pressure of the Framework Agreement of 1994, North Korea again joined the NPT, a second time.

North Korean Economics

It is to be recalled that North Korea had agreed to "shut-down" the Yongbyon reactor and had joined NPT under the 1994 Framework Agreement. In exchange, Washington, along with South Korea and Japan, had promised the speedy completion of two civilian nuclear reactors by 2003 that would provide North Korea with much needed electricity. The work on the reactors started in 1999. Only the foundation was laid down till 2001, while North Korea largely remained energy-starved. To make up, North Korea started trading its military assets, including missile technology. As it later came to light, Pakistan transferred advanced nuclear bomb technology to North Korea in return for advance-finished missiles and their manufacturing technology. Yemen and other Middle East Asian and North African States negotiated missile deals, which USA rightly suspected were to be used by terrorist outfits ultimately against oil and world domination interests of USA. Alongside this background, after the happenings of 11 September 2001 in which terrorist suicide bombers toppled three buildings in New York, Pennsylvania and Washington, killing more than 4000 persons in one stroke, the USA linked North Korea with terrorist outfits targeting American diplomatic missions[10] for ousting USA from Asia and Africa. The US President Bush in 2002 started a war on terrorists and on the States that sponsored terrorism in one way or the other.

The Shaking Time for North Korea

George W. Bush as President of USA replaced the Democratic Party President Clinton of USA in January 2001. Bush had sought election mandate for firmly dealing with terrorism in its effect on American interests and security. Terrorists were against continued US policies and presence in the Middle East. Yet, the US government did not promptly take any drastic step against terrorism while the terrorists were suspiciously alert and aggressive. The terrorist attack in USA of 11th September, however, brought a new diplomacy of open confrontation in international political dynamics between the USA and terrorist sponsoring States. The United Nations and the world politic vigorously condemned the terrorist attack, but at the same time, Islamic fundamentalist organizations were elated by their hi-tech success of hijacking commercial passenger aircraft and crashing them on predetermined important locations that were of American pride. The spirit that something should be done against the perpetrators of the terrorist attack 9/11 shook the American administration. In January 2002, in a message to the Congress, President Bush vowed to crush the international 'axis of evil' composed of Iraq, Iran and North Korea. However, no direct evidence of link between the *Al Qaeda* terrorists of 9/11 attacks and Iraq was established and the reactions in favour of the knocking out terrorists were openly centered on Osama bin Laden, who was operating from Afghanistan. Afghanistan was already under censor by the Security Council for various terrorist attacks in and outside Afghanistan.[11] A direct action to capture Osama bin Laden and Taliban terrorists in Afghanistan, led by USA under UN resolutions of sanctions started. Threats of using nuclear and chemical weapons in and against States participating in UN action against Osama bin Laden and Taliban terrorists were issued. The result was that international attention in addition to capture Osama bin Laden and destruction of Taliban terrorists in Afghanistan, shifted to WMD possessing States particularly in violation of NPT. Iraq and North Korea came under international and particularly the US scrutiny. Through extended events in this direction, the UN Security Council in early 2003 asked Iraq to destroy WMD under UN supervision. Iraq co-operated but no evidence of WMD in Iraq was confirmed. In this context, UN Security Council did not take any direct military action against Iraq. Ominously, however, the USA and UK, supported by Spain, took military action in Iraq, insisting that latter did possess nuclear weapons, and these States bypassed UN and the world opinion against this 'war'. North Korea was suspected to be the source of sophisticated Soviet made arms and missiles with the use of which the terrorists from Iran, Iraq and Afghanistan were familiar. As discussed ahead, North Korea already posed threat to peace in Korean peninsula.

DIPLOMACY OF DOCTRINES AND CONFRONTATION

New US Diplomacy of Doctrines

President Bush of USA came with the doctrine of "pre-emptive strikes" in September 2002, against WMD possessing States without regional location. This categorical assertion raised and led to the reaction against nuclear dangers present on the Korean peninsula also. As the US and UK led unilateral war on Iraq progressed, the US Defense Secretary, Rumsfeld stated that the USA was capable of fighting wars on two fronts at the same time, that is, Iraq and North Korea in 2003. This meant opening of theatres of a new kind of war designed to 'dispossess these two sovereign countries of their WMD' or to at least destroying the capabilities of both Iraq and North Korea 'to fabricate and deploy such weapons'. War with North Korea on the same lines as with Iraq was predicted in early 2003. The Bush administration had already refused to honour explicitly the 1994 Framework Agreement with North Korea in February 2002[12]. This was interpreted by North Korea to mean that it was free to re-embark on its nuclear weapons and missile development programmes.[13] It promptly withdrew from NPT again in January 2003. It received nuclear technology from Pakistan in exchange for advanced missile technology given to Pakistan.[14] It was a mutual deal through which Pakistan prepared its offensive against India while North Korea went ahead to successfully counter US intervention.

American commentators around January-April 2003, feared that poverty-starved but nuclear-capable North Korea would begin proliferating nuclear technology to non-state terrorists outfits in Asia and Africa; so it deserved strict censor. On the other side, USA was charged by the international media for working out "stealth imperialism" in Asia. As 2002 had come to a close, a war with North Korea was predicted as a certainty.[15] The causes had been apparent as the happenings developed date-wise thus:[16]

(1) On 14 November 2002 the US President George W. Bush declared that November oil shipments to the North Korea under FA of 1994, will be the last unless North Korea agreed to put a halt to its nuclear weapons programmes.

(2) On 11 December, North Korean-made Scud missiles were seized aboard a ship bound for Yemen, provoking American outrage.

(3) On 12 December, North Korea threatened to reactivate nuclear facilities for energy generation, asserting that the Americans' decision to halt oil shipments left it with no other choice and it blamed the US for wrecking the 1994 F.A. pact.

(4) On 13 December, North Korea asked the UN's International Atomic Energy Agency (IAEA) to remove seals and surveillance equipment from its Yongbyon atomic power plant.

(5) On 22 December, North Korea itself started removing monitoring devices from the Yongbyon nuclear reactor.

(6) On 24 December, North Korea began repairs of the Yongbyon plant.

(7) On 10 January 2003 North Korea announced its withdrawal from the Nuclear Non-Proliferation Treaty (NPT).[17]

(8) On 28 January, in his annual State of the Union address, President Bush declared North Korea is "an oppressive regime [whose] people live in fear and starvation". He accused North Korea of deception over its nuclear ambitions and said "America and the world will not be blackmailed" and promised 'pre-emptive nuclear strikes".

(9) On 29 January, North Korea countered Mr. Bush's speech as an "undisguised declaration of aggression to topple the DPRK (North Korean) system". At the same time, however, it reiterated its demand for bilateral talks on a non-aggression pact.

(10) On 5 February, North Korea declared that it has reactivated its nuclear facilities and their operations are now going ahead "on a normal footing".

(11) On 6 February, North Korea warned the United States that any decision 'to build up its troops in the region' could lead the North Korea to make a pre-emptive attack on American forces.

(12) On 9 April, the United Nations Security Council expressed concern about North Korea's nuclear programme, but did not condemn Pyongyang for pulling out of the NPT.

(13) On 12 April, in a surprise move, North Korea signaled that it might be ready to end its insistence on direct talks with the US, announcing "if the US is ready to make a bold switchover in its Korea policy for a settlement of the nuclear issue, [North Korea] will not stick to any particular dialogue format".

(14) On 18 April, North Korea announced that it has been "successfully going forward to reprocess" the fuel rods of the Yongbyon nuclear reactor lying closed under FA of 1994 for nuclear bombs.

Prevention of Confrontation

The above chain of events made a confrontation between the US and North Korea foreseeable, looking at the drastic US-UK unilateralism in the matter of Iraq. However, world opinion was against such a war outside UN sanctions and resumption of bilateral talks between North Korea and the USA was suggested which, as a trial, the USA also accepted,[18] but with China playing the host. China was to be not only the 'proactive host but also the key interpreter of the mood and methods of these two adversaries' being associated with both of them in active diplomacy of the past. The bilateral meeting for North Korea and US understanding was held in Beijing on April 23, 24 and 25, 2003, hosted by China. The US Assistant Secretary of State for East Asian affairs, James Kelly, and the deputy Director General of North Korea's American Affairs Bureau, Li Gun, led the talks. North Korea wanted from the US at this bilateral meet the resumption of dialogue, which would lead to (1) guarantees that its sovereignty would be respected, (2) the US would not resort to military force to resolve the political impasse in the Korean peninsula, and North Korea also wanted an undertaking from Washington that it would not try to hinder North Korean economic growth by continuing with the economic blockade; (3) North Korea further wanted an assurance from the Bush administration that it would not undermine the diplomatic links between the two Koreas, which with mutual understanding and desire had been assiduously cultivated by North and South Koreas in the last five years. For the USA, in 2003, North Korea's nuclear establishment and 'programmes', both plutonium-based and uranium-derived, became targets of diplomacy. Its agenda of the talks with North Korea henceforth vitally became a pursuit for "nuclear free Korean peninsula".

President George W. Bush was keen to include in his ongoing "global war against terror" such "regimes" also that were suspected to possess weapons of mass destruction (WMD).[19] On 24 April, some American officials said that at the first direct talks Pyongyang has told them that it now has nuclear weapons, the talks ended a day early on 25 April amid mutual recrimination, after the US declared that North Korea has made its first explicit admission that it possessed nuclear weapons. North Korea charged the US for bringing their bilateral talks to a confrontation and to the "brink of a nuclear war".[20]

In April 2003, the USA-UK led unilateralism in Iraq had generated too much of adverse world opinion. Iraq had insisted that it had no WMD, which was controverted both by USA and UK, while on the other hand, North Korea had openly admitted possession of nuclear weapons, and the solution of the matter through dialogues continued to be an open matter. Therefore, a unilateral adventure in North Korea,[21] on the pattern of Iraq, was contrary to common sense. Moreover, unlike as in case of Iraq, there was open threat of dropping of nuclear missiles on US soil by North Korea. Soon after the failure of bilateral talks on 25 April 2003, the US Secretary of State, Colin Powell, observed that North Korea had made an offer to US officials, during the talks in Beijing, to scrap its nuclear programme in exchange for some major concessions from the United States, though the exact nature of those concessions was not specified. Colin Powell indicated that Pyongyang still wanted normalized relations with and economic assistance from the US; and that Washington was studying the offer. The confrontation was diplomatically avoided by both North Korea and the USA. The next multilateral meeting was ultimately held on 27-29 August 2003, and in the meantime following noteworthy steps or events took place:[22]

(1) On 12 May 2003 North Korea scrapped a 1992 agreement with the South Korea to keep the peninsula free from nuclear weapons; this was last remaining international agreement on non-proliferation to which North Korea was committed.

(2) On 2 June 2003 the North Korean officials admitted to a visiting delegation of US Congressmen that the country now possessed (finished product) nuclear weapons and had "just about completed" reprocessing

8,000 spent fuel rods which would allow it to build plutonium bombs.

(3) 9 June, North Korea declared that it would build a nuclear deterrent, "unless the US gives up its hostile policy".

(4) 18 June, North Korea declared that it is further "increasing its nuclear deterrent force for self-defense".

(5) 1 August 2003 North Korea agreed to six-party talks on its nuclear programme, and confirmed that the US, South Korea, Japan, China and Russia will be other involved parties; Since then five-six nation talks have been held by 2005.

Agenda and Issues for Six-Nation Talks

It can be remembered that in April 2003, the Bush administration made it abundantly clear that the way to move forward in North Korean crisis would be through multilateral talks. Both North Korea[23] and the USA wanted to avoid a military solution for their own compulsions. It was against this background that China succeeded in convening the August 2003, multilateral meeting. The policies of the two sides were also well-known: A goal of a nuclear-weapons-free Korean peninsula, which would include the US presence in South Korea too, was agreed upon as a principle and it was expected that USA would be required to readjust to the feasibility of a US-DPRK non-aggression pact to ease North Korean security concerns. South Korea had felt concerned and left alone when American troops in South Korea were moved further south of Seoul, beyond short-range missiles of North Korea. A remark by US Deputy Defense Secretary, Paul Wolfowitz, made in July that US troops in South Korea were within target range of North Korean short-range missiles and that the US mainland was within the target zone of Pyongyang's long-range missile programme was on record. Fear was generated for USA when Washington had claimed that the Yongbyon nuclear plant was to be used to produce weapons-grade plutonium. The facility was said to have 8,000 spent fuel rods stored in a cooling pond. According to the Western intelligence, apart from other resources, these rods alone had enough plutonium to make five or six lethal plutonium bombs.

On 27-29 August 2003, the first six-nation talks were held in Beijing on nuclear programme of North Korea. It was repeated often in media that US regarded North Korea as one of the 'Axis of Evil' open for possible further action. The United States had been adamant to try for and dispossess the Democratic People's Republic of Korea (DPRK) of its capabilities to make and deploy weapons of mass destruction (WMD), most notably nuclear arms. This was a sensitive issue for both sides.[24] The DPRK did not give up its own sovereign right to defend itself, in the event of a "pre-emptive nuclear strike" by the US. It was apparent to the USA that North Korea was negotiating from a position of strength and that could not be taken lightly.[25] It had already declared in June earlier about its deterrent nuclear force. No solution of the problem emerged as this difficult multiparty dialogue ended. But, the participants were, by and large, willing to keep this new dialogue process going. The dates and venue for the next round were to be decided upon in due course. The consensus was seen on the goal of a nuclear-weapons-free Korean peninsula, which would include South Korea alongwith its allies. Russia, Japan and South Korea, the other members at the talks feared that US and North Korea nuclear confrontation would harm them and Korean peninsula. The US discomfiture and sense of isolation over unilateral action leading to Iraq's occupation by the law-unto-themselves alliance forces against international public opinion was apparent when the US desired to continue multilateral talks on the Korean nuclear issue, sidetracking[26] its power of 'pre-emptive nuclear strike'. The chief Chinese delegate, Wang Yi, observed that "while some disagreement still remains", the meeting had "brought about progress" in the matter. Noting that "future talks are not ensured to be always smooth", he said, "the six parties might find ways of peacefully solving the Korean nuclear issue, so long as we make concerted efforts".[27] The meeting failed to bridge the gap between Washington and Pyongyang and no formal joint communiqué was issued at the end of the conference. Delegates only agreed to meet again.[28]

Follow-on Steps

Following the failed first six-nation multiparty talks of August 2003 various linked developments took place. In October 2003 North Korea declared that it has reprocessed the spent nuclear fuel of restarted reactor and that it was inclined to "physically display" its nuclear deterrent. It further agreed to resume talks on the nuclear crisis with the six-member States, and gave out that it was prepared to consider the US offer of a security guarantee in return for ending its nuclear programme. In November 2003, the KEDO project was suspended; it was an international consortium in existence under the Framework Agreement of 1994, for constructing two 'tamper-proof' nuclear civil power plants in North Korea. In December, North Korea offered to "freeze" its nuclear deterrent programme provided US agreed to 'a list of concessions'. However, President Bush rejected the offer, asking North Korea to dismantle its nuclear deterrent make-up altogether. Following this, North Korea showed its willingness for a resumption of August 2003, six-party talks. In January 2004, North Korea allowed a group of US experts, including a top nuclear scientist, to visit its Yongbyon nuclear deterrent facility.[29] Further, 25 February 2004 was agreed upon for the next round of six-party talks on the Korean peninsula nuclear crisis.

The Second Round of Talks

The agenda of the February 2004 talks included "denuclearising the Korean peninsula" and not just the DPRK. The USA sought the complete, verifiable, and irreversible dismantlement of all nuclear programmes, both plutonium and uranium-based and nuclear weapons."[30] The capability of North Korea with regard to chemical or biological weapons continued to be outside the framework of the six-party talks. Meanwhile, the US investigations had surprisingly revealed that the nuclear network in violation of NPT run by Pakistani scientist, Abdul Qadeer Khan, was extensive and he had provided the DPRK with the technology and equipment necessary for uranium enrichment, reprocessing of nuclear spent fuel alongwith blueprint for plutonium bomb in early1990s, while North Korea had in return provided ballistic missiles related technology and components to Pakistan. North Korea did not make a secret of its asymmetrical capability: possession and deployment of special forces, missiles and weapons of mass destruction (WMD). Thus the real nature of nuclear profile of North Korea was now clearly known to the US and the nuclear stakes were very high at the meet. North Korea was also not risking its nuclear deterrent achievements without securing an international guaranteed nuclear umbrella cover. North Korea declared that it was worried by the US strategic doctrine, which allows it to make pre-emptive strikes against countries regarded by it as its enemies, particularly in the declaration of 'axis of evil' that included North Korea. The second round of the six-party talks on the North Korean nuclear programme in February 2004 ended in Beijing on a hopeful or positive note: the parties agreed to resolve outstanding issues through dialogue and focus was made on setting up through consensus a "working group" that could, among other tasks, facilitate the convening of the next round of talks. North Korea had at the talks offered to abolish its military nuclear programme but was to maintain a 'peaceful' nuclear capability. North Korea was offered energy aid in return for freezing and dismantling its nuclear weapon programmes. The USA had demanded a "complete verifiable and irreversible dismantlement" of nuclear programmes of North Korea while forsaking its own intention of invading or attacking North Korea.

The Matters of Crux

North Korea's plutonium-based and uranium-derived 'programmes' continued to be targets of US diplomacy and the solution of the issues has been evasive. The six-party talks mechanism with North Korea aimed at dismantling North Korea's nuclear facilities and programmes remained in place. North Korea had charged USA of double standards with reference to a disclosure of alleged nuclear experiments by South Korea in 1982 and 2000, in criticizing North Korea but showing understanding with South Korean views. The next, third round of six-party talks scheduled for September 2004 were stalled when North Korea failed to participate citing 'hostile' policies of USA. The official KCNA news Agency of North Korea reported: "It is self-evident that the resumption of talks can no longer be discussed unless US drops its hostile policy based on double standards towards DPRK and that the latter can never dismantle its deterrent nuclear force".[31] At the same time, the general conference in Vienna of 137-nation International Agency,[32] ignoring the claim of North Korea that it has withdrawn from nuclear Non-Proliferation Treaty (NPT) in January 2003, called upon North Korea "to promptly accept comprehensive IAEA safeguards and co-operate with the Agency in their (safeguards') full and effective implementation".

CONFRONTATION WITH USA

Confused Diplomacy of US

The US diplomacy in general, including towards North Korea, during the decade after collapse of Soviet Russia, remained incoherent inspite of professed pious objectives. The objectives continued to be guided by perspectives of self-interest and not of equity and comity of nations. The Clinton Administration had sagaciously understood the changes in international politics and cold war confrontations naturally resulting from the demise of Soviet Union and had singled out North Korea as a residuary of cold-war politics. But, in the meantime there was emergence or upsurge of Islamic fundamentalism due to creation of several Islamic States out of broken Soviet Russia,[33] in the Middle East Asia. This had given rise to a new identity for Islamic States somewhat fanned by anti-West attitude. There was attempt to unite them as a new force in 1990s in which Pakistan played a visible leading role. The USA and UK got perturbed for danger to the continuation of their oil interests and diplomacy in the region, particularly after termination of oil exploitation concession by Iran to USA by 1980. The intra-Islamic States war between Iraq and Iran (1980-88) with USA helping Iraq was confusing but invasion of Kuwait by Iraq was illegal. These two wars inverted the role or position of USA in oil resource areas. The Kuwait War was fought with UN sanctions without veto of

Soviet Russia while the cold war era was in existence. President H.W. Bush Sr. in 1991 was hard hitting and saved the Anglo-American interests in the Persian Gulf area by foiling the designs of Iraq. The 1990s also saw the growth of globalization and free-trade economics alongwith "an end-game of the Cold War"[34] but these were tackled by the US President Clinton with understanding of the directions of the winds. The Framework Agreement of 1994 between USA and North Korea depicted the understanding of the changed world political and economic patterns. In Asia-Pacific region, the USA also does not like to understand that Korea, both South Korea and North Korea, and China have a deep, long-drawn hatred of Japan for the invasions, murders, enslavement and raping done since 1905 and particularly during the II World War. This feeling has not been removed by the diplomacy under which USA has since close of Second World War become political protector of Japan, South Korea and Taiwan. President George W. Bush (2001), being a Republican, has followed the policies of his Republican father, President H.W. Bush, bridging a gap of six or eight years but ignoring the social, economic and diplomatic changes of this period. Bush, after the 9/11 terrorist bombings, declared with concern an unrelenting global war on terrorism. Terrorism has its birthplace and confinement in North Africa, Central Asia and fundamentalist Islamic States, while the cold war politics since 1950s had global ramifications. Mixing the two, which have had different origins, though both of them have in common the dangers arising out of the uses WMD, is however a questionable wisdom. President Bush declared North Korea with Stalinist communist regime to be one of the 'axis of evil' against which pre-emptive nuclear strikes could be made. While Iran and Iraq have had, to some extent, Islamic fundamentalist backlash for their support, it was different position with North Korea, that of being danger to South Korean existence. The USA has taken easy the acquisition of nuclear weapon technology by North Korea from Pakistan. Feeling unsafe from North Korea, the US Secretary of State[35] dubbed Stalinist North Korea as an "outpost of tyranny" prompting North Korean foreign ministry in March 2005 to rule out resumption of (fourth) six-nation disarmament talks till USA dropped its 'hostile' attitude towards the country. It also indicated that it was preparing since March 2005 for an underground nuclear test. The USA took the line of asking China to make North Korea desist from pursuing the test.

A New Element

The North Korea had been conducting government to government talks with South Korea for border-easing by opening border town travel, fertilizer deals and calling the Korean peninsula as 'our nation'. There had been a peaceful attempt to unite or bring closer the two parts of the peninsula. The US experts saw in the resumed North and South Korea talks in mid-May 2005, after a seventh-month gap, as a campaign to drive a wedge in the US-South Korean alliance. It used the diplomacy of terming North Korea as a sovereign State to counter the moves of North Korea. There was pressure on both USA and North Korea. Latter was becoming an open nuclear power alongwith direct overtures to South Korea for common peace and prosperity. At the same time, North Korea was having poverty and energy crunch, the US embargoes were hurting its economic growth. In such arms and political economics, the North Korean and six nations met for thirteen days in August 2005, for 'agreement on basic statement of principles' for disarmament talks and failed to agree. North Korea insisted on pursuing its peaceful nuclear programme after abandoning its nuclear weapons and USA insisted on total abandonment of nuclear programme by North Korea and refused any economic package as incentive.

A Step Forward

In a surprise breakthrough reached at the end of a six-day 'fourth' round of talks of August-September 2005: (1) North Korea agreed to abandon its nuclear weapons and enrichment of uranium programmes and to rejoin the NPT, (2) North Korea accepted inspections by IAEA, (3) The USA agreed to normalize bilateral ties with North Korea; it affirmed and assured that it has no nuclear weapons in the Korean peninsulas and it has no intention to invade or commit aggression on North Korea based on 'axis of evil' concept, (3) Parties made a commitment of joint efforts for lasting peace and stability in the region of north-east Asia, (4) The directly related parties, that is, North and South Koreas particularly, will negotiate a permanent peace regime on Korean peninsula, (5) The six parties agreed to take coordinated steps to implement the consensus reached in the fourth round talks in a phased manner, following the principle of "commitment for commitment, action for action" and to keep up the pursuits through next fifth round of talks.

Distrust Prevails

The fourth round talks between the six parties had concluded in a strange form of agreement for the sake of doing something for evading a military showdown. After the fourth round talks were over, both USA and North Korea showed distrust of each other's motives and sincerity. North Korea emphasized on 'action for action' while USA made it clear that a "complete verifiable and irreversible dismantlement" or "shut-down" of the 5-MW research Yongbyon atomic reactor, which, apart from supplying electricity, could alongwith yield "weapons-grade" plutonium, was basic matter. No incentives were offered to North Korea as in "Agreed Framework" of 1994. The South Korea has its own fears. It is noteworthy that United States Defence Secretary, Donald Rumsfeld, has reassured South Korea on protection under the American "nuclear umbrella" against any hostile military moves by North Korea. The US first made this commitment under the existing1953 Mutual Defence Treaty with South Korea made following the Korean War.[36] The distrust continues in mid-2006 as well. There are only feelers for holding a next round of talks.

ENDNOTES

1. Cuba and China are Communist States but not of Stalinist category.
2. Korea was annexed by Japan in 1925 and was divided between Soviet and US occupation zones after Second World War.
3. Born on April 15, 1912.
4. North Korea was the lone non-European Stalinist State in the ring of Iron Curtain.

5. For this his Secretary of State, Madeleine Albright, visited Pyongyang, the capital of North Korea.
6. That is 'path towards the status of a state with nuclear weapons'.
7. See, John Cherian, 'A Korean Crisis": *Frontline*, Vol. 20, Issue 02 (2003); P.S. Suryanarayana, 'Nuclear Brinkmanship' *Frontline,* Volume 20-Issue 01 (2003).
8. [However, the North Korean government claimed that it had processed plutonium from the 8,000 fuel rods that had been stored, until recently, at its Yongbyon nuclear reactor. Pyongyang had said in October 2002 that it had a programme to build nuclear weapons with an explosive core made of uranium.]
9. Composed of USA, South Korea and Japan.
10. Reference here is to the 7 August 1998 terrorist bomb attacks on United States embassies in Nairobi, Kenya, and Dar-es-Salaam, Tanzania, which claimed hundreds of lives. Also, Gaddafi's government of Libya had accepted responsibility for the 1988 bombing of Pan Am Flight 103, in which 270 people had died.
11. The UN Security Council repeated its concern, vide Resolution 1193 (1998) of 28 August, 1998, at the continuing presence of terrorists in the territory of Afghanistan. It condemned attacks on UN personnel in Taliban-held areas, the killing of two Afghan staff members of the World Food Programme and the UN High Commissioner for Refugees in Jalalabad, and of the Military Adviser to UNSMA in Kabul. It also condemned the capture of the Consulate-General of Iran in Mazar-e-Sharif. Further, by resolution 1214 (1998), of 8 December, the Council had demanded that the Taliban stop providing sanctuary and training for international terrorists and their organizations and that all factions in Afghanistan should cooperate in bringing all indicted terrorists on its territory to justice.
12. One of the things that George Bush did as President in February 2002 was to express his disapproval of the growing closeness between the two Koreas and Bush castigated North Korea by including it in the "axis of evil".
13 It may be recalled that North Korea, had negotiated with Clinton Administration a missile test moratorium, in September 1998, in exchange for the partial lifting of US economic sanctions, alongwith non-monetary compensation, such as satellite launches and food aid.
14. Washington has been accusing Pyongyang of causing missile proliferation. Western intelligence sources claim that North Korea has supplied Pakistan with its Nodong missile of upto and more than 2000 km range in exchange for uranium enrichment technology.

15. Media made such assessments and the Former US Defence Secretary, William, also predicted war with North Korea, taking place by the end of the year 2003.
16. Based on: "Timeline: North Korea Nuclear Crisis", *BBC News Service*: Wednesday, 25 February 2004.
17. The IAEA had passed on 5 January 2003 a resolution demanding that North Korea readmit UN inspectors and abandon its secret nuclear weapons programme "within weeks", or face possible action by the UN Security Council.
18. The US had said on 7 January 2003 that it was "willing to talk to North Korea about how it meets its obligations to the international community". But it "will not provide *quid pro quos* to North Korea to live up to its existing obligations".
19. "Bush for Pre-emptive Strikes": News from Washington, January 26. The US President, George Bush, has signed a top-secret directive, authorizing pre-emptive strikes against nations close to acquiring nuclear weapons. The directive, okayed last May, authorized the Pentagon and the CIA to launch such strikes, *Time* magazine said, adding the Energy Department's nuclear weapons experts are "training Special Operations Group personnel in attacking nuclear facilities." But the magazine said, "in the current crisis with North Korea, the US so far is committed to diplomacy to pressure Pyongyang to give up atomic weapons programme".—PTI: *The Hindu*: 27 January 2003.
20. P.S. Suryanarayana, 'Nuclear Brinkmanship': *Frontline,* Volume 20-Issue 01.
21. In the UN Security Council, any resolution against North Korea would have been vetoed either by China or Russia or both. Further, in case of war there was no guarantee that China would not have come to the side of North Korea as it had done in 1950-53 Korean War.
22. Based on: "Timeline: North Korea Nuclear Crisis", *BBC News Service*: Wednesday, 25 February 2004.
23. North Korea was conscious of new strategic doctrine of the US, which allows it to make pre-emptive strikes against countries viewed as its enemies. Further, the official North Korean news agency KCNA, in July of 2003, said that if the US "dropped its hostile policy towards the Democratic People's Republic of Korea (DPRK) and legally committed itself to non-aggression, the latter would be ready to dispel the American concerns".
24. North Korea has said that Washington's demand that it dismantle its nuclear programme is aimed at "disarming" the country, before

launching a military attack against it. The North Koreans have not forgotten that the US was on the brink of using nuclear weapons against their country during the Korean war of the early 1950s.

25 The missile expertise of North Korea has been internationally acknowledged: its missiles can hit targets all over Japan. Seoul is within the range of North Korean guns. Its long-range missiles are capable of reaching targets in USA.

26 Former US Defense Secretary, William, had predicted war by the end of the year [2003], if the situation was not resolved diplomatically.

27 See: P.S. Suryanarayana, 'Eluding Consensus': *Frontline:* Volume 20-Issue 19, 13-26, September 2003.

28 Later, in the second week of January 2004 a statement issued by the official North Korean agency said that the North Korean government had at some time declared that economic sanctions over North Korea against its nuclear programme would mean war. "Sanctions mean war and a war knows no mercy. The US should opt for dialogue with the DPRK," and not for sanctions.

29. In their Report the Delegation told US Congress that the delegates visiting Yongbyon were shown what appeared to be weapons-grade plutonium but they did not see any evidence of a nuclear bomb. Subsequent investigations made by USA revealed that Pakistan had been supplying for money the reprocessing nuclear spent fuel and nuclear bomb-making technologies to North Korea, Iran and Libya since 1990s. Pakistan transferred the blame to nuclear scientist, A.Q. Khan, and pardoned him for the crime.

30. See, P.S. Suryanarayana, 'Consensus on Dialogue': *Frontline*: 13 March 2004.

31. Reuters reporting from Seoul: *Times of India,* Lucknow Ed. 19 September 2004.

32. Held in Vienna on 24 September 2004; AP report from Vienna: *Times of India,* Lucknow Ed. 25 September 2004.

33. The Soviet Union had kept under its wrap a Pandora's box, which got opened, in the form of Islamic fundamentalism after its demise causing much trouble for US diplomatically.

34. North Korea being the lone Stalinist State remnant from the ring of Iron Curtain.

35 Statement of Madame Condoleezza Rice made in mid-March 2005 in Japan.

36. "US assures South Korea of Nuclear Umbrella": P.S. Suryanarayana reporting from Singapore, *The Hindu,* 25 October 2005.

7

Iran and Nuclear Proliferation

Iran has been a centre of international diplomacy and politics since the Second World War. Iran has extensive underground oil reservoirs and that has been the cause of its international problems. It has always to be in a defensive mode; it is flayed forcefully by world's big powers. Hitler wanted to occupy Iran in the course of Second World War but British and Soviet Russian armies pre-empted Iran and both were reluctant to leave their domination over Iran after war was over. Then, with principle of self-determination, Iran became a true sovereign State, thanks to the United Nations Charter, but has been struck with oil diplomacy of big powers. The West also wanted Iran as member of military alliance against expansionist designs of Soviet Russia during the early cold war period. The oil exploiters want Iran to be in a militarily weak position, not strong enough to defend itself against any blockade of oil outflow independently of the ongoing oil diplomacy. The Charter of the United Nations works to keep a balance among the nations who would have fought battles to decide as to who should keep Iran under occupation. Islamic fundamentalist States, which are Arab or *Sunnis*, keep a distance from *Shi'ite* Iran. No doubt, a sociological approach is required to know the worth, capacities, turbulences and compulsions that work upon the existence of Iran as a nation. Iran has needed strong survival oriented diplomacy particularly in the context of its necessity or desire to nuclearize itself. Iran is a member of NPT, is subject to hostility of USA that has its forces in Iraq and Afghanistan, both on its borders. Iran has the use of nuclear bombs, if possessed, against Israel as a champion of

Arab and Islamic States. This is a serious matter of contemporary international politics. Iran has the passive backing of both Russia and China, though neither would defend Iran in case of confrontation with the West, since it is as yet not regarded as a mature and responsible State. India has economic and business interests in Iran and is a probable source of much needed natural gas for it.

IRAN AND THE WORLD

Iran in World Geo-Politics

Iran or Persia has had unique geographical position. Apart from being a coveted rich resource of petroleum since nineteenth century, it has had an obstructing position in the ambitions of Russia to gain entry into Indian Ocean via Persian Gulf. Both of these aspects have attracted imperial powers of Europe to gain control over the rulers and territory of Iran. To ward off European geo-politics, Iran has to be an intrinsically powerful State but religious fanaticism extending back to several centuries coupled with mercantile shrewdness of UK and later of USA, have kept Iran a weak and meek State. Despite being oil rich, Iran has to go for nuclear power reactors for operating its oil refineries and industrial complexes. At the same time, the deep-rooted foreign policy of Iran for leadership of Islamic States involved confrontation with Israel State. Iran perhaps needed nuclear umbrella or else a nuclear arsenal against threats from oil-diplomacy nuclear States present in the Persian Gulf. The USA, one among such States, does not rule out the use of nuclear weapons in any confrontation anywhere in the world. One has to go into the past of Iran and its relationships with once Ottoman Empire till the end of First World War and then as close geographical neighbor of Soviet Russia providing vital airbases to USA during the intense cold war era. This seems to be a point in order to understand the strategic importance of Iran in world diplomacy and politics. Iran had been through a lot of prehistory and history before reaching the contemporary times. It has seen many civilizational changes of the world passing with time through its soil.[1]

Modern Iran State, Genesis

Now in first decade of twenty-first century, though now a controversial international State on nuclear issue, Iran under the Shah had been a fond allied country of USA during 1950-80. But, down the historical lane, with all modern knowledge, expertise and technological advancements, the inner soul or justification of the present existence of man or a nation remains as was preached in ancient *Upanishad* or *Bhagwat Gita*. That is our present is determined by our past and that our present shall determine our future. If Iran has religious fundamentalism, experiences of exploitation of its natural resources by dominating foreign powers, this shall reflect in its present or contemporary aspirations and steps validly taken for dealing with the problems facing it. In precise, the question to be answered is as to why Iran has to go nuclear when it has natural mineral oil in abundance with which it can manufacture electric energy or purchase all its requirements. Naturally, the political, economic, religious and sociological past becomes relevant for proper perspective. To proceed, Persia or Iran has been a constituent of Ottoman Empire since 16th century. Under King Osman (1288-1326), Turks had adopted Islam and had become Islamic crusaders. This empire included the Iran plateau with *Shi'ite* population also.[2] The Ottoman Empire in 1815 after Napoleonic war included Rumania, Bulgaria, Serbia, Albania, Greece, Iraq, Iran, Syria Lebanon, Jordan, Egypt, Armenia, among other territories bordering Russian Empire. Dissolution of the Ottoman Empire started in the 19th century.[3] Russia had designs over northern areas of Ottoman Empire, including northern parts of Persia. Russia tried to establish a protectorate over Turkey, in 1830 but Britain and France frustrated this. Crimean War (1854-56) was successfully fought by Britain and France to prevent Russian expansion into Ottoman Empire. By the Treaty of Paris of 30 March 1856, Turkey a non-Christian State, was recognized to be an independent State under modern international law system and England took over the responsibility of protecting its borders. Under British pressure, Persia (Iran), a vassal State, had gained autonomy by 1878 within Ottoman Empire.

OIL DIPLOMACY OF WEST IN IRAN

Oil Diplomacy over Iran

By the end of 19th century, Persia was recognized as an independent State, away from being a vassal State of Turkey, but subject to some extra-territorial rights for Britain that extended to the protection of British nationals under a treaty of unilateral obligation known as 'capitulation'[4] alongwith oil and mineral exploration rights. The third party Anglo-Russian Agreement of 1907, that not included Iran, recognized these rights for their mutual benefits on Iranian territory particularly with reference to oil rich regions of Iran for oil exploitation by the two.[5] During the Second World War, the troops of both Britain and USSR occupied Iran to defend it against the advancement of Nazi armies of Hitler. This was done without consent of Iran, without declaring a war on Iran and the whole situation was not called an occupation of Iran, though in 1945-46 both most reluctantly withdrew their armies from Iran. However, Iran continued to remain under British 'sphere of influence', thereby meaning that Iran was not open to other States for diplomacy. It may be mentioned in the context of 'spheres of influence' that the Kellogg-Briand Pact (1927) on renunciation of wars was essentially a policy agreement between France and USA on the matter of aggressive wars.[6] Britain had agreed to be a party to the Pact on the condition that it was granted liberty of action in "certain regions of the world, the welfare and integrity of which constitute a special and vital interest for our peace and security". Regions were not defined but the British 'Monroe doctrine' extended to Canada, Ireland, Egypt, Turkey and Persia Kingdom. The Pact was not to affect British and US Monroe doctrines. Most of the Middle East, Indian sub-continent, and China were recognized to be under British 'spheres of influence' by European powers till 1945.[7] In 1927, Iran unilaterally terminated the unilateral extra-territorial and capitulation rights claimed by Britain,[8] but for other States, Iran had continued to remain under British 'sphere of influence'.

In parenthesis it is noted that world over, particularly in developed States, the movement has been from manual labour to coal energy to oil energy to nuclear energy. The replacement of coal energy by oil in mid-nineteenth century as industrialization process increased, focused aggressive interest of Russian Empire on bordering northern areas of Ottoman Empire. Oil diplomacy asserted itself in later half of nineteenth century. Oil producing Armenia, parts of Azerbaijan and Turkmenistan were annexed by Czarist Russia and later by its successor USSR. In reaction and for furtherance of its own interests, Britain made Turkey and Persia a sort of protectorates or areas under 'sphere of influence' and the Russian southward advance was resisted or compromised from time to time. To mention again, Persia was in late nineteenth century recognized as an independent State with membership of international community only on acceptance of some extra-territorial rights extending to protection of British nationals under treaty of unilateral obligation known as 'capitulation' by the Shah of Iran in favour of Britain.

Neo-colonialism in Iran of the West

Capitalism of the West in early twentieth century adopted a new approach as alternative to annexing a kingdom or State. That was, to give an agreed share to the king on the exploitation of minerals or oil on annual basis by the States of the West. The British established the Anglo-Persian Oil Company in 1912 on this principle. A further concessionary agreement between the Iran and the Anglo-Iranian Oil Company was made in 1933. The agreement was negotiated to settle a dispute between Iran and the UK, which had been before the Council of the League of Nations, wherein UK had charged Iran for violation of its treaty obligations. After the conclusion of the concessionary agreement between Iran and the Company, latter got wider range of oil producing rights in Iran. The Company was nationalized around 1950 and its refineries were seized by Iran and British workers were asked to leave. Oil production stopped, the matter was taken to International Court by Britain, where Iran as a State was not held to be a party to the agreement and so not bound by the concessionary agreement. Thereafter, to tide over the situation of oil production stoppage due to the tussle, help was sought by Iran of USA for settlement. It was agreed at State levels in 1953 that pending negotiations, the Anglo-Iranian Oil Company will remain nationalized but Bahrain Petroleum Company and Arabian American Oil Company (ARMCO) formed by Standard of California and the Texas Oil Company of USA were to operate the nationalized Anglo-Iranian Oil Company. The oil production started again thereafter in Iran.

USA replaces UK in Iran

Subsequently, an oil accord was signed by Iran with USA at State level on August 5, 1954, that was to run for 25 years with the right to renewal for another 15 years with the process beginning in 1957, and Iran, for all practical purposes, became a US protectorate through complex arrangements for enforcement of the accord.[9] Under the accord, a 'consortium' of 8 oil companies was incorporated in Netherlands, namely Secony-Vacuum, Standard of New Jersey, Standard of California and the Gulf Oil Company with 32% share stock (each holding 8%,) French 'Compagnie Francaise de Petrole' holding 6%, Royal Dutch Shell 14% and British Anglo-Iranian Oil Company holding 40% of Stocks. This consortium shared with British, French, and American and Dutch corporations a variety of oil exploration and producing and exporting contracts for Iran oil. The consortium agreed to pay in addition to some agreed amounts 50% income tax annually on exports.[10] As a concession, the State run Iranian National Oil Company was to operate only the Kermanshah fields and refinery, limited to serving the local market only without right to export. The Anglo-Iranian Oil Company was to be paid $70,000,000 over ten years by Iran and another $ 500,000,000 by the consortium in compensation.

Iran and World Reaction to Neo-colonialism

The developments under the Charter of the UNO, particularly by the end of 1950s, followed the path of self-determination and liquidation of empire systems. The development of people of new undeveloped States from grass root level and democratic form of government were made watchwords for the hundred or more such States that were without industrialization and technical know-how. It was emphasized that autocracies were retrogressive form of government polity as compared to democracies in the civilization timescale. The new States came into existence but the USA and the former imperial powers coupled the formation of new States out of their empires with continued association in economic field in the name and form of assistance and co-operation. Naturally, for economic reasons, the new States became or continued to remain suppliers of raw materials to the developed, industrialized States and in return these got manufactured goods. Side by side, the USSR and China with their dogmas of Marxism worked to convert the new States to communist totalitarian one-party democracy form of polity, before these were given technical and industrial expertise by them. However, the General Assembly of UNO with representation of new States with 'one State-one vote' system disturbed such a balance by mid-1960s. The new States wanted, in the name of humanity and the high principles enshrined in the Charter, that the developed States should come forward and for humanitarian development gratuitously and generously help the undeveloped States in raising the gross national product and per capita income. The argument taken up was that the richness and stability of industrialized and imperial States was built on the exploitation of labour, natural resources and raw materials cheaply or rather freely acquired from the colonies, vassal States, occupied territories or subordinated kingdoms. The continued prosperity of the former imperial States after giving independence to their territorial possession under the above system was expressed as neo-colonialism and was condemned. It was regarded as a new civilization element that new international relationships should be accompanied by measures to help the new or undeveloped States in raising their gross national product and per capita income alongwith indigenous industrialization.[11] The West controlled oil industry of Iran, Iraq and other States of the

Gulf region also came under censor of the vice of neo-colonialism associated with them. In the transitional turbulent period, there was resistance to the nationalization or expropriation of foreign property by new States and also the indigenous industrialization, by denying energy resources, finances and knowledge of technical expertise. The denial processes led to commercial inequities, new forms of diplomatic configurations[12] and later for demands for new energy sources, viz., the nuclear reactors, for meeting energy needs.

UN for Permanent Sovereignty over Natural Resources

The efforts of UN to reduce technological and industrial gap between rich and poor States and for giving incentive to indigenous industrial growth of undeveloped countries took a shape with the decision of UN General Assembly to establish[13] the United Nations Conference on Trade and Development (UNCTAD), a standing or continuing body. This objective was to be achieved without disturbing or reducing military strength and balance between developed and undeveloped States. The UNCTAD was followed by various discussions and formulations between North (developed States) and South (undeveloped States). A boost to new States was provided by UN resolutions on elimination of use of economic, political or any other type of measures to coerce another State in order to put restraint on or to obtain from it the subordination to others in the exercise of its sovereign rights. The Security Council[14] of the UN and the General Assembly[15] adopted the resolutions confirming "Permanent Sovereignty over Natural Resources', including radioactive elements, to be exercised by all the States alongwith the right to nationalize such resources for making their optimum or proper use. The resolutions laid a duty on other States to refrain from use of military, economic or other coercions aimed at the territorial integrity of the State exercising the mentioned rights. These developments made the States, including Iran, conscious of their natural wealth, including oil and other energy resources to the obvious disadvantage of the West. Those States like Iran which had radioactive natural resources, also desired to use such materials commercially or for converting these for nuclear power resources, though might not be for making nuclear weapons that involve a high-technology background and a powerful enemy to be tackled.

A pious culmination of the above process was further reached by the adoption by the UN General Assembly of (1) the proclamation for "The Establishment of New International Economic Order"[16] accompanied with "The Programme of Action on the Establishment of a New International Economic Order",[17] both of which made no progress. However, the resentment of the States of South, including Arab and other Islamic States of Middle East and North Africa, whose oil was being exploited by the States of North moved in a wrong direction also when the latter made no compromises. These States resorted to terrorism and 'hostage taking', even by flouting diplomatic immunities, for extracting economic aid or ousting foreign companies from their soil. On the other hand, States of North developed rigid business terms for monetary debit and credit transactions through World Trade Organization system developed by 1993 for globalization of markets, free trade and sanctity of business transactions. The WTO system has replaced aid to the States of the South with trade with the States of North for their development. Iran is also caught in this web. Semi-developed States have welcomed the WTO system but it has strangulating effect on less developed States including Iran, which in all circumstances leaves much leverage to the developed industrial powers. The WTO system operates through International Monetary Fund (IMF) for balance of payment transactions between trading States but IMF operations are totally controlled by few States of the West.

The US and Iranian Hostilities, Nuclear Offshoots

It was mentioned that in the years 1950-80, USA and monarchial Iran had close international relationship. According to US documents[18] declassified in 2005, in 1970s "the Iranian uranium enrichment programme, the shut-down of which the US now demands, was recommended by former President Gerald Ford's top officials, including his Secretary of State, Henry Kissinger, current Vice President, Richard Cheney and

Defense Secretary, Donald Rumsfeld". Kissinger justified[19] his endorsement of the recommendations by observing that "they (Iranians) were then an allied country (under the Shah) and this was a commercial transaction. We did not address the question of them one day moving toward nuclear weapons". The hostilities between US and Iran, though at first related to oil concessions, have had several other related reasons. In 1980s, one was that in order to have favourable or subservient Iran government's responses, USA was maneuvering Iranian internal politics. In Iran, an 'Islamic Revolution' in political ruling system had taken place in 1979 and the pro-US Shah Mohammed Reza Pahalvi of Iran went to USA in exile.[20] In order to compel return of deposed Shah for attrition, on 4 November 1979 hundred of fanatic students stormed into the US embassy and consulates, took control of the premises and also took 53 hostages. Iran government ignored and maintained an attitude of indifference. A resolution in Security Council urging Iran to end the crisis was adopted and when it was not heeded, a resolution in Security Council for adoption of sanctions against Iran was brought and that was vetoed in January 1980 by USSR. Proceedings in International Court of Justice were boycotted by Iran, though in its judgment on 24 May 1980, the ICJ held Iran responsible for violating international law and obligations owed by it to USA. However, it was a humiliating experience to US on the whole. What price USA ultimately paid for ending the matter is another story, but unfortunately for USA and the world the episode established nefarious worth of the acts of terrorism in forcing international actions of States. This is how Iran became a terrorist State for the West for all the times to come. Eventually, a US sponsored invasion of Iran by Iraq took place in 1980 aimed at deprivation of Iran of the oil rich province Khuzestan, lying along the common border with Iraq near Persian Gulf, and the Abadan refineries on the Persian Gulf. The Iraq-Iran war, fought for 8 years, ended on an even note in 1988 under a UN sponsored armistice. However, the economy and oil producing capacity of Iran was badly shaken. This was regarded as US diplomacy of vengeance. In another episode, it is widely believed that between 1984-86 US administrations had to seek and receive co-operation, in reverse gear, of Iran in the matter of securing release of hostages held in Lebanon by the Hizbollah party. Under this diplomacy of co-operation, US sold substantial arms secretly as a deal to Iran as a price in order to obtain release of hostages. Further, as Israel had special fears from the Hizbollah party, the pressure on US to depend on Iran in order to help its natural ally, Israel, by keeping in control the Hizbollah party with the help of Iran continued for a long time. Perhaps, in return with US looking the other way, Iran managed to get nuclear reactors from Russia and China for power generation, while Pakistani private bank BCCI and Pakistan got entry into Iran for clandestine nuclear centrifuge deals for upgrading uranium to dual use fission-uranium, which could be used both ways either as fuel for power generating nuclear reactors or for making low-yield nuclear weapons. Pakistan got the status of a go-in-between the two States, USA and Iran, for protection of the interests of the former. However, in the net result, the strangulating effect of oil diplomacy against Iran forced it to develop or acquire nuclear reactors for its energy requirements alongwith the technology for enrichment of uranium to reactor grade. The Russian built reactors use uranium enriched fuel and not thorium based fuel; and Non-Proliferation Treaty does not prohibit indigenous manufacture of fuel for nuclear reactors. The technologies for producing weapon grade uranium and reactor grade uranium fuel are practically the same; ultimately, it is only a matter of intention, fair or fraudulent, depending on the ultimate use of the product.

Iran-Iraq War (1980–88), use of a WMD

The eight or ten-year war between Iran and Iraq began on 22 September 1980, when Iraqi armed forces invaded in a pre-emptive strike in western Iran along the joint border of the two countries. As for the causes, it is believed that President Saddam Hussein of Iraq wanted to seize control of the rich oil-producing Iranian border province of Khuzestan with Abadan refineries and to reassert sovereignty of Iraq over both banks of the Shatt al-'Arab, a river formed by the confluence of the Tigris and Euphrates rivers that historically was the border between the two countries. Politically, Iraq was also concerned over attempts by Iran's new Islamic revolutionary regime to incite rebellion among Iraq's Shi'ite majority. At this time, the government of Iran after the revolution was rather in a disorder and its regular armed forces were demoralized, Iran not knowing how to adjust to the changed political organization of the country . The war upto 1981 saw initial success of Iraq followed by substantial advances by troops of Iran into Iraq. Later in 1982, Iraq voluntarily withdrew its forces from all captured Iranian territory and began seeking a peace agreement with Iran. However, Iran persisted and continued the war in an effort to overthrow President Saddam Hussein. It was known that Ayatollah Ruhollah Khomeini, a founder of Iran Republic, and President Hussein of Iraq bore strong personal animosity toward each other. Soon a situation of stalemate was reached. Both nations made sporadic air and missile attacks against each other's cities and military and oil installations and they also attacked oil tankers of each other in the Persian Gulf. Iran also attacked tankers of Kuwait and other Gulf States. It is also a fact of international diplomacy that the interests of USA and Iraq coincided where devastation of Iran was concerned.[21] This had prompted the United States and several western European nations to enter and station warships in the Persian Gulf on the pretext of protecting oil tankers of neutral States. The world community condemned Iraq when it used chemical gas weapons, a WMD, against troops of Iran in violation of international law. Iraq had been forced to sue for peace since the mid-1980s, but in August 1988 the deteriorating economy of Iran and the Iraqi gains on the battlefield also compelled Iran to accept a United Nations-mediated ceasefire that it had been resisting for long.[22]

After, 11 September 2001 episode, USA had charged that Iran was supporting Osama bin Laden and Taliban, though it is generally believed that the Shi'ite clergy in Iran would never show any sympathy for the Wahabi variant of Sunni religion that the Taliban followed, unless there was a political necessity.

Principles of diplomacy, however, emphasize that enemies of USA should combine and this might have happened here. Taliban were a creation in Afghanistan of US-Pak diplomacy against Soviet Russia. In 1990s, it is known that the relations between Iran and the Taliban regime have always been embittered and had almost broken down into open hostilities in 1998. After 9/11 episodes, USA was advised by Israel that Iran was rendering vital arms support to the Hizbollah Party, latter being a constituent of the ruling coalition in Lebanon State but which was considered to be a terrorist organization both by Israel and the US. Earlier, US President Clinton had ordered on 4 January 1995 freeze of the assets in USA of West Asia 'terrorist groups' including Hizbollah that threaten to disrupt peace process in West Asia. However, the description of the attacks on the Israeli military by Hizbollah force in a territory, which the Lebanese believe to be a part of their country but to be in an illegal occupation of Israel, as 'acts of terrorism' is confusing and not easily understandable. Perhaps the term terrorist attack is diplomatically stretched a bit far for attacks on Israeli military forces on the borders of Israel and Lebanon. Both of the above mentioned aspects, the 9/11 attack and conflicts on Israel-Lebanon border, made Iran a matter of direct strategic concern to USA, and USA took upon itself the task of cleansing terrorist incidence upon itself and its supporter, Israel. Thus Iran factor became a target of bellicose US diplomacy.

NUCLEAR IRAN AND NPT

The Nuclearization of Iran

It is not very clear when Iran thought, if at all, of acquiring or developing a nuclear arsenal. In Iran an 'Islamic Revolution' in political ruling system had taken place in 1979 and Shah of Iran went to USA in exile. The relations between USA and Islamic Republic of Iran since then have been tense, of action and reaction and of diplomatic chess game. The US has been fearful in 1990s that Iran might have developed nuclear fuel with the secret transfer of nuclear technology[23] by A.Q. Khan of Pakistan in 1991 and 1992. In 1995, US is said to have proceeded to set a nuclear verification facility in Pakistan to monitor nuclear explosion and nuclear testing ability in neighboring areas, including Iran, China and India. Iran has had an ongoing dispute with UAE over the possession of three islands in Persian Gulf, and Iran has abstained from taking them over because of strong US-UK naval presence in the Gulf. Further, on the other side, Iran was starved of hi-tech machinery and energy for operating its oil refineries and for general industrialization since 1970s onwards as and when the American run oil refineries closed down by 1979. The world understanding was that Iran has been a sufferer of neo-colonialism and has been economically and diplomatically coerced to depend on the West concerned for the protection of its oil interests. The Monarchy of Iran had regarded the royalties received from oil companies basically to be personal income but then after the political revolution took place in Iran in 1979 and Shah of Iran safely went to USA to live in exile, the attitude of government towards development of the country by oil sale income radically changed. Now, the income from this source was no longer royalty for personal income of Shah. The relationship of USA with Iran had alongwith changed drastically and some of the sore points were referred to earlier in this lecture. Now, after the UN General Assembly denounced in 1994-96 the proliferation of Weapons of Mass Destruction (WMD) including nuclear arsenal and asked have-not States not to acquire and develop them,[24] interestingly the USA became active as a self-styled promoter and enforcer of the GA resolution prohibiting the States of proliferation of WMD in general.

Nuclear Curbs on Non-Big Five

The USA had reacted with admonitions against Pakistan, India, Iran, Iraq, Libya and North Korea from time to time, though not against Israel, for their nuclear policies. Curbs were placed by USA on arms and military aircraft supply to Pakistan in 1990 for developing nuclear technology clandestinely in violation of NPT principles and not by indigenous research and development. The US President, Clinton, had radically restructured the US nuclear policies in the post-cold war era of 1990s. He had sought indefinite extension of NPT in 1995, alongwith reassurances to the developing States of assisting them in their pursuits of acquiring civil nuclear reactors for generating power while he insisted that all States joined the proposed Comprehensive Test Ban Treaty (CTBT). Israel and India which were developing nuclear weapons by indigenous research without smuggling nuclear materials or violating NPT, reiterated in February 1995 to retain their options in making nuclear weapons. Pakistan said that it would follow Indian stance and will join CTBT only after India did so. After their respective 1998 nuclear tests by India and Pakistan both States had to undergo severe restrictions on import of nuclear related technology, equipment and machineries placed by USA, England, Japan and several other States. Again, the States Iraq and Iran, from the point of view of decades old international politics or oil-diplomacy of the West, which had been inimical and were obstacles to the oil interest pursuits of the West, were presumed to be interested in acquiring or developing nuclear weapon technology and so came under censor. Stalinist North Korea became nuclear in 1990s and was determined to unite South Korea under its national policy of one Korea, which was contrary to US anti-communism policies,[25] and so became an evil State. As for Libya, though it was friendly to Britain, it also had two decades old record of hostility towards Israel as part of Arab fight for Palestinian Arab State. The US President Reagan had accused Libya of running a reign of terror directed against American nationals and had called President Gaddafi to be the "mad dog of the Middle East". On 15 April 1986, American fighter aircraft had raided two cities Tripoli and Benghazi of Libya in reprisal for so-called Libyan terrorist activities.[26] A nuclear Libya was obviously a risk factor with reference to Arab causes particularly when so developed in violation of its NPT obligations.

USA up against Iran in 21st Century

By the beginning of twenty-first century, CTBT had failed after US did not join it but the UN General Assembly resolution banning proliferation of weapons of mass destruction

(WMD) was in force. Further, as part of the move for general disarmament in the world, the United Nations had firmly moved for "Prohibition of the Development and Manufacture of New Types of Weapons of Mass Destruction and New Systems of Such Weapons"[27], on the report of the Conference on Disarmament. The 'Prohibition' extends to radiological weapons, lethal chemical weapons and other emerging new types of Weapons of Mass Destruction (WMD), nuclear or conventional, that have characteristics comparable in destructive effect to those of 'weapons of mass destruction' already identified in the definition of weapons of mass destruction adopted by the United Nations in 1948. The UN has called upon all States, immediately to follow the recommendations of the Conference on Disarmament. The USA has taken these developments as legal obligations for some States. After 11 September 2001, episode, USA had charged that Iran and Iraq were supporting Osama bin Laden and Taliban whom US regarded responsible for the 9/11 terrorist event. Both of the States denied any such involvement. It was known gradually that with the blessings or protection of Taliban régime of Afghanistan, Osama bin Laden was actively financing, encouraging and masterminding the Islamic fundamentalist terrorism. He had also challenged the presence and policies of USA in Saudi Arabia, Arab States and the Middle East. The UN that had condemned 9/11 terrorist activities had recognized that Bin Laden was an outlaw menace and had sanctioned armed action in Afghanistan in 2002. However, in absence of proper and sufficient evidence of the possession or preparations for production of WMD, the moves of USA and UK for UN action against Iran and Iraq had failed by early 2003. Later, USA and UK had concentrated on Iraq alone, might be for tactical limitations, and had initiated unilateral armed action, ignoring UN and world opinion, on the territory of Iraq and had vowed to end the WMD acquired by Iraq; and to oust the political regime of President Saddam Hussein. By July-August 2003 the operation against Iraq leading to its occupation was complete though no WMD were found on the territory of Iraq.[28] The country was completely devastated and was without any civil supplies system and was without administration except for the rule of occupation forces. This had a telling effect on the morale of Iran, Libya and Pakistan,[29] other possessors of WMD, all of which reacted as these would not have reacted otherwise.

The US Offensive on Iran

President Bush had declared Iran to be one of the 'axis of evil' presumably on the intelligence reports that A.Q. Khan of Pakistan had sold and supplied know-how and necessary expertise for making nuclear arsenal to Libya, Iran, North Korea and possibly also to Iraq and Syria.[30] The use of A.Q. Khan could have been a 'sting' operation, in American slang. Rather surprisingly, according to declassified documents[31] in 2005 the "Ford administration of 1970s even recommended to Iran at one point to make the nuclear project a joint one with Pakistan" while commercially supplying nuclear know-how to its then ally, Iran. Examining the cases of 'axis of evil', North Korea was already under negotiations with USA separately on nuclear disarmament. The Bush administration had refused to honour explicitly the 1994 Framework Agreement with North Korea in February 2002,[32] and war with North Korea on the same lines as with Iraq was predicted in early 2003. In the matter of Iraq it was declared by USA and UK that Iraq possessed a nuclear arsenal and these two had begun unilateral action in March 2003 in disregard of international law. Under this operation Iraq was badly devastated by bombing and missiles, occupied and President Saddam Hussein was 'captured' and was put on trial under a 'restored' national regime. When USA and UK failed to find any nuclear arsenal in Iraq after occupation, it was conjectured that Iraq might have transported the nuclear facilities and nuclear arsenal to Iran. The hostilities, to re-emphasize and recapitulate, between US and Iran related to withdrawal of oil concessions granted to USA by Shah regime of Iran by the new government of Iran. As already mentioned in Iran an 'Islamic Revolution' in political ruling system had taken place in 1979 and the pro-US Shah Mohammed Reza Pahalvi had gone to USA in exile.[33] The USA had unsuccessfully maneuvered the internal politics of Iran in 1980s in order to have a changeover to a favorable or subservient regime here.[34] The pro- US Shah of Iran had been deposed and in sequence the unparallel case or incident of taking fifty three US embassy and consulate staff as hostages following anti US stance had taken place in 1979-80. This nefarious historical event became the starting point of dreadful international terrorism sponsored by Islamic States having its effects in India also. Rather in retaliation to the hostage taking of 1979 by State backed Iranian mobs, a US backed invasion of Iran by Iraq had taken place in 1980. Iraq on its part also feared that the new regime of Iran was out to replace the existing regime of Saddam Hussein by a Shi'ite regime in Iraq. The Iraqi invasion, 1980, was also interpreted by the world as an activity aimed at deprivation of Iran by conquest of the oil rich province Khuzestan, along the common border near Persian Gulf and the Abadan refineries, both areas in which USA had commercial interest. The war was fought for 8 years but ended on an even note and ended in 1988 under a UN-sponsored armistice. However, the economy and oil producing capacity of Iran was badly shaken, leading to poverty and energy resource shortages. This was regarded as US diplomacy of vengeance. Further, as Israel had special fears from the Hizbollah party of Lebanon, there was pressure on US to treat Hizbollah party as a 'terrorist organization supported by Iran'. However, in mid-1980s the color of diplomacy had changed a bit for few years when Iran became otherwise useful to USA first with reference to Nicaragua[35] and secondly for the control of Hizbollah party of Lebanon.[36] The USA directly or indirectly supplied arms and allowed Iran to receive nuclear reactors from Russia and China alongwith nuclear technology from Pakistan. Iran had joined NPT and it is believed that the details of the deals of Pakistan on prohibited proliferation of nuclear technology were known to USA or else this was, to use American slang, part of 'sting' diplomacy. Thus, it was generally understood that the USA diplomatically tainted Iran as a terrorist State, possessing WMD and so worthy of being chastised as one of the 'axis of evil'.

NUCLEAR WEAPONS IN IRAN

Iran in 'Axis of Evil'

To recapitulate, the inclusion of Iran among the 'axis of evil' by the USA in January 2002 seems to have been guided by several considerations: (1) Oil diplomacy in which Iran disassociated, not extended or repudiated in 1980 the old oil contracts with US companies in the exploitation and export of its oil resources; (2) Iran had sought the help of Russia and China in the procurement of atomic reactors for replacing oil in generation of energy but was charged to be developing nuclear weapons, (3) US assessment is that Iran was in league with Arabs in the politics against Israel and was at one time trafficking Islamic militants into Syria, from where these crossed over to Lebanon to blow up Israeli security forces, and Iran was also accused of shipping arms to Palestinian militants,[37] (4) Iran was threatening stability in Gulf region which was detrimental to American interests, and (5) Iran was participating in the hostages taking diplomacy raging in the area. On 30 April 1995 under its US Trade Sanctions Act, 1995 the US had, in a much delayed action, announced trade sanctions on Iran under which US trade, export and investments were banned; the US Iran-Libya Sanctions Act of 1996 had followed. This was done in order to prevent Iran generating economic resources and finances required to pursue above-mentioned Iranian designs. The US also pressed other nations to follow suit but this did not succeed: Both Russia and China had continued to bid for the development of nuclear power plants in Iran; Pakistan a dependable ally of USA secretly provided Iran with uranium enrichment technology for handsome price; Japan and several European States continued to import oil from Iran; and Iran found other suppliers of wheat and equipments for oil production, a trade loss for the USA.

When Iraq stood devastated and destroyed by unilateral US and UK-led unilateral invasion, July 2003, Iran seems to have had reasons to get panicky, it denied having possession of nuclear bombs and invited IAEA to examine and give it clean chit on the question of possessing any nuclear arsenal. The moot question that has prevailed even in 2006 is whether US will act unilaterally as it did in Iraq or will get support of UN Security Council. Iran has maintained that it has not been pursuing nuclear weapons and has not violated the NPT. All the uranium enrichment works that it has were related to production of fuel for energy producing atomic reactors. But, USA contested the claim and had charged that Iran currently possessed nuclear weapons in violation of NPT. Scenario further enlivened when Libya, on 19 December 2003 renounced its weapons of mass destruction programme. Libya went on to officially confess that it was pursuing nuclear weapons production plan and this being a violation of the NPT, it signed an additional protocol to the Nuclear Non-Proliferation Treaty (NPT), allowing snap inspections of its nuclear facilities by IAEA.[38] The IAEA had acted swiftly making inspections and investigations both in Libya and Iran, but in case of Iran by presuming its statement that it had no nuclear bombs as incorrect.[39] The US independently accused Iran of pursuing a clandestine programme to develop nuclear weapons and wanted the matter to be brought before the UN Security Council, which could impose sanctions on Iran. It can be mentioned that there is a loophole under the nuclear Non-Proliferation Treaty (which came into effect in 1970) that countries without nuclear weapons are allowed to develop nuclear reactors for power and are allowed to make or manufacture indigenously the fuel for the reactors. However, the enriching of uranium beyond nuclear reactor grade to weapons grade is not a difficult scientific or technological proposition and as long as a State can keep such activities a secret, the State can do so but by violating the NPT in case it has joined the treaty. The non-signatories to the NPT, like India, can indigenously develop nuclear weapons but without obtaining nuclear expertise, equipment, uranium or technology from NPT Parties.

An IAEA report of November 2003 of investigations, based on limited inspections in Iran, did not find any evidence that nuclear weapons were being developed but did accuse Iran of concealing some of its nuclear research based programmes[40] The United Nations nuclear agency had added that it was seriously concerned by Iran's failure to declare aspects of its nuclear programme. The UN inspectors discovered high-tech enrichment equipment, called the gas centrifuge system, on an Iranian air force base. The find appeared to signal a link between Tehran's suspect nuclear program and its military use. The gas centrifuge system equipment is used to process uranium, which then can be used for nuclear fuel or warheads, depending on the level of enrichment.[41] The IAEA confronted Iran with evidence that suggested that it had concealed its nuclear programme for nearly two decades. Iran in October 2003 acknowledged running of an enrichment program but asserted that it is only for producing fuel indigenously for generating power from nuclear reactors and to avoid foreign dependnce. Tehran has insisted that its nuclear reactors are largely based on Russian technology using uranium based fuel, are for peaceful purpose and are needed to meet Iran's growing energy demand.[42] The United States and other nations, however, accused Iran of secretly trying to make nuclear weapons. Mohamed ElBaradei, Director of the UN International Atomic Energy Agency, had singled out for particular explanation Iran's failure to declare that it was researching on advanced centrifuge designs, known as P2, capable of producing highly enriched uranium.[43] Later, Iran made a limited admission that it had acquired expertise from abroad.[44] Investigations had revealed that Dr A.Q. Khan of Pakistan was the source of transfer of nuclear technology both to Libya and Iran but that the transfers of nuclear-tech to Iran took place before these were made to Libya, since the nuclear technology given to Iran was less sophisticated. The IAEA investigators had concluded that it was so because it appeared that A.Q. Khan simply gave Pakistan's surplus equipments to the Iranians. Pakistan had also developed new centrifuges, which meant that the old ones went into the black market. One of them, which were transferred to Iran, was apparently contaminated with enriched uranium. After this was established by the United Nations International Atomic Energy Agency (IAEA), Iran thereafter had no option but to admit either that it had processed the fuel itself or had got it otherwise by accident. It chose the second explanation, but simply said that it got the parts through a third party. This opened up the question as to from where it came. The IAEA investigations revealed before February 2004 that a Pakistani-led nuclear trafficking network existed which extended to at least seven nations and that A.Q. Khan operated this Pakistani nuclear trafficking network.[45] The technical analysis by IAEA had detected the hand of Dr Khan in the designs.[46] Independently of this, A.Q. Khan, on television, admitted in the first week of February 2004 that he, not the Pakistani government, had supplied nuclear technology to Libya, Iran and North Korea and had asked the President of Pakistan for forgiveness, which was given.[47] Even in 2005, the USA continued to suspect Pakistan for close ties leading to nuclear cooperation with Iran though 1980s. However, Pakistan throws the blame for nuclear proliferation to Iran on the disgraced scientist A.Q. Khan personally.

The Stalemate

The United Nations IAEA had said it was seriously concerned by Iran's failure to declare some aspects of its nuclear programme. It had said in a report that Iran had not declared designs it possessed for a centrifuge that could be used to make bomb-grade material. Iran had also experimented with polonium, a radioactive substance that can trigger a nuclear blast.[48] The matters did not come to rest with the confessions of personal responsibility by A.Q. Khan and exoneration of Pakistan for nuclear proliferation. USA linked Iran with terrorism[49] and insisted that Iran should scrap and close down the nuclear plant for this reason while Iran insisted that those uranium enrichment facilities were for providing nuclear fuel for its energy producing civilian nuclear reactors and did not involve violation of NPT.[50]

Iran, in August 2004 announced that it has contracts with Russia to build more nuclear reactors using uranium for producing electricity, though US has expressed concerns that the waste by-products could be used by Iran to manufacture nuclear bombs. This was followed by a demand from Britain, France and Germany, the EU trio, that Iran should halt all parts of enrichment of nuclear waste in the atomic fuel cycle that can be used to make a nuclear bomb. These nations submitted a draft resolution to UN International Atomic Energy Agency, calling upon Iran to immediately freeze its uranium enrichment programmes. Iran rejected the European demands of hardline diplomacy, reiterating that its atomic ambitions are peaceful. It denied any plan to develop nuclear arms and insisted that its programme was intended only to produce electricity and the enrichment facilities would be used only to produce low-enriched fuel used in nuclear power plants and not for producing highly enriched fuel required for nuclear bombs. It also asserted that it has already mastered the nuclear fuel cycle but was using it for peaceful purposes only.[51] In turn, the USA squarely accused Iran of pursuing nuclear bomb plans. European Union States offered incentives, like fuel, to Iran for halting nuclear enrichment and ruled out any US war with Iran on its nuclear plans. The question was whether Iran should halt 'all' uranium enrichment activities as part of self-denial, which it resisted. While the matter was before IAEA, President G.W. Bush, in an interview when asked if he would 'rule out the potential for military action against Iran', said that US would not give up any option, including war.

After Iran had submitted to the inspection of its nuclear plants for scrutiny by IAEA in October 2003 for obtaining a clean chit against the US charges of possessing nuclear weapons, the IAEA had become active in making investigations as already discussed. The IAEA had welcomed in February 2004 Iran's agreement to suspend enrichment activities and to stop the assembly and testing of centrifuges, as a step that could help in building confidence.[52] Further, in February, Iran had signed[53] the 1967 Protocol of IAEA. This was taken to mean that Iran was moving towards greater compliance with the IAEA in order to avoid the danger of UN Security Council sanctions at the behest of the USA. Normally, the IAEA has right to conduct searches or inspections of the nuclear facilities of its members at short notice but it is not authorized to make unannounced inspections. Under the Protocol the Inspectors get broader search powers, including the right to demand information on non-government facilities and the right to check radiation levels in wider territorial areas and the

Government has greater obligation to report all matters relating to its nuclear fuel cycle.[54] The inspections carried out under the provisions of protocol are not random and intrusive, which Iran was trying to avoid. Under the protocol any suspicion about possible undeclared nuclear sites have to be made known to the host government, which is given every opportunity to clarify the situation, and inspections are only insisted upon as a last resort. On 8 March 2004 Mr. ElBaradei, Chief of IAEA, said at the Vienna that Iran had violated the Nuclear Non-Proliferation Treaty (NPT) for many years and he singled out for particular concern failure of Iran to declare that it was researching on the advanced centrifuge designs, which are capable of producing dual use highly enriched uranium.[55] On 13 March 2004 in Vienna the IAEA had in a resolution censured Iran for omitting key atomic technology from an October declaration. But, the resolution stopped short of threatening UN sanctions against Tehran which the US had been pressing for asserting that Iran had violated NPT by developing nuclear weapons.[56] It is to be remembered that Iran had invited IAEA inspections only to help in dispelling suspicions that it had something to hide in the matter and extent of its nuclear programme against the US accusations.

The said resolution of IAEA had set sparks of reaction. Iran forthwith suspended key inspections of its nuclear facilities after the IAEA accused Iran of keeping nuclear activity secret. On 6 April 2004 Iran held that researches and building of a nuclear conversion or enrichment plant near Isfahan, accordingly, were a totally separate issues from the commitment to the suspension of uranium enrichment, and that the new facility will process uranium ore into gas, a step towards enrichment for production of uranium fuel for reactors and not for nuclear weapons.[57] After a meeting of 7 April 2004 between Mr ElBaradei, Head of IAEA and the Head of Iran's Atomic Energy Association, Gholam Reza Aghazadeh, all the doubts of Iran about insincerity of and spying activities by UN inspection team were removed. Thereafter the inspection work by the UN team was resumed in April 2004. Iran announced it would "voluntarily" suspend centrifuge work from 9 April

2004 and it also pledged to accelerate the process of co-operation with the UN team of inspectors and clarify where needed all concerns about its nuclear programme by June.[58] Asserting its right to develop nuclear energy, Iran declared in August 2004 that it was going ahead to build more nuclear power plants with the collaboration of Russia with which Iran has contracts[59]. Under bilateral agreement between Iran and Russia, a 1000 megawatt nuclear reactor is being built at Bushehr on Persian Gulf coastline of Iran. The nuclear reactor would use thorium based low grade uranium fuel and will be active by 2006. Under the agreement, the fuel supply for the reactor will be maintained by the Russian Federal Energy Agency.

Iran and European Union

Following the Paris Agreement of November 2004 between the E.U.-3, composed of Britain, France and Germany supported by the High Representative of the European Union, and of Iran, Iran suspended enrichment activity both at Esfahan and Natanz. These two plants were subsequently sealed by the IAEA. The EU sought to pursue a reconciliatory approach towards Iran so that diplomacy was given its due role in place of confrontation. The EU-3 was to negotiate[60] a package of trade, technology and security issues or incentives in lieu of guarantee from Iran that its nuclear programme is of peaceful purpose only. In the meantime, it came to light that Iran had not reported the existence of a key underground uranium enrichment facility at Natanz[61] to the International Atomic Energy Agency (IAEA). The Esfahan facility essentially converts uranium into material for enrichment at Natanz. This said[62] secret activity of Iran would be a violation of the Nuclear Non-Proliferation Treaty (NPT) by Iran if the enriched uranium would be used for making nuclear weapons. The existence and presence of these facilities was leaked out by Iranian exiles to Western authorities. This factor had some effect on negotiations. But, the EU-3 failed to submit the package proposals by July 2005. Interestingly, Iran threatened to resume the sensitive nuclear enrichment work from Monday, 1 August 2005 giving

24 hours to the EU to submit the relevant proposals for ending the nuclear standoff. This step on the part of Iran involved breaking of UN seals on the Esfahan nuclear plant. This was taken by USA and EU to be a "barely acceptable pressure" on their stance. The IAEA Chief intervened and demanded that the seals can be broken only in presence of UN inspectors and for that two days' further time was necessary. Iran resumed the operation of unsealed facilities from 8 August 2005, after a gap of nine months. Iran had argued that it was entitled to master all aspects of the nuclear fuel cycle[63] so long as all its facilities were monitored by the IAEA under its Statute.[64] The IAEA 35-member board acted differently and at its meeting on 11 August it passed a resolution expressing "serious concern" and calling Iran to stop enrichment work at Esfahan, since the IAEA was seized on the outstanding issues relating to Iran's nuclear programme that were yet to be resolved, and that the IAEA was not yet in a position to conclude that there were no undeclared nuclear materials or activities in Iran. Significantly, the IAEA did not refer the case to the United Nations Security Council for sanctions.[65] Iran responded by saying that the core issue was open to negotiations with EU-3 States.[66] The trade-economy package that the EU-3 placed on the negotiating table in August 2005 were vague and fell short of Iran's expectations. Iran removed the IAEA seals on the process lines and hexafluoride (HEX) stored at the Uranium Conversion Facility (UCF) at Esfahan. This resumption of uranium conversion activity, though pursued under safeguards, has triggered the loud call from the West for referral of the actions of Iran to the Security Council. As mentioned on 11 August 2005 the IAEA Board had adopted a resolution of by consensus, urged Iran to resume its voluntary suspension all enrichment-related activities, but it did not recommend a referral to the Security Council. The resolution also asked the Director-General to submit a status report on Iran before 3 September. On September 19, the IAEA board met to consider the report of Director General and to decide a future course of action following Iran's refusal to revert to the suspension of uranium

conversion and repeating of the argument that Iran is not obliged to put uranium conversion under safeguards and the suspension of enrichment process had been voluntary. The meeting of IAEA board of 24 September 2005 finally resolved that Iran's "non-compliance" with the safeguards agreement and continued "concealment" of its activities warranted referral of the matter to the Security Council. However, the final resolution by votes deferred any decision to a later meeting of the board scheduled in November 2005. The resolution was against the wishes of USA, India voted for the resolution so that confrontation might be ultimately avoided by change of minds while China and Russia abstained from voting and might have thus reserved their right to veto in the Security Council against any UN armed intervention. Late in November 2005, Russia proposed for a solution that Iranian uranium could be enriched as fuel for nuclear reactors of Iran on sites in Russian territory. But, the fact remained that "Iranians have resumed conversion and no alternative proposals have been accepted". The uranium matter of Iran is hot, though not boiling hot now, it so appears. The EU-3 States got fed up by January 2006 with their efforts signified end of their two and half years attempts to convince Iran or barter with it the plans of Iran to abandon its uranium enrichment, research and development programmes. EU-3 expressed their suspicion that Iran intended to use its uranium to produce fuel for nuclear weapons and in a joint statement[67] said: "We believe the time has now come for the Security Council to become involved". But the way to UN Security Council depends on the decision of the Board of Governors of IAEA, which is the nuclear watchman of UN. On part of Iran its President, Mahmoud Ahmadinejad, reiterated: "We have repeatedly said the Iranian nation does not need nuclear weapons. We are civilized nation" and that "According to Agency (IAEA) regulations and the NPT, all member nations can have nuclear technology and no excuses or strategies can infringe on these rights, even inspections (by the Agency) must not stop them from having their rights".[68] The oil diplomacy persists alongwith this confrontation, the oil prices have climbed up to a record high in January 2006. Iran is fourth biggest exporter of crude oil of the world and its exports would be disrupted causing ripples in world economy if any armed action against it takes place on the nuclear issue.

ENDNOTES

1. Early Iran, Persia, had its first kingdom ruler Cyrus (550 BC), of the then royal house of Greeks called 'Achaemenians' and a sort of 'World State' was established by the Achaemenians. They had become part of Syric civilization of Judas, Zoroastrians, Mahayana Buddhists, fire and idol worshippers. Alexander the Great of Macedonia, a city state of Greece, devastated this "World State" of Achaemenian in 4th century BC, and Persian kingdom became part of the Hellenic Greek "World State" and Iran provided the land route for Greek expansion into India for more than four centuries. After the reign for about a thousand years by the Hellenic civilization, Hijazi Semitic nomad barbarians from Arabian Plateau, called by Greeks and Romans as 'Saracens' conquered the Iranian Plateau in around 4th century AD and brought back the Syric world with them along with the teachings of Christ, in the form now known as Orthodox Christian Church. Thereafter, Saracens became the "Orthodox Christian universal state' that incorporated Iran plateau and parts of Russia. Saracens, by middle of seventh century, embraced Islam and became fanatic developed military power. Persia by 750 AD came under Saracen universal state and became Islamic platform. In the same year, Baghdad, in present Iraq, became the spiritual capital of Islam, after the descendents of Prophet's uncle Abbas took over Umiyad dynasty. The Umiyad dynasty had turned Khalifa`it (Caliphate) into kingship. Later, in 16th century, Khalifa`it (Caliphate) went to Turkish Ottoman Empire and Constantinople became both spiritual and temporal capital of Islam. Those who resisted this change were called Shia Muslims, their leaders, including Imam Ali, were cruelly executed by new Khalifa in the city of Karbala, near Baghdad. Karbala is the holy shrine of Shia sect of Muslims since then. At present, Shia faction of Islam is in majority in Iraq and Iran. However, most of the modern Islamic States being Sunni, the Shi'ites are victims of local religious fanaticism as in Pakistan. The boundaries of Persia under its Kings or *Shah* have changed from time to time, but since 1945, its boundaries are confined to the State of Iran only.
2. It was mentioned that in 1571 AD, Caliphate was passed on to Ottoman Emperor Salim I and after Najaf massacres of Shi'ites including Imam Ali leading to the foundation of Karbala shrine

located now in Iraq, revered by Shi'ites of all over the world, Iran became Shia majority area.

3. Serbia became autonomous in 1815 and independent by Treaty of Berlin of 1878 alongwith Montenegro and Rumania. Greek revolt took place in 1821 and independence of Greece was recognized at the London Conference in 1831, Bulgaria became autonomous in 1878.
4. Under capitulation rights, the personal and property rights of Christians were to be governed by laws of Britain and not by Islamic law.
5. In general, the European powers recognized the respective spheres of interest with regard to unoccupied territories in Asia or Africa and avoided conflict. This did not involve the consent of host or local State.
6. Also known as 'Pact of Paris' or 'Treaty for Renunciation of War'. 15 States signed it on Aug. 27, 1928. The USSR also joined the Pact on 1 April 1929. The Pact did not apply to entry of troops under an alliance, defensive wars, etc.: See, F.L. Schuman, *International Politics*, 250-52: Fenwick *International Law*, Ed. 2, 234.
7. North coastal States of Africa constituted French 'sphere of influence'; while Philippines, Thailand, Taiwan, South Korea or Saudi Arabia are or have been regarded to be under US 'sphere of influence' apart from States of Monroe doctrine.
8. Egypt, Turkey and Persia Kingdom at different times declared not to be bound by British doctrine or qualification to the Pact.
9. Already in Saudi Arabia, the US companies have had the exclusive rights to export oil and King Ibn-Saud and his 40 sons received $3000,000,000 annually by 1958 from the American oil companies.
10. See: F.L. Schuman, *International Politics*, 317 and 379.
11. The concept of 'New International Economic Order' took shape as a result of this attitude but was sidelined later by the super economic powers by 1980.
12. For example, Union of American or African States, unity of Islamic States, non-aligned movement and even division between Soviet brand and Chinese brand of communist States.
13. UN GAOR, Resolution 1955 (XIX) of 30 Dec. 1964.
14. SC Resolution 330 of 21 March 1973.
15. GA Resolution 3117 of 21 December 1973.
16. UN GAOR, Resolution 3201 (S-VI) of 9 May 1974.
17. UN GAOR, Resolution 3202 (S-VI) of 16 May 1974.

18. "Iran N-Programme at the behest of ex-US President": PTI report from Washington of the news-story appearing in *The Washington Post*: *Times of India,* Lucknow Ed., 28 March 2005.
19. Ibid.: f n, above.
20. A year later in 1980, Iran was attacked by Iraq and the war with Iraq was widely perceived to be having the extensive backing of the USA.
21. The war efforts of UN in Iraq were openly financed by Saudi Arabia and other Arab States and the war was tacitly supported by the United States and the Soviet Union, Iran's only major allies were Syria and Libya. *The New York Times*, in a report on August 18, 2002, highlighted another dimension of the clandestine US support for Iraq. The Reagan administration, it said, provided, "critical battle planning assistance at a time when American intelligence knew that Iraqi commanders would employ chemical weapons in waging the decisive battles of the Iran-Iraq war."
22. See: "Gulf War (1980-90)": *Encyclopedia Britannica*, 2002.
23. The Administration of President Ford in 1970s is reported to have suggested for a joint Pakistani-Iranian reprocessing plant and the experts held that "the deal was attractive in terms of commerce, and the relationships (with Iran and Pakistan) as a whole was very important". Quotes attributed to Charles Naas, the then US Deputy ambassador to Iran, appearing in *The Washington Post*, vide, "Iran N-Programme at the behest of ex-US President": PTI report from Washington of the news-story on official declassified documents appearing in *The Washington Post*: *Times of India,* Lucknow Ed., 28 March 2005.
24. *General Assembly Resolution.* 51/37 of 10 December 1996, entitled, "Prohibition of the Development and Manufacture of new types of Weapons of Mass Destruction and new Systems of such Weapons".
25. This attitude or international situation is parallel to China trying again and again to take over Taiwan but for US protection to Taiwan. Direct confrontation between USA and China shall be inevitable if that will involve a nuclear world war.
26. This US action was criticized world over. In the UN, the censor resolution was vetoed by US, UK and France but on 21 November, 1986, the UN General Assembly described the attack as violation of international law and had affirmed the right of Libya to receive appropriate compensation from USA for the material and human losses inflicted by the air attack.
27. General Assembly Resolution 51/37 of 10 December 1996. Prohibition of the Development and Manufacture of New Types of Weapons of Mass Destruction and New Systems of Such Weapons:

The General Assembly,

Recalling its previous resolutions on the prohibition of the development and manufacture of new types of weapons of mass destruction and new systems of such weapons,

Taking note of paragraph 77 of the Final Document of the Tenth Special Session of the General Assembly,

Determined to prevent the emergence of new types of weapons of mass destruction that have characteristics comparable in destructive effect to those of weapons of mass destruction identified in the definition of weapons of mass destruction adopted by the United Nations in 1948,

Noting that the item entitled "New types of weapons of mass destruction and new systems of such weapons: radiological weapons" was considered in the Conference on Disarmament during its 1994, 1995 and 1996 sessions, ...

(1) Reaffirms that effective measures should be taken to prevent the emergence of new types of weapons of mass destruction;

(2) ...

(3) Calls upon all States, immediately following any recommendations of the Conference on Disarmament, to give favourable consideration to those recommendations;

(4) Requests the Secretary-General to transmit to the Conference on Disarmament all documents relating to the consideration of this item by the General Assembly at its fifty-first session;

28. Actions against Iraq examined and discussed in detail in a next chapter, below.

29. Pakistan gave unqualified support to the USA in combating Taliban and Osama bin Laden and closing down Islamic fundamentalist organizations operating on the borders with Afghanistan and from its territory, handing over named terrorists to USA, etc. All this was done contrary to the wishes of the people of Pakistan and internationally it was viewed as complete surrender by Pakistan (President Musharraf) to USA (President Bush), of course, Pakistan received massive economic support in return from USA.

30. In January 2002, in a message to the Congress, President Bush vowed to crush the international 'axis of evil' composed of Iraq, Iran and North Korea.

31. "Iran N-Programme at the behest of ex-US President": PTI report from Washington of the news-story from declassified official documents appearing in *The Washington Post*: *Times of India,* Lucknow Ed., 28 March 2005.

32. One of the things that George Bush did as President in February 2002 was to express his disapproval of the growing closeness between the two Koreas and Bush castigated North Korea by including it in the "axis of evil".

33. A year later in 1980, Iran was attacked by Iraq and the war with Iran was widely perceived to be having the extensive backing of the USA or was a proxy war.

34. See paragraph 7.07, *supra*.

35. The USA had been charged in March 1983 to June 1986 by Nicaraguan Sandinista Government for intervention by way of massive infiltration of trained military units from neighboring States and of bombings by violation of its airspace, causing loss of several thousand lives, for training, arming, equipping, financing and supplying contra-rebel forces from across the border in professed order to overthrow dictatorship or oppressive government and to install a democratic government in Nicaragua. See also the Case Concerning Military and Para-Military Activities in and against Nicaragua, (Nicaragua v. U.S.) *ICJ Reports* (1984) 169 [Final verdict given on 27 June 1986] and the Case Concerning Border and Trans-border Armed Action (Nicaragua v. Honduras) *ICJ Reports* (1988) 91.

36. Earlier it was observed: "it is widely believed that between 1984-86 US administrations had to seek and received co-operation, in reverse gear, of Iran in the matter of securing release of hostages held in Lebanon by the Hizbollah party. Under this diplomacy of co-operation US sold substantial arms secretly as a deal to Iran as a price in order to obtain release of hostages. Further, as Israel had special fears from the Hizbollah party, the pressure was on US to depend on Iran in order to help its natural ally, Israel, by keeping in control the Hizbollah party with the help of Iran. This situation continued for a long time. Perhaps, in return with US looking the other way, Iran managed to get nuclear reactors from Russia and China for power generation, while Pakistani private bank BCCI and Pakistan got entry into Iran for clandestine nuclear centrifuge deals for upgrading uranium to dual use fission-uranium, which could be used either as fuel for power generating nuclear reactor or for making low-yield nuclear weapons."

37. US Defense Secretary, Donald Rumsfeld, raised the stakes still further by alleging complicity of Iran in the escape of erstwhile Taliban and Al Qaeda elements facing the military action in Afghanistan. Already, Iran had been accused of shipping arms to Palestinian militants after the Israeli defense forces interdicted a vessel carrying 50 tons of lethal weaponry in the Red Sea. The US,

under Israeli pressure, seemed to have accepted Sharon's account of some collusion between Arafat and the Iranian regime.

38. The interception of a significant shipment of components in Italy around October 2003 led President Gaddafi to decide on the elimination of non conventional weapons programs of Libya, as US officials have said.

39. USA had charged that Iran did have nuclear bombs but it was hiding them just like Iraq.

40. 'Iran Signs up to Nuclear Checks': *BBC World News,* Thursday, 18 December 2003.

41. 'U.N. Inspectors find Link to Iran Nuke Program', *Washington Post,* February 19, The Associated Press, 19 February 2004.

42. 'Iran Signs up to Nuclear Checks': *BBC World News,* Thursday, 18 December, 2003.

43. 'Iran Set for UN Nuclear Censure': *BBC World News,* Tuesday, 9 March 2004.

44. 'On the Trail of the Black Market Bombs': *BBC World News,* Thursday, 12 February 2004.

45. 'UN Inspectors find Link to Iran Nuke Program', The Associated Press, *Washington Post,* 19 February 2004.

46. "Nuclear Proliferation: Is Pakistan doing enough?" *BBC World News*: Saturday, 7 February 2004.

47. 'Pardon for 'Hero' Selling Nuclear Secrets' Anchor NBC's Tom Brokaw NBC News from Rawalpindi, *Washington Post,* 6 February 2004.

48. 'Iran Nuclear Omissions Worry UN': *BBC World News,* Tuesday, 24 February, 2004.

49 All that the US has given by way of evidence of a concerted link between the Iranian government and Al Qaeda is assertions that it intercepted radio communications emanating from Iran and directed at the perpetrators of the bombings in Saudi Arabia. According to the US, these intercepts of radio communications provide proof that an Al Qaeda operative named Saef al Adel had, from a base in Iran, masterminded the Riyadh bomb blasts, which killed 34 people. See, in general: P.S. Suryanarayana, 'Nuclear Brinkmanship': *Frontline,* Volume 20-Issue 01.

50 'Iran Agrees to Nuclear Timetable', *BBC News*, Tuesday, 6 April 2004.

51 Reuters reporting from Tehran, 13 September, 2004, "No Rethink on N-tech: Iran" *Times of India,* Lucknow Ed., 14 September 2004.

52. 'Iran Nuclear Omissions Worry UN': *BBC World News*, Tuesday, 24 February 2004.
53. The document was signed by Tehran's outgoing representative to the agency, Ali Akbar Salehi, and by IAEA Chief Mohamed El Baradei. The signing of the protocol on 18 Feb 2002 was a formality as Iran had agreed earlier in 2002 to act as though it was already in force. Since then, Iran had been allowing the IAEA inspectors all the access that they requested.
54. 'Iran Signs up to Nuclear Checks' *BBC World News,* Thursday, 18 December 2003.
55. 'Iran's Nuclear Stance Criticized' *BBC World News*, Monday, 8 March 2004.
56. The US accuses Iran of systematically hiding evidence of nuclear weapons development.
57. 'Iran Uranium Plant Sparks New Row', *BBC World News*, April 2004.
58. In June 2004, the board of governors of IAEA was to have its next meeting to discuss Iran's progress regarding nuclear inspections. The IAEA had a June deadline to present a judgment on Iran's nuclear activities. Later, the IAEA chief said that inspection report will come out by end of 2004.
59. "Iran to build more nuclear reactors with Russian help": AP news from Tehran, *Times of India,* Lucknow Ed., 23 August 2004.
60. The standoff between the West and Iran over its nuclear programme prompted Iran to negotiate with Germany, France and Britain in 2004. Iran also signed the additional protocol to the NPT, under which the IAEA could make surprise inspections of any of its real or suspected nuclear facilities.
61. It is understood that in December 2002, US satellite images showed the construction of the fuel facility at Natanz and the heavy water research reactor at Arak in Iran.
62. Iran has claimed that Natanz and Arak facilities are part of its peaceful nuclear programme which includes a long-term strategy for establishing 6000 MW of nuclear power by 2020 and are not required to be declared to IAEA. Latter did not accept this claim. Iran has since cooperated with the IAEA in inspections to verify that its nuclear activities at the plants are indeed peaceful.
63. Iran has natural uranium ores, though not in big quantities.
64. Article IV of the NPT gives any signatory "an inalienable right to develop, research, produce, and use nuclear energy for peaceful purposes", and the right to acquire technology for this purpose from other signatories.

65. Any 'referral' to the Security Council follows from Articles III B 4 and XII C of the IAEA Statute: Article III B 4 concerns the functions of the Agency and states: "... [I]f, in connection with the activities of the Agency, there should arise questions that are within the competence of the Security Council, the Agency shall notify the Security Council, as the organ bearing the main responsibility for the maintenance of international peace and security...." Article XII C of the Statute concerns safeguards and, inter alia, the functions of the Board. It states: "... The inspectors shall report any non-compliance to the Director-General who shall thereupon transmit the report to the Board of Governors. The Board shall call upon the recipient State or States to remedy forthwith any non-compliance, which it finds to have occurred. The Board shall report the non-compliance to all members and to the Security Council and General Assembly of the United Nations."

66. For some details also see: "Iran's Nuclear Gambit": Atul Aneja from Bahrain, *Frontline,* Vol. 22, No. 18, 27 August 2005.

67. Reuters reporting from Tehran: "Iran, West in War of Nerves over Nukes", *Times of India,* Lucknow Ed., 14 January 2006.

68. AFP reporting from Tehran: "Iran won't be Bullied, says Ahmadinejad", *Times of India,* Lucknow Ed., 15 January 2006.

8

Nuclear Pakistan and Proliferation

Intricately Balanced Nuclear Diplomacy

Pakistan has acquired nuclear expertise for reasons that it calls national objectives. Pakistan as a player in international relations and diplomacy has been an anomaly. Its diplomacy has been confusing except for the tenacity to achieve parity with India and bargaining with the West. Pakistan exists by justifying to its people and international community that it is not less important than India, from which it was carved out in 1947. For that it maintains that Kashmir ought to be its part and not of India and forces other States of the world to recognize its point of view. It tries to match its military power with India on all platforms. Pakistan has been highly useful to the USA during its cold war with Soviet Russia and had been allowed airbases on Pakistan territory to be used in any war between the two. This situation has also been encashed by Pakistan and military and economic grants and aids have abundantly flowed into Pakistan from time to time. Pakistan had been useful to USA in ousting Soviet influence from Afghanistan, since USA could get entry into Afghanistan through Pakistan only. Later, Pakistan organized Taliban forces for USA to oust pro-Russian regime from Afghanistan. In its hostilities towards India, Pakistan found communist China as a natural ally even though, for several reasons, USA was hostile to communist China in international diplomacy. Pakistan also helped USA in upstaging the friendship between Communist China and the USA, leading to recognition of communist China as a *de jure* regime of China. Later, perhaps as *quid pro quo* Pakistan obtained nuclear bomb technology from China and a probable though not dependable, ally in a dream war against India. Interestingly, Pakistan supplied nuclear bomb technology to North Korea that North Korea aims to use on the USA. In 2002, Pakistan sacrificed Taliban, its child, to the US interests. Pakistan remained a frontline ally of USA but continues to be an important Islamic fundamentalist State.[1] What emerges as a great success of Pakistani diplomacy is the friendship with communist China while latter was target of US anger; its nuclear deals with Stalinist North Korea while latter was unbearable to US and South Korea; its nuclear proliferation contrary to principles of NPT to a number of States, Libya, Iran, Iraq or North Korea among many others, when US has been ardent supporter of NPT and all these States had been at the same time targets of US wrath; or its continuation as Islamic fundamentalist State, yet remaining best ally of USA. At one time, Pakistan tried to be the leader of Islamic States of North Africa and the Middle East on the basis of 'Islamic nuclear bomb'.

THE PAKISTAN STATE

Pakistan is a State that came into existence in 1947, but without a history and a national philosophy to back it. Pakistan has been a separated portion of India and its history is only a history of separation and break-away from a past. In order to understand its diplomacy as a nuclear power since 1999, when it declared itself to be a nuclear State, it is necessary to have a sociological approach that figures out why and how Pakistan survives and pursues its policies. It has a peculiar territorial situation and a narrow but meaningful and not to be ignored status in world politics, e.g., cold war, Islamic unity or international terrorism, of which it has been neither a prime mover and nor a contributor. It has withstood time as a partner of big giants, USA and China. The form of government in Pakistan has alternated between civilian democracy and military dictatorship but the Pakistani diplomacy of crusade against India, now involving nuclear missiles, has always flourished. International law, international turmoil and politics have just come into its way to keep it standing, so as to say in Indian parlance.

Pakistan at Origins

Pakistan, a Muslim State, was born as reward for loyalty to the British rulers of India during struggle for Indian independence, which had developed during 1930s. The loyalty to the British was of a few prominent Muslims, who had led the Muslim League political party in India during British era. British rulers treated the freedom movement led by Mahatma Gandhi as a hostile Hindu insurgence. British patronage was extended to sectarian Muslim and backward class politics. When patriots claimed that India was a nation deserving independence, the Muslim League opposed the call for independence by the political argument adopted in 1940 that India was constituted of several nations and that at least a Hindu nation and a Muslim nation could be identified. Backward class movement was set to explain that the majority Hindu community was itself socially and culturally divided. The British also highlighted that there were also more than eight hundred princely States on the Indian sub-continent which had accepted British suzerainty, saying that India could not be one nation. The British rewarded Muslim League in June 1947 by partition of British India into Pakistan as a Muslim State and India as residual State for other communities. The Indian Independence Act of 1947, enacted by British Parliament left it to princely States to become independent or to join India or Pakistan. The future of Indian backward class of people was left to Indian and Pakistani sovereigns.

Pakistan, in August 1947 had a migrant political leadership led by Muslim League emigrants from India into West and East Pakistan. Pakistan does not accept Indian history as part of its history, though it was part of Indian sub-continent. It does not take pride in the Muslim dynasties or Moguls who ruled India, or Muslim historical monuments and does not treat them as part of Pakistan's cultural past. These Muslim rulers and monuments are taken to be part of Indian history and are alien to the culture of Pakistan. At the same time, it does not regard scores of Hindu or Buddhist shrines or institutions of past which had thrived on its territory as constituting its history, since Pakistan strictly confines itself to the pride of being a new or frontline Islamic State.

Politically, Pakistan began with a scratch. At the time of its creation, it had five provincial governments, a military establishment of British army on west and east borders of British India with Indian military paraphernalia since the end of the First World War, and an Indian civil service of Muslims but it had no national or federal authority. The British established the federal government for Pakistan in August 1947 by the Indian Independence Act. The leaders of Muslim League migrated from India to form and lead the federal government while the provinces had local Muslim League leaders. Thus Pakistan was born with an inner conflict between indigenous provincial and migrated federal leadership and a conflict for supremacy between civil government and dictates of military. It is noteworthy that both of these took a few years to organize themselves as the British had left an option to their personnel to opt either for Indian civil service or Pakistani civil service and Indian military service or Pakistani military establishment. In the meantime, the Provincial Governments of Sind, Punjab and East Pakistan did provide the stability for Pakistan. Further, while Pakistani army was mainly composed of Punjabi, Baluchi and Pashtuni section of population, the civilian rulers were migrants from India, mainly as members of Muslim League political party, or migrated civil servicemen.

The Pakistani Armed Forces

The army of Pakistan grew in size, strength and influence because of assistance from the USA when in 1953, the US in its efforts to build a airbase bulwark south of the Soviet Union capable of bombing large industrial and military production areas, signed several military agreements with countries in Middle East Asia, including Pakistan. Efforts were made by the federal government to make fresh recruitment of as many officers and other military cadres from Punjabi areas of

Pakistan, while influential Pashtuni communities had in the past dominated the military. This led to recriminations between top military men and civilian government that was making fresh recruitments to the armed forces of Pakistan. In a country, which was driven by ethnic and sectarian divisions, there were distinguishable civilian and military bureaucracies during 1950s and the latter was turning hostile to the former, leading to a military coup.

Minorities in Pakistan

Pakistan was a created Muslim State. It was part of British dispensation that all 'other religious communities' would go to India unless the individual members of those communities chose to remain there. Pakistan has felt it to be a natural sequence to indulge in ethnic cleansing. Pakistan completed ethnic cleansing of its territories early: (a) First by communal riots forcing almost its entire Hindu population to flee out of its territory, and later by squeezing out processes. (b) Secondly, by a linguistic division and cleansing of Pakistan of Bengali speaking Muslims as a result of the 1971 war with India after which Pakistan disintegrated into Urdu speaking mainland, Pakistan, and Bengali speaking State of Bangladesh. The last resulted in exodus of Bengali Muslims in West Pakistan to leave for Bangladesh. Millions of non-Muslim Bengali speaking refugees in India from East Pakistan were also repatriated by India to the new Bangladesh State. (c) By adopting a cautious squeeze out attitude towards Christians. (d) By creating a second-class citizenry since 1980s, Pakistan has created intra-Islamic problems for Muslims who have migrated from India and have settled in its province of Sind, designated as muhajirs as well as its attitude towards some lesser, unclear or impure Muslims who are treated as second rate Muslims. It has also occasional Shia-Sunni sectarian flare-ups, the majority of Muslims in Pakistan being Sunni. Gradually, Shia Muslims are getting the feelings of being a minority community who deserve international concern if not protection. Pakistan has maintained inner unity among Muslims by finding a common cause, that is, the annexation of borderline Jammu and Kashmir area of India, which had a majority Muslim population with a Hindu ruler at the time of partition of India. The sovereign ruler of Kashmir had legally acceded to India but this aspect was in diplomacy ignored by Pakistan and the policy has been adopted by it solely at religious level, that is, a Muslim majority area at its border should be a part of Pakistan.

Democratic Rule I to Military Dictatorship I to Democratic Rule II

The standing of ruling political elite soon eroded in Pakistan in 1948 after the death of Pakistan's founder and Muslim League leader, Mohammad Ali Jinnah and the assassination in 1951 of his successor, Liaquat Ali, shortly afterwards in a failed coup. This inner conflict was fully covered up by establishment of a perennial military dictatorship by another coup of 1957, by General Ayub Khan. The military rule imposed martial law in the country. Since then the civil service has played only a second fiddle[2] in the administration and politics of Pakistan. Gradually, military dictatorship has also passed on to Punjabi and refugee repatriate citizen officers of Pakistan army, leaving influential Pashtuni communities and Baluchi aristocracy non-influential in the military establishment. The decade of development of Pakistan under General Ayub Khan had brought some stability and growth to the country alongwith strong military alliance with the West. These factors led to the desire of giving a military showdown to India in the matter of Kashmir. Indian defeat at the hands of China[3] in Chinese invasion of India of 1961 acted as a big incentive to the Pakistani diplomacy of befriending communist China. But, the defeat of Pakistan in the 1965 war with India led to the army's invincibility being challenged by an increasingly vocal civilian opposition.[4] A civilian democratic government, after a decade's lapse, was established with Zulfikar Ali Bhutto, an Ayub Khan's protégé as Prime Minister. Soon Bhutto had deserted him and established the Pakistan People's Party. Later, in 1969, there was a second military takeover spearheaded by General Yahya Khan, the new army chief appointed by Bhutto. It is observed that the 1960s had well-established politically in Pakistan the desire to humiliate India in war and to annex Kashmir as a pivotal policy and that constituted emotional, religious or *jihadi* justification for all future governments, civilian democratic or military dictatorships of Pakistan to date in 2006.

Military Dictatorship II to Democratic Rule III to Military Dictatorship III

After 1964, when China had become nuclear power, Pakistan found in China a natural ally against India, it also had an impressive record of victory over India (1961) and had an eye on adjacent Indian territories. China under Mao had a general 'pan-communism' policy of expansion into States that were becoming independent on breaking of empire systems. China had reciprocated to Pakistani overtures. Subsequently, President Nixon of USA used Pak-China relationship in 1970 and around for making its own inroads of peace and understanding with nuclear communist China irrespective of Taiwan question. Pakistan had made a diplomatic coup and USA had reciprocated with generous arms and other aids, paving the way for second Pakistan attack in 1971 on India to wrest Kashmir from India. The defeat of Pakistan resulted in separation of East Pakistan and formation of Bangladesh a new State instead. Again, the army came into disrepute and civilian government with Pakistan People's Party leader Zulfikar Ali Bhutto as Prime Minister was formed. The government of Bhutto was toppled on July 5, 1977 by the chief of staff of the army, General Zia-ul-Haq, in a military coup. The General took over as Chief Administrator of Martial Law. In early September 1977, Bhutto was arrested and was charged with exterminations and attempted murders. Soon on March 18, 1978, he was sentenced to death that was confirmed by the Supreme Court on review. Bhutto was hanged on April 4, 1979. For this coup, Bhutto was regarded to be responsible himself.[5] He had restored the influence of the army by seeking its participation in administration. Army and the air force were deployed in a big way in Balochistan Province to fight a feudal-tribal-Marxist guerrilla force. Also he had encouraged young political Pakistan People's Party cadres to join the force, as officers while senior generals did not look upon this development favourably.

On Sept. 16, 1978, General Zia-ul-Haq proclaimed himself as President of Pakistan. The power of General had a providential boost in 1980s after US President, Ronald Reagan, planned war against Soviet forces in Afghanistan[6] and in this project, Pakistan became 'frontline' State and dictator General Zia-ul-Haq became a principal partner. The project enriched Pakistan by renewed US aid to Pakistan of $4.2 billion for the years 1987 to 1992, apart from this massive military equipment meant by US to be carried to the *mujahideen* via Pakistan to Afghanistan were diverted into hands of Pakistan civil militia active in Indian territory of Kashmir. Pakistan became the US army depot for the Afghanistan war and Pakistan itself received huge military supplies. Apart from this, Pakistan became a long term partner of USA in breaking Soviet influence in world politics. Pakistan was allowed secretly to supply nuclear bomb technology capability to various States, like North Korea, Iran or Libya for money or barter. From Korea it received missile technology in exchange. The favourable military dictatorship government of Pakistan was tolerated with appreciation by the USA in preference over a scheming democracy. The nuclear proliferation into Pakistan from China was tolerated, if not encouraged, by the West because latter had become a partner in its anti-Soviet diplomacy.

Military Dictatorship III to Democratic Rule IV

However, coming back to turbulent history of 1970s, there had been world pressure in late 1970s for restoration of democracy in Pakistan, desiring to make military rule a transitional phase. Perhaps this was the only possible disapproval by the West of the Pakistan-China accords. General Zia played his cards carefully. The constitutional history of Pakistan[7] thenceforth made interesting reading. In July 1978 General Zia announced the formation of a civilian cabinet of administrators, technocrats, and some political leaders drawn from the Muslim League and the religious parties. On 16 September 1978, he proclaimed himself President of Pakistan with the approval of his civilian cabinet. A national referendum was held in December 1984 for approval of the Islamization measures already taken by the government, which were cleverly coupled with an endorsement of General Zia's presidency for an additional five years. To ensure his supremacy, the eighth amendment of the constitution gave to the President extraordinary discretionary powers to be exercised in supreme interest—to dismiss an elected Prime Minister and to dissolve the national assembly.[8] This was to maintain overall dominance of military oligarchy over civilian government and bureaucracy.

Under the new provisional Pakistani constitution in February 1985 elections for the national and provincial assemblies were held in which political parties were not allowed to participate, but there was a high turnout of voters despite a boycott of the elections by the opposition. General Zia chose Muhammad Khan Junejo,[9] as Prime Minister, a Sindhi politician who had already loyally served in Zia's Cabinet. Martial law in Pakistan was lifted in December 1985. Soon in 1986, Benazir Bhutto, the daughter of Zulfikar Ali Bhutto, returned from abroad and revived the PPP. In May 1988, Zia dismissed the Junejo government and dissolved the national and provincial assemblies holding that it was corrupt, weak, and inept. In June 1988 a caretaker government was set up, with Zia additionally acting as the head of government. Under the revived 1973 Constitution, the elections were announced to be held in November 1988. But in the meantime, on 17 August 1988, President Zia was killed in an airplane crash alongwith his leading generals and the US ambassador to Pakistan. The chairman of the Senate, Ghulam Ishaq Khan, a long-standing Zia supporter, took over as acting President and the elections to the national assembly as scheduled earlier by Zia were held in November 1988. The military rule was lifted; the new President used these powers to appoint a Prime Minister to form a civilian government under the amended 1973 constitution. A new constitution, fifth, was proposed and adopted in 1988 by the consensus of President Ghulam Ishaq Khan and the elected National Assembly with Benazir Bhutto as Prime Minister.[10] The PPP, led by Benazir Bhutto, had won as a majority party without absolute majority and she became Prime Minister with the blessings of the President. The National Assembly elected Ishaq Khan, President in December 1988. Benazir Bhutto had to accept the old policies of military rule including Islamization and the commitment of Pakistan to the Afghan mujahideen for the favour of continuing as Prime Minister, though in fact without real powers. She was distrusted both by the President and the military and she was dismissed in November 1990. A Punjabi industrialist, Nawaz Sharif was made Prime Minister. The relations between Sharif, and President Khan also became tense and Khan dismissed Sharif as Prime Minister in April 1993. Interestingly, President Khan dissolved the National Assembly and promised to hold new elections in July, but the Supreme Court held his actions as unconstitutional and reinstated Sharif and his government in May 1993.

In the bitter power struggle that followed in 1993, a deadlock was reached in July, forcing both Sharif and Khan to resign. An interim government took over under the army chief of staff, General Abdul Waheed, and elections for national government were soon held in October 1993. The PPP won a clear majority of seats in the National Assembly, and Benazir Bhutto was elected Prime Minister. Bhutto had bad equation with prime movers in Pakistan politics, like Muslim fundamentalist leaders that included President also, army and so on. The opposition in National Assembly led by Nawaz Sharif successfully projected her and her administration as corrupt and deviating from anti-India stance. The President Farooq Ahmed Leghari, by his powers under eighth amendment, ousted her in December 1996 on charges of corruption, promoting lawlessness, arbitrary killings, misrule and disrespect of judiciary among others, in 'supreme national interest'[11] after a three year old term. This was a third time exercise of the supreme power by President of Pakistan to dismiss a democratic government.

Elections to National Assembly followed. In February, 1997, Nawaz Sharif became the Prime Minister for 32 months, which was up to October 1999. Nawaz Sharif had been a bargainer. He tried to make constitutional reforms, particularly, by taking away Presidential powers of sacking the Prime Minister and dissolving National Assembly,[12] thereby creating big distance between military and administration. Though, later when in October 1999, Mr. Sharif tried to fire Musharraf latter had seized power in a military coup, had appointed himself Chief Administrator of Pakistan and had promised to bring "true" democracy to Pakistan.[13] In terms of military primacy over democratic process, it might be added that Prime Minister Sharif's political power appeared to have become strong enough to secure a long-term future for the civilian administrations. In 1998 he assigned to the army substantive roles in the country's decision-making process,[14] had sacked army chief General Karamat and had replaced him by General Musharraf. It was the first time that an army chief of staff had stepped down in Pakistan at the behest of civil administration.[15] Moving further, Pakistan had in 1998 declared itself to be a nuclear power and had invited crippling economic sanctions from international community including Security Council of UNO, which condemned its violations of NPT principles and the later WMD Convention. Military authorities of Pakistan made no secret that its nuclear arsenal will be used against India and they bartered missile technology from North Korea against their nuclear technology soon thereafter. Military establishment had been itching for a war with India and earlier it had not been possible for Prime Minister Benazir Bhutto[16] to bridle and pacify military on this point, she had rather played their tunes. Nawaz Sharif had been positive on this score by having secured a dominating position over army. Prime Minister Sharif had declared Pakistan to be a nuclear State and maintained his finger on the 'nuclear button', that is, Prime Minister Sharif had taken up the controls over the use of nuclear arsenal.

Kargil Blunder and Nuclear Blackmail of India

Kargil war of 1999 was a blunder both of India and Pakistan: India had left its snowy peaks unguarded during winter while Pakistan had overestimated its duping, blackmailing powers and armed strength. General Musharraf had, without knowledge of Prime Minister Nawaz Sharif, started and pursued the army plan of sending army troops in 1999 in plain dress to occupy Kargil in winter when Indian patrols used to withdraw. But, a book, *Pakistan's Drift into Extremism* authored by a Pakistani officer, Hassan Abbas, who had served Benazir Bhutto and Musharraf as well, asserts that "Former Pakistan PM, Nawaz Sharif, granted formal approval to the Kargil plan to capture Indian peaks along the Line of Control" but was informed about the operation that had already begun only on March 27 or 28, 1999.[17] Under this operation, Pakistan had infiltrated over 1,000 troops into Indian held Kashmir during winter who had occupied Indian peaks when under snow. When Pakistan came close to war with India over Kargil in Kashmir, though Sharif was Prime Minister but General Musharraf was regularly seen briefing the media and making appearances on Pakistan television. Quietly, Musharraf and other senior generals were reportedly to have gotten increasingly angry at the efforts of Prime Minister to find a diplomatic way out from the crisis. The moves of PM Sharif led to the belief in international forum that the Pakistan military was without full political backing of the government in making the Kargil adventure. Pakistan, under humiliating circumstances and international pressure, eventually ordered a full withdrawal of troops from Indian territory of Kargil. The Kargil plan, according to a study,[18] was the third in the series, with the earlier two having been rejected by then Pakistani rulers, including Zia-ul-Haq, on the grounds that it could lead to full scale war with India. Musharraf was "taken in" by the enthusiasm of his closest generals and "became the strongest advocate of the operation". Former US Deputy Secretary of State, Talbott, has in his book noted that[19] when Sharif had visited Washington in 1999 to discuss Kargil with Clinton, Sharif had insisted that "I am prepared to help resolve the current crisis in Kargil but India must commit to resolve the larger issue (of Kashmir) in a specific time frame." President Clinton rejected the line of approach of Sharif as one of blackmail. To quote Talbott,[20] Clinton said "I am not—and Indians are not going to let you get away with blackmail, and I will not permit any characterization of this meeting that suggests I am giving in to blackmail". President Clinton also pointed it out that beyond the unconditional surrender of Pakistan over Kargil and return to its previous positions, was the danger of a nuclear war.

Democratic Rule IV to Military Dictatorship IV

When, in October 1999, Mr. Sharif tried to get rid of General Musharraf, the latter seized power in a coup and promised to bring "true" democracy to Pakistan.[21] The supreme court of Pakistan later validated General Musharraf's assumption of power for a period of three years. The coup was, however, widely condemned by the international community. It called for elections and an immediate restoration of civilian government. Pakistan was also suspended from the Commonwealth. After three-year military dictatorship, Musharraf formally installed a highly controlled civilian rule in the country, after holding an election in October 2002. On the eve of general elections, the military also chose to make fundamental amendments in the constitution by a Legal Framework Order. Zafarullah Khan Jamali was appointed as Prime Minister, who did not have any independent voice and accepted the role of army in the politics of the country. He resigned in June 2004 after a period of strained relations with the President. Under the new [projected] arrangement, Mr. Aziz of the Pakistan Muslim League and a senior minister in the cabinet of Jamali was to be the Prime Minister in due course. Mr. Aziz was then (July 2004) a member of the Upper House and, under Pakistan's Constitution, only a member of the Lower House can become the Prime Minister. Mr. Aziz has been professional economist having experiences of the IMF and World Bank economic philosophy. However, the roles of military and of nuclear bomb in Pakistan's diplomacy towards India did continue as matters of course.

NUCLEAR PAKISTAN

Pakistani Nukes and World Response

As noted above, at the time of Kargil adventure (1999) Pakistan possessed nuclear bombs, though not with a perfected delivery system. The 1998 nuclear tests by India followed by similar nuclear tests by Pakistan brought about brisk and renewed international rethinking on NPT and as to what international community should do to deal with the problem. The UN Security Council had condemned India and Pakistan for carrying out nuclear tests and urged both nations to stop all nuclear weapon programs. As a sequence, for deterrence, United States and other western countries imposed various kinds of economic and military sanctions and demanded the two countries to disarm. The United States had ordered sanctions against both India and Pakistan by freezing more than $20bn of aid, loans and trade, Japan ordered a block on about $1bn of aid loans and several European countries acted likewise. The G-8 governments imposed a ban on non-humanitarian loans to India and Pakistan. The sanctions had marginally affected Indian economy but had crushing blow on Pakistan economy. However, both States had ignored the call to disarm and had stuck to their nuclear armament policies. Since the Kargil war (1999) and the international sanctions on Pakistan after its nuclear explosions (1998), President Musharraf has been additionally worried of the increasing Israeli and Indian cooperation in defense equipment dealings, though this cooperation had continued all through 1990s. He had been worried that President Bush was prepared to let Israel sell hi-tech defense equipment to India and that could tilt the military balance between the two rivals to disadvantage of Pakistan. Pakistan had no delivery system for nukes. It badly needed from USA its F-16 fighter planes[22] with capabilities for targeting nuclear warheads on India, which it was unable to get[23] till 2005. But, Pakistan immediately bartered nuclear bomb technology with North Korea, ignoring the horrific relationship between North Korea and the USA, for advance missile technology to become at par with India.[24] It may be recalled and mentioned that it was known that both countries had possessed nuclear weapons long before 1998. India had overtly tested a nuclear bomb in 1974 by underground explosion. Pakistan, by contrast, had deliberately maintained a policy of nuclear ambiguity. It had started its nuclear programme soon after 1971 that had prompted India to revise its stand on nuclearization, and it is believed that Pakistan had built a workable nuclear device in 1982 and by the end of the 1980s the claim of Pakistan that it had become a *de facto* nuclear power[25] was widely accepted in the international community as genuine.

Pak-US-China Axis

It would be worthwhile to have a look into the development of this strange nexus. This relationship has often kept Indian diplomacy shaky and generally on tiptoes. The 1965, 1971 and Kargil (1999) wars with India were initiated by Pakistan on supposed strength of this nexus. In 1971 war, American Seventh Fleet had entered into Bay of Bengal and USA would have intervened if India had proceeded to dissect West Pakistan into more small States, since American airbases meant against Soviet Russia were intensively located there. Why China kept away and quiet remained a matter of disappointment for Pakistan. How did this axis develop? The events leading to this are discernible. While Pakistan continued to occupy part of Kashmir to the discomfiture of India, Pakistan had in 1950s opted for giving full support to US in the cold war era by permitting its territory to be used for air-bases for any nuclear war between USA and USSR, thereby exposing its territory to the high risk of retaliatory attack from USSR. This diplomacy led to intensive US economic and military grants and support to Pakistan and alienation of India from USA. When India led the non-alignment movement against the cold war confrontation, in this process USA rewarded Pakistan by remaining indifferent to Indian causes and thereby indirectly supporting Pakistan in the matters connected with Kashmir. Concurrently, Pakistan aligned itself and configured with the Islamic and Arab nations of the Middle East. It claimed superior brainpower and leadership of

Islamic group and evolved it as diplomacy helpful to the causes of the West. Pakistan has successfully played up Palestinian cause against Israel while Israel has full USA-UK axis support. Obviously, USA had valued military alliance with Pakistan more important than participation of Pakistan in Islamic alliance even when it is at the cost of its relations with Israel. Then, impressed by Chinese victory over India in a war of aggression against India in 1962, Pakistan became intensely friendly with China henceforth. China had successfully become a nuclear power in 1964, and had a general pan-communism Maoist policy of expansion into States that were becoming independent by the breaking of the empire systems.

Apart from this, the more important factor that brought the two States together was their respective interest in Kashmir part of India. Pakistan had illegally continued its occupation of the part of Indian Kashmir through which traditional land route connecting China with British India passed while China had quietly occupied in 1950s and had constructed its highway connecting South China with West China that passed through north-eastern Aksai Chin[26] part of Indian Kashmir. China has reciprocated to the Pakistani hand of friendship and as mentioned above, the two States developed a clandestine alliance of mutual help and coordination particularly in commercial transactions relating to military hardware. This was against the general policy of USA towards Communist China but was tolerated perhaps because Pakistan became useful as a springboard for USA contacts with China. Subsequently, President Nixon of USA used Pak-China relationship in 1970 and around for making its own inroads of peace and understanding with nuclear communist China irrespective of Taiwan question. China had earned respect from USA by its nuclear deterrence capabilities. Gradually in 1970s, Pakistan obtained active Chinese participation in the development of its own nuclear programme contrary to international standards laid down under the NPT and this was again fully tolerated by the USA. The Chinese cooperation with Pakistan in updating and strengthening its military capabilities in various sectors continues with profound American tolerance and approval. In 1996, the US intelligence findings[27] placed before the US Congressional Research Service (CRS) in a Report-Study were that China has transferred more than 30 complete M-11 nuclear warhead capable ballistic missiles to Pakistan. It was 'probable'that Pakistan has developed "nuclear warheads small enough to be launched by the M-11 missiles". These M-11 two stage missiles are of short-range upto 400 km and capable of delivering 500 kg warheads. The US intelligence officials expressed their belief that the transfer of these missiles to Pakistan "could exacerbate a possible nuclear armed clash between Pakistan and India over the Kashmir area". Recently in 2004, China agreed to sell four frigates to Pakistan. For Pakistan navy during the talks between the visiting Pakistani Chief of Naval Staff and the head of the General Armament Department of the Chinese People's Liberation Army, Mr. Li, the two further discussed ways to increase the military cooperation between the two nations. Mr. Li praised the Sino-Pakistan relationship and their armed forces and said that the two sides shared comprehensive friendly ties that had "great potential".[28] The USA has quietly watched the nuclear and military co-operation between the two, irrespective of China being a communist State that occasionally gives out threats for forcibly annexing Taiwan for making it a part of the mainland. Perhaps as a counter reaction to all this in 2005, USA made the move for strategic partnership with India, recognizing India as a potential regional South Asian power in the changed world diplomacy scenario.

Pakistan with North Korean Missile: Prospects

Pakistan has worked hard to supplement its US supplied F-16 nuclear bomb capable fighter aircraft fleet with efficient nuclear warhead missile system as barter deal with North Korea. Pakistan has, in addition, F-22 fast attack nuclear capable missile frigate-crafts. Pakistan has resolved to "maintain minimum credible deterrence as the cornerstone of its security", of course, it has by 2005 marked Israel and India as its potential enemies. Pakistan is confident that it can strike targets deep inside whole of India, though it is wishfully desired that Pakistan shall not use Islamic nuclear bomb to wipe out Islamic population of India. It is no secret that most of the areas of India of strategic or economic importance have cream of Islamic population, like, Ahmedabad, Hyderabad, Secunderabad, Bhopal or the area comprised in New Delhi-Aligarh-Agra-Lucknow-Rampur-New Delhi belt that Pakistan will have to devastate with at least twenty nuclear bombs in a war in order to grab Kashmir. Israel is also now within the reach of Shaheen-II missiles of Pakistan, only five or so nuclear bombs will be needed to wipe out Israel. However, USA is a common ally and is expected to ditch Pakistan if there is a tie between the two. Pakistan has no other apparent enemy States outside NATO of which it is a non-member important ally. Its missile arsenal with North Korean assistance has the following:

HATF-I is of a range of 280 Km;

HATF-III (Ghaznavi) with range 290 Km.;

HATF-IV (Shaheen-1) for range of 700 Km.;

HATF-V (Ghauri) covers 1500 Km.; while

HATF-VI (Shaheen-II), a two-staged solid fuel missile, has a range between 2000-2500 Km.

Economic Rejuvenations of Pakistan, Cashed Opportunities

Every nuclear war oriented State requires a strong economic base, since maintaining nuclear war paraphernalia is a heavy economic burden. The enquiry is as to how Pakistan could be so strong economically. Some observations on this score are pursued here:

(1) As mentioned earlier, severe economic and military aid sanctions following six nuclear tests in 1998 by Pakistan in Chagai area in Balochistan were imposed on it by various States. This was ominous for Pakistan, since its armed strength was built on large-scale military aid supplies provided by US President Ronald Reagan as part of the US struggle against Soviet forces in Afghanistan during the 1980s.[29] In the same period Pakistan was hosting considerable number of refugees from Afghanistan also that involved financial burden. But with the end of the Afghanistan occupation by Soviet Russia and the Cold War in early 1990s, the

US assistance was not so generous and Pakistan had continued to face a large burden of Afghan refugee population. Pakistan had ceased to be of strategic importance to the USA, yet for reasons of diplomacy the acquisition of nuclear technology from China, contrary to obligations of NPT, was tolerated by the USA.[30] It is interesting historical fact that during 1990s Osama bin Laden was prime associate of USA in the Afghanistan war and had patronized the social and political structure of Pakistan. But then by 1998, Bin Laden had become anti-US and wanted to oust USA from Islamic Middle East and this move was tacitly or diplomatically welcomed by Pakistan, leading to an increasing diplomatic isolation from the USA.

(2) The 11 September 2001, suicide attacks in the United States brought an unexpected rapprochement between Pakistan and the West when Pakistan changed sides. Musharraf agreed to cooperate with the US's campaign against Osama bin Laden, his *Al Qaeda* network and the Taliban rulers of Afghanistan. The capture of Osama bin Laden and Taliban leader, Mullah Mohammed Omar, was actively being pursued by USA since then and so 'President Musharraf faced intense pressure from Washington to help US forces in Afghanistan to capture or kill Bin Laden and other top *Al Qaeda* and Taliban leaders hiding in the Pakistan-Afghanistan border tribal region'.[31] In this diplomatic crisis, Pakistan chose American line by forsaking Bin Laden.

(3) USA had suddenly realized that it needed Pakistan on its side if it was to punish the Taliban in neighboring Afghanistan.[32] The road to Afghanistan was through Pakistan and Pakistan had prepared the Taliban cadres in its training camps for terrorists and it had full inside knowledge of the new US enemies. Sanctions against Pakistan for embarking on nuclear programme were slowly lifted by the US in exchange for greater

and greater involvement of Pakistan in the new war in Afghanistan, which also had the sanction of Security Council. General Musharraf was 'wooed and feted' by US President George W. Bush, who now badly needed him in his war on terror and the 'axis of evil'. Musharraf became, almost overnight, a pivotal player on the world stage of diplomacy, an ally direly welcomed in Washington and London alike and was extolled to the status of a statesman of international standing. USA also became soft on Pakistan's bellicose attitude against India on Kashmir matter. Pakistan withdrew and diverted Taliban and Pakistani mercenaries operating in Afghanistan into Kashmir to fight and create terror. This relieved Taliban and pro-Osama bin Laden pressure from allied forces engaged in fighting terrorism in Afghanistan. It is to be kept in mind that Osama bin Laden was and is even now a prophetic leader of Islamic fundamentalism and Taliban outfit was a creation of Pakistan and Bin Laden, its cadres having been trained in Bin Laden financed training centers within Pakistan and Afghanistan situated around their common international border. The defense cooperation between Islamabad and Washington was revived[33] in 2002. Pakistan had already identified a number of hi-tech military hardware it would like to buy from Washington, a long-term demand for its belligerency against India. No doubt, there have been some economic gains for Pakistan since 2002 but at the same time there is obvious realization that these gains have come at a high cost. Much of the gains are due to the sudden decision of Pakistan to side with the United States-led coalition in the "war" against terrorism and Osama bin Laden. At the same time Bin Laden had made claims of possessing nuclear skills believed to be of Pakistani origin. The US leadership genuinely feared that this could be used to make 'rogue nuclear devices'[34] to nurture further suicide attacks in its territories. As such, it was feared that if Islamic fundamentalist terrorist elements, well entrenched in Pakistan, seized power then the nuclear arsenal of Pakistan would fall in the hands of Bin Laden. Pakistan, therefore, in 2002, feared either pre-emptive attack from USA to take control of its nuclear facilities or Israeli surprise air attack on its nuclear facilities. In the then prevailing panic, some spokesmen of Pakistan made statements that if any of such attack happened to which India was or was not a party Pakistan will fire all its nuclear bombs on Indian targets, a clear nuclear terrorist blackmail.

In sequence, in 2004, USA bolstered the national and international position of the Pakistan President Musharraf with an announcement that Pakistan would be termed or treated as a "major non-NATO" ally of USA.[35] The proposed designation was clearly an emphatic expression of gratitude by Washington for the role played by Gen. Musharraf in the fight against terrorism since 11 September 2001. Under the new status, future military to military relations between Washington and Islamabad would become closer. Among others, Israel, Japan and Egypt are also "non-NATO" allies of the US. The country could henceforth have access to advanced weaponry of USA for the first time since 1990. At the same time, it was a US diplomacy of bridling and harnessing Pakistan, which was openly declaring use of nuclear weapons against its neighbor in the event of India going in on 'hot pursuit' of Pakistani infiltrators and terrorists training camps on Pakistani territory or even if Israel took pre-emptive steps to destroy nuclear installations and reactors of Pakistan. But, as a "major non-NATO" ally, Pakistan will have to take into confidence USA before it embarks on any military adventure.

Pakistan: A "Major non-NATO Ally"?

For earning the status of a "major non-NATO ally" of USA, Pakistan has had to come to terms with USA[36] (1) to provide "five airbases to American forces and landing rights to their fighter aircraft anywhere in the country during emergency as part of its cooperation in the fight against Taliban and Al Qaeda"; (2) grant two-thirds of its airspace as air corridor to the US-led coalition forces; (3) provide on an average 0.4 million liters of fuel per day to the US forces and other services on the bases used by them, of course, on payment basis;[37] (4) provide landing facilities to the US coalition warships at Pasni, west of Karachi, while curtailing its own naval operations at Pasni. Further as follow-up, the USA had one week after bestowing "major non-NATO" ally status to Pakistan lifted or waived the 'democracy sanctions' imposed on Pakistan after General Musharraf had usurped political power in 1999 on a coup and that had taken place before 9/11 tragedy of 2001. This development will help the US by "having sticks" on Pakistan in order to fight international terrorism of Taliban and *Al Qaeda*. As reward, USA had "written off" by an agreement $495.4 million debt in July 2004, while in April 2003 it had written off one billion dollar debt.[38] The American Ambassador to Pakistan, Nancy Powell, who signed the agreement alongwith Secretary of Pakistan Economic Division, observed,[39] "Our continued commitment to Pakistan is a vote of confidence in the economic stewardship of the Pakistani government and intelligence, energy and resourcefulness of the Pakistani people". From Indian point of view the economic packages for the people concurrently or indirectly help Pakistan in its nuclear and bellicose stances against India. The developments also show the confidence of advantageous US diplomacy in the stewardship of President Musharraf in maintaining a much-controlled civilian government. USA had felt too much embarrassment by the attitudes of democratic former Prime Minister Sharif in 1999 and also before that.

Projected 2002 Pakistani Nuclear War with India

Since the Kargil war (1999) and the international sanctions on it after its nuclear explosions (1998), President Musharraf has been worried with the increasing Israel-India cooperation in defense equipment dealings particularly since late 1990s. He has been worried that President Bush was prepared to let Israel sell hi-tech defense equipment to India and that could tilt the military balance between the two rivals to disadvantage of Pakistan. It badly needed from USA its F-16 fighter planes[40] with capabilities for targeting nuclear warheads on India, which it was unable to get.[41] The Pakistan President Pervez Musharraf, after witnessing the test-firing of the Ghauri missile by Pakistan in June 2004 said that the world had come to accept the reality of Pakistan's nuclear status that was a major achievement. He rejected "roll-back syndrome" in the wake of world and domestic reactions and asked people to develop the self-confidence from the fact that Pakistan has become a nuclear power.[42] After all, on top of everything, General Musharraf is also one of the few (seven) men in the world who have a finger on a nuclear button. This nuclear self-confidence drafted Pakistani diplomacy of acquiring Kashmir through strength.

To recapitulate, in order to regain American patronage against India and Israel, the diplomacy of President Musharraf had taken a major U-turn as the involvement of USA in Afghanistan had increased. As a logical extension of the aftermath of the 9/11 terrorist strike in USA, there has been tremendous pressure on the Pakistan establishment by the USA to cut its relations with fundamentalist outfits.[43] In this process, Musharraf has lost the 'strategic depth', via Islamic fundamentalism, both for the claim of leadership of Islamic States and of popularity in Afghanistan. On the contrary, since 2002 it has earned the wrath of the *Al Qaeda* and the Taliban. The remnants terrorist outfits of these two organizations in Pakistan had continued to have strong links with religious and militant outfits in the country. The government has had little choice but to tolerate these militant organizations and their highly efficient and effective infrastructure that these had built in Pakistan over the years. These outfits have dared to defy Pakistan Government directives and have carried out terrorist killings with vengeance repeatedly in India and in Pakistan as well. The Pakistani policy of diverting the terrorists into India has been in censor. India, after the grim experience of Kargil invasion by Pakistan (1998), has been maintaining about 0.4 million strong army deployed on the 720 km of Line of

Control (LOC) and 120 km international border in Kashmir part of India in order to counter cross-border infiltration. More troops were sent by India as a deterrent after Pakistan trained terrorists had attacked Indian Parliament on December 13, 2001. Because of these factors, General Musharraf has not been able to pursue a cohesive policy on Kashmir, since his U-turn in Afghanistan diplomacy, with the result that militant outfits operating from its territory have become sore and embarrassing liability for it. Thus Pakistan had the overpowering compulsions of counter-balancing Afghanistan diplomacy by diverting the terrorist militant outfits into India for maintaining peace within. The Indian border vigilance has been overwhelming deterrent for Pakistan in fulfillment of its diplomacy. As a concrete lasting step against infiltration across the border, India has had taken up fencing work along 820 km border in a big way. It is to act as a major preventive against *en masse* infiltration. The fencing comprises of four strands, is equipped with live wire, electronic sensors, spikes and in case of actual infiltration it will send alarms.[44] However, the risk of cross border terrorism for India continues with little abatement. Contrary to Pakistani assertions, as late as July 2004, the US Deputy Secretary of State, Richard Armitage, maintained,[45] "All terrorist camps have not been dismantled (in Pakistan)".

Soon after 9/11 terrorist attacks in USA that killed more than three thousand people, the terrorist activities increased in India in 2001. This was taken as exultation and increased self-confidence of the same brand of terrorists. During October, 38 people were killed after an attack on the Kashmir State Legislative Assembly in Srinagar. After the attack, the Chief Minister of Indian State of Jammu and Kashmir, Farooq Abdullah, called on the Indian government to launch a war against militant training camps across the border in Pakistan. A month later, 14 people were killed in an attack on the Parliament of India in Delhi. India, international media and also USA, blamed Pakistani-backed Kashmiri militants for all these acts of terrorism in India. Increasing pressure of terrorists along with open encouragement, free and assisted passage to militant groups through Pakistan and cry of Pakistani leaders for the urgent need to settle Kashmir matter with Pakistan[46] had made India critical. All these developments had become serious threat to Indian security. Consequently, after a series of terrorist events it had deployed about 0.3 million of troops in forward positions on its border. A dramatic build up of troops along the Indo-Pakistan border had ensued and tension along the line of control developed. A heavy fighting lasting for more than a year broke out across the border in October 2001 in which both countries started shelling military positions beyond the international border and the Line of Control in Kashmir. The world recognized the seriousness of terrorist onslaught in India while India condemned Pakistan for cross-border terrorism and declared that Pakistan was abetting terrorism in India as a matter of its international diplomacy. Military exchanges between the troops of both States had raised fears in 2002 of a wider conflict and the USA was drawn in, since a war between India and Pakistan would have adversely affected the assumed tasks of USA in Afghanistan for which collaboration of Pakistan was necessary. This American interest affected Pakistani diplomacy by way of adverse US diplomatic pressure on Pakistan and this proved to be helpful to India.

Danger of a Nuclear Conflict

In January 2002 President Musharraf, under his new found diplomacy, made a Kashmir specific statement pledging that Pakistan would not allow terrorists to operate from Pakistani soil. He called on the Government of India to resolve the dispute over Jammu and Kashmir with Pakistan through dialogues. India responded with the statement that it would wait for action to back up his words. In January 2002 onwards simultaneously, a relentless build-up of troops along the border continued and villagers on both sides of the border fled their homes as both governments had advised nationals to leave the region. A Pakistani militant attack on a bus and army camp in Jammu in Indian Kashmir in May 2002 had placed relations between the two countries at their lowest point, though without a regular war. In 2003, India accused Pakistan's embassy in Delhi of channeling funds to Kashmiri militant supporters and terrorists. Both sides expelled the other's acting high commissioner and soon India broke off diplomatic ties with Pakistan and Prime Minister A.B. Vajpayee feared that the time for a "decisive battle" was imminent. President Musharraf did likewise and declared that Pakistan would respond to any Indian attack with "full force" and would definitely use nuclear weapons. The Indian Government made a 'no first use' of nuclear weapons pact offer to Pakistan but it also made clear that it could take the first nuclear attack from Pakistan and thereafter completely destroy it by its nuclear arsenal. At the same time, India maintained that if a war ensued, then alongwith the risks of a nuclear conflict, India would be prepared to use its superiority of conventional armaments against Pakistan.[47] Both countries recognized the nuclear risks but remained adamant.[48] War was averted, in part due to a 'flurry' of international diplomacy led by US Secretary of State, Colin Powell. Indian Prime Minister Vajpayee had clarified: "Pakistan's nuclear program is India-specific... But we are concerned about other States as well."[49]

The subsequent flow of events since January 2002 showed that India took a highly specialized diplomatic position, that is, linking its military preparedness and build-up to the persistent terrorist threat from Pakistan. The terrorist threat had direct connection with allied action against Bin Laden and Taliban in Afghanistan. This brought in the USA on its side weaning away the traditional American diplomatic support to Pakistan. Further, since Islamic fundamentalists also troubled China along its western frontiers linked with Pakistan through a road on Pakistan occupied Indian Kashmir, Pakistan had also lost probable support of China in its much-harped armed conflict with India. Pakistan was having much trouble in placating the Islamic fundamentalists on its own soil. In this context, President Musharraf shifted the internal public attention from Kashmir to the newfound status of Pakistan in the world as a nuclear power. Pakistan, when faced with the disapproval by its allies of its nuclear policy and peddling[50] of nuclear bomb know-how to North Korea, Iran and Libya, justified its actions on the ground of developing armaments parity with

India while USA and other States recognized that India has nuclear weapons not only because of Pakistan, but also because of fears arising from China. In turn, China can use[51] its nuclear arsenal only against USA, Japan or India. Cumulative effect of world situation and diplomacy was that Pakistan responded favorably with the offers of Indian Prime Minister to take up confidence building measures[52] by better trade relations and communications between the people of the two countries. Pakistan was already under tremendous pressure from the USA to prevent cross border infiltration activities. Remarkably, in mid-2004 Pakistan changed its general priorities from annexation of Kashmir to acquiring developed nation status at par with South Korea, Japan and Thailand in place of comparing its economic stability with Indian economic achievements. By April 2005 President Musharraf had become shaky and uncertain of the merits and achievement of his objectives in the perspectives of world politics and was drifting towards pacifism, though he found Kashmir issue with India as conducive to its internal unity. He visited to pay obeisance at the famous Dargah of Sufi Saint, Khwaja Moinuddin Chisti of thirteenth century, at Ajmer in India and 'prayed for peace and prosperity of our peoples and for improvement in relations between the two countries' adding that 'there can be no progress without peace' and 'I hope my prayers are answered'.[53] He conceded that 'strategy of coercive diplomacy is no more an option' and 'there is a realization that the military option is not the option any more (for solution of Kashmir problem)' and generally speaking there 'was a time when ...we used to talk geopolitics more than economics. Now the world is so focused on economic development' that a major change in attitudes has taken place in the world.[54]

NUCLEAR PROLIFERATION BY PAKISTAN

Though Pakistan was not a signatory of the NPT, it has had the rare and singular distinction of supplying in violation of NPT and WMD Convention, nuclear technology to two signatory members of NPT, Libya and Iran. The investigations had revealed that Pakistan had supplied since early 1980s for consideration this technology to the two countries, which had, to its embarrassment, submitted their territory to inspections by IAEA since August 2003. It can be recalled that the President Bush of USA had vowed to eliminate the WMD of nations falling under 'axis of evil', these were Iraq, North Korea and Iran,[55] after the 9/11 terrorist incident of 2001. North Korea had already started negotiations on nuclear issues with the USA in continuation of the Framework Agreement, 1994, made earlier.[56] As Iraq stood devastated and destroyed by July 2003, Iran seems to have reasons to get panicky, denied possession of nuclear bomb and invited IAEA to examine and give it clean chit on the question of possession of nuclear bombs. Iran has maintained that it has not been pursuing nuclear technology for weapons and has not violated the NPT. All that it has acquired, developed or possessed, is related to energy producing atomic reactors. But, USA contested the claim and had charged Iran of possessing nuclear weapons in violation of NPT. Soon, Libya on 19 December 2003 renounced its weapons of mass destruction programme. Libya officially announced that it was pursuing nuclear weapons and this being a violation of the NPT it expressed regret and signed an additional protocol to the Nuclear Non-Proliferation Treaty (NPT), allowing snap inspections of its nuclear facilities by IAEA.[57] Libya had a history of strained relations with USA, international terrorist organizations were known to have links with it and Libyan President Gaddafi was vocal supporter of Arab causes and was afraid of US reprisals that may follow on Libya after the Iraq war. The IAEA had acted swiftly making inspections and investigations both in Iran and Libyan States, but in case of Iran, by taking incorrect its statement that it had no nuclear bombs.[58] The US openly accused Iran of pursuing a clandestine programme to develop nuclear weapons and wanted the matter to be brought before the UN Security Council, which could impose sanctions on Iran.

Pakistani Involvement in Libya

Libya did not make the source of its acquired nuclear capabilities a secret. The IAEA reported that the designs of nuclear weapons, which Libya had obtained from a Pakistani network, had originated in China. According to the news report, the packet of documents that included some texts in Chinese was in details and had step-by-step instructions for assembling an implosion type nuclear bomb that could be fitted atop a ballistic missile. It also contained technical instructions to manufacture components for the device, according to officials and experts.[59] Libya only made minimal progress towards building a nuclear weapon and had nothing in its arsenal to carry the device to the targets. At the same time "This design would be highly useful to countries such as Iran and North Korea," a former weapons inspector with the United Nations, has been noted as saying in the media. The UN gave objectionable information for checking to Pakistan in October/November 2003 received from IAEA investigations into the clandestine nuclear programmes of Iran and Libya both taking place via Pakistan.

One of the things that came up in the course of investigation was the role of A.Q. Khan of Pakistan. Abdul Qadeer Khan, founder and head of State owned Khan Research Laboratories at Kahuta, the top nuclear facility of Pakistan, was retired by President Musharraf on the advice of USA in March 2001 in order "to prevent him from transferring any more nuclear secrets".[60] Since then he was holding the post of scientific adviser to the Pakistan Government. Pakistan Government sacked him from his post as scientific advisor on 31.01.2004 after the US supplied evidence against him in October 2003. This evidence was accompanied with the threat or remarks that "Islamabad would be in dock internationally and risked losing the $ 3 billion US aid package Washington had just cleared".[61] Khan was known in Pakistan as the successful assembler of the country's atomic bomb by purchasing parts from various sources, he held a place of pride in the country. Since 1980s, he had purchased tritium purification and production facility from Germany as also plutonium, centrifuges, spark gaps and oscilloscopes that are necessary for nuclear explosive devices from Belgium and other European States for further transactions in nuclear commodities black-markets. He acknowledged in a televised statement on Wednesday, 4 February 2004, that he had passed nuclear secrets to other States, and specifically said that he acted without authorization from his government, thereby he denied complicity of government[62] and asked for forgiveness. A day later, on 5 February 2004 President Musharraf pardoned Khan.[63] This assumption of full responsibility by A.Q. Khan for nuclear proliferation absolved Pakistan as a State for the nuclear proliferation through military aircraft and naval carriers that had taken place. But it has unsettled the obvious course of fixing responsibility for the nuclear 'trafficking network' issue under the NPT.

What was That?

The IAEA probe after Iran and Libya renounced their nuclear programme revealed in February 2004 that a Pakistani-led nuclear trafficking network existed and it extended to at least seven nations. A.Q. Khan operated this Pakistani nuclear trafficking network. The probe further revealed that Khan was suspected to have visited several countries, apart from Libya, North Korea and Iran, seeking customers and materials for his black market trade.[64] Khan has now admitted[65] before TV of supplying on personal basis nuclear expertise and equipment to three States, namely Libya, Iran and North Korea. He is believed to have offered it to Iraq and Syria also. Iraq rejected the offer in 1990 suspecting it to be a US 'sting operation'. Syria too is believed to have rejected Khan's offer.[66] Among other nations, Mr. Khan had visited were Sudan, Mali, Nigeria and Niger. Visits to these States are significant because all these States are known to have or suspected to have raw uranium deposits[67] required both for nuclear reactors and for making nuclear bombs. The investigators disclosed that they had traced that the nuclear smuggling ring controlled by Pakistani scientist, Abdul Qadeer Khan had businesses from Africa, Asia and Europe. In February 2004, Khan confessed on television that he had been selling Pakistan's nuclear secrets.[68] At once the world media became active and various States also began to examine the possible role and association of the vendors of their country in this nuclear trafficking business of A.Q. Khan.

It appeared that the scientists, engineers and suppliers from Holland, France, Belgium and Switzerland had particularly helped in sustaining the international nuclear commodities black market and so indirectly these had supported or sustained A.Q. Khan's proliferation network.[69] Further, a "Sri Lankan businessman with close connections to Malaysia's business elite" also emerged as central figure in the international investigations into the clandestine Khan network while latter sold Pakistani nuclear technology to Libya, Iran and North Korea.[70] The "US, British and UN investigators found that a company[71] in Pakistan was prepared to sell everything needed to make a nuclear bomb—plans, equipment and fuel for $ 50 million, with no questions asked about how it might be used".[72]

Western diplomats and intelligence officials said that the expansive reach of the nuclear commodities black market network had the character of a global enterprise that supplied nuclear technology and processing parts to Libya, Iran, North Korea and possibly other States also, surprised them. Soon, US and other Western intelligence agencies joined the UN investigators. "Dr. Khan was not working alone. Dr. Khan was part of a process"; "There were items that were manufactured in other countries. There were items that were assembled in a different country" said Mohamed ElBaradei, Director of the Vienna-based UN International Atomic Energy Agency.[73] The US and UN investigators had stated that Khan's nuclear trading network represented the most brazen and notorious case of nuclear proliferation that would ever be discovered. Using suppliers and middlemen scattered across three continents, Asia, Africa and Europe, the network delivered all machines and technology required for enriching uranium, a key ingredient in production of nuclear weapons. In the case of Libya, at least, the network had provided blueprints for the bombs also. The designs were later handed to US, British and IAEA officials by Libya in Tripoli and were later scrutinized in the United States. Khan supplied what one US intelligence analyst called the 'one-stop nuclear package', that is, "the entire kit: the weapons design, a full-up centrifuge and the Rolodex of suppliers" that Khan had developed while building Pakistan's nuclear bomb.[74]

Meanwhile, Pakistani officials in October 2003 disclosed that they had launched their own probe of Khan's activities after the Bush administration presented what one senior official described as "mind-boggling" evidence that Khan was peddling nuclear technology and expertise to Iran, Libya and North Korea, and had attempted to do the same with Iraq and Syria. The US officials presented evidence of Khan's alleged attempts to sell nuclear secrets to Saddam Hussein when he was President of Iraq and reported that Khan had traveled to Beirut for a clandestine meeting with a top Syrian official in the mid-1990s. President Musharraf claimed that soon after he received this information from USA, he had removed A.Q. Khan from the top government position of scientific advisor. Khan was known in Pakistan as the creator of the country's atomic bomb and had a distinguished national and international standing.

Pakistani Probe results

On the review of the progress of Pakistani investigations of nuclear proliferations by the Government, daily *The News* of Pakistan reported "investigators had made an independent confirmation of the IAEA allegation that Khan had direct ties with international black market dealers who sold non-peaceful N-technology".[75] Also, President Musharraf and Prime Minister M.Z. Jamali asserted that "the nuclear programme would not be rolled back at any cost, they said that action would be taken against the proliferators" and "denied any official involvement".[76] The fact remained that Pakistani scientists and officials manning Khan Research Laboratories had successfully stolen nuclear secrets and had sold them for profit to Iran, North Korea and Libya, for personal gains and if not for Pakistan. A 'US Senate Committee' heard that Pakistan was "very vulnerable to the dirty bomb". The terrorists[77] "could steal some of the vast stocks of unsecured radioactive material" to launch a 'dirty bomb'. Before the Committee it was testified by a witness that Pakistan boosts Islamic extremists in the region, and provided them fertile ground for terrorist recruitment. Greater instability (in South Asia) also meant that nuclear weapons could fall into wrong hands.[78] President Musharraf's stand that the State was not involved in proliferation activity to Iran was re-iterated by former Army Chief General General, Aslam Beg, from 1988 to 1991. Top scientists, while admitting proliferation of N-technology, had maintained that it could be possible only with his approval, considering the tight army control over Pakistani nuke facilities. General has, however, remarked, "I was never confronted with any such situation".[79] Later, Iran made an admission that Iran too had acquired expertise from abroad.[80] Investigations had revealed that the Iran nuclear operation pre-dated the one with Libya and was less sophisticated. The IAEA investigators had concluded that it was so because it appeared that Dr Khan simply gave the Iranians surplus equipment. He had over-ordered some parts for his own needs, so he had something to sell. He had also developed or acquired new centrifuges, which meant that the old ones could go on the market. One of them, which ended up in Iran, was apparently contaminated with enriched uranium. This was found by the United Nations nuclear agency, the International Atomic Energy Agency (IAEA). Iran thereafter had no option but to admit either that it had processed the fuel itself or had got it by accident. It chose the latter explanation, but that opened up the whole question of where it came from. Iran had simply said it got the parts through a third party. But technical analysis by IAEA had detected the hand of Dr Khan in the designs. A.Q. Khan on television later admitted that he, not the Pak government, had supplied nuclear technology to Libya, Iran and North Korea.

Probes by International Media

The international media made its own researches and conclusions. Before the televised admission of A.Q. Khan and pardon given to him by the Pakistan President, every media person worked on the presumption that whatever A.Q. Khan had done was with full approval of his government and the profits went to refurbish the dwindling Pak economy. "What is missed out in these disclosures is that Khan needed the nuclear black market for Pakistan's own nuclear effort. Shibadur

Rahman, in his book *The Long Road to Chagai*, has given the details of how "Pakistan paid various European firms up front and had no difficulty in buying all equipment, processes, materials needed to set up its uranium enrichment project at Kahuta." ... The black market "continues to be necessary to sustain Pakistan's nuclear programme and it is possible even now that China is a beneficiary (of the black market). Otherwise it is difficult to understand China providing Pakistan with various missiles without an adequate *quid pro quo*".[81] The international media had zeroed on the role that the Pak army might have played, which had tight control over the N-programme of Pakistan. It is noted by media that the transfer of Pakistan's nuclear technology to other countries took place in late 1980s and early 1990s. In this period, army had full political control in Pakistan. Moreover, there were allegations that 'the governments of President Musharraf and former Prime Minister Benazir Bhutto shared nuclear technology with North Korea".[82] By the beginning of February 2004, the investigations took new dimensions when the *Washington Post* said that "Khan has told the investigators that Musharraf, former premier Benazir Bhutto and ex-army chiefs, Mirza Aslam Beg and Jahangir Karamat, were all involved in nuclear proliferation in addition to him and his colleagues, according to a friend of Khan and a senior Pakistani investigator". An Editorial in *The Times of India*[83] made the observation: "The myth that Dr. A.Q. Khan's proliferation activities were conducted without the knowledge of the Pakistani army chiefs and prime ministers and further that the US administration was fully satisfied with this explanation stands demolished." The editorial gave lucid four points to substantiate its conclusions and cited the role and relationship of BCCI (Bank of Credit and Commerce International) owned by a Pakistani, Agha Hasan Abedi, in the nuclear proliferation activities and achievement of US policies, keeping in view the then international politics and compulsions. The editorial also drew its conclusion from the Report of Senator John Kerry Committee, which was a US Senate Foreign Relations sub-committee. It is interesting that Senator Kerry in the report[84] said that BCCI was involved "in the sale of nuclear technologies". The following make further interesting reading in the editorial:[85] Agha Hasan Abedi was close to the Pakistani ISI leadership; the BCCI was involved in Iran-Contra deal sponsored by CIA; the "BCCI had cultivated many prominent US personalities—among them, former defense secretary, Clark Clifford, directors of CIA, Richard Helms and William Casey, former president, Jimmy Carter". The editorial continued: "Between 1984-86, the US sold arms to Iran illegally to secure release of hostages held by Hazibullah in Lebanon. ... A part of proceeds of arms sale to Iran was diverted as aid to contra-rebels in Nicaragua. ... Pardons were given to the guilty in the Iran–Contra affair ... that the trial of Clark Clifford, the front man for BCCI operations in USA, was dropped". Further, "Two former Assistant Secretaries of State of the Bush (Sr.) administration, Harry Rowan and Henri Sokoslki, have disclosed (before the Committee) that General Aslam Beg told them in 1990 that if the US were to cut off aid to Pakistan, it might be forced to share nuclear technology with Iran at a price", and so on.

The Modus Operandi

From the media reports of statements of diplomats familiar with the Pakistan's operation, it had become clear by January 2004, that Khan had devised the method of 'one stop shopping' for shoppers of nuclear devices. Khan and his closest associates were the "salesmen" who filled orders for Libya and other customers. Some officials with knowledge said that companies or individuals in at least seven countries, including Pakistan, were involved, either as middlemen or suppliers. Among the countries known to media and investigators, to be thus involved were Malaysia, South Africa, Japan, the United Arab Emirates and Germany. A company in another European country, Switzerland, was also involved. "The black market's trail stretched all the way to Europe", US officials said, adding that that the key to the black market was a small family run company in the Swiss canton of St. Gallen. It was there, officials told the network, that "Swiss engineers helped design 14 key parts of the centrifuge sent to produce the bomb's fuel enriched uranium."[86] "It was a remarkable network that was able in the end to provide a turn-key gas centrifuge facility and the wherewithal to make more centrifuges"; "The technology holder was always Khan. Suppliers came and went, but Khan was always there", according to former IAEA inspector, David Albright, a physicist who analyzed in details the *modus operandi* of nuclear procurement networks of Iran and Libya.[87] In the case of Libya, representatives of Libyan leader Gaddafi contacted the Pakistanis, who relayed the requests to middlemen. The middlemen, in turn, found suppliers to produce the necessary components. Finished parts were then shipped to a firm in the Persian Gulf emirate of Dubai, which arranged for delivery to Libya. The commodities produced for Libya ranged from electronics and vacuum systems to high-strength cobalt metal bearings used in manufacturing gas centrifuges, which are in turn required in making enriched uranium.

A.Q. KHAN AND THE NUCLEAR CURTAIN

A.Q. Khan, who held the prestigious position of scientific advisor to Pakistan, has officially[88] admitted supplying of nuclear expertise and equipment to Libya, Iran and North Korea. He is believed to have offered nuclear merchandise to Iraq in 1990 and to Syria after the Gulf War of 1991. Saddam Hussein is believed to have refused the offer, believing it to be a 'sting operation' of USA.[89] The refusal by Saddam Hussein led to the conviction in USA that Iraq had already possessed nuclear technology and that Iraq had also acquired a few scud class missiles capable of carrying nuclear warheads to Israel. A few of them it did fire during Kuwait war but never with nuclear warheads. Syria was not interested in Khan's nuclear deals. Till the public admission by Khan that the nuclear proliferation activity was done by him at a purely personal level, the world media and the concerned State governments believed that whatever Khan had done or was doing was sanctioned by Pakistan and that he was conducting the clandestine activities to the knowledge of his employers. The "UN investigators are increasingly certain Pakistan government leaders knew the country's top atomic scientist was supplying nuclear technology and designs to other nations, particularly

North Korea, according to diplomats familiar with a probe of the world's nuclear black market" ... "Despite denials by the Pakistani government, the investigators now were certain that some, if not all, of the country's decision makers were aware of Khan's dealings, especially with North Korea, which apparently helped Islamabad build missiles in exchange for help with its nuclear arms programme, said one of the diplomats."... "However, Andrew Koch of *Jane's Defense Weekly*, said that he ran into evidence that senior military officers knew of Khan's sideline four years ago when he attended a military exhibition in Karachi..."[90] From the nature of transactions it was firmly believed that Pakistan army and air force could only have moved or transferred the nuclear equipments from Pakistani laboratories to the territories of recipient States. Although, Pakistan had initiated action against A.Q. Khan at the end of the year 2003, on the persistence of USA, the world media believed that USA must have been a silent privy to the transactions and that it was a 'hand in glove' diplomacy of USA, the glove being Pakistan or Khan. The questions that have been raised in world media interlink USA, Pakistan, BCCI[91] and A.Q. Khan in one-way or other.

However, there are certain points of statecraft and diplomacy that should be kept in mind in understanding the curtain dropped by USA and Pakistan via A.Q. Khan in the matter of nuclear proliferation.

First, it is normal for vigilant States to keep under spying ring the armaments of potential enemy. Such States work to come up to the mark and excel the potential enemy. Thus concerned, USA and Soviet Russia have spied against one other. The USA has kept China and North Korea under surveillance; China and Pakistan have joined to keep India under observation; and, India is supposed to know all about Pakistan's nuclear progress alongwith the clandestine shipments of missiles or nuclear equipments passing through its ports or through the land route connecting Pakistan with China.

Secondly, the spying results are heavy weight State secrets and are kept under heavy wrappers and are not easily revealed and are not generally known. The State run spying agencies, like, ISI, CIA or others work for decades, arrange things to suit their masters but never let public know as to what a president, dictator, prime minister, foreign minister or defense minister desired from the spying agency to decipher or arrange. That is, what Kennedy, Nixon or Carter, Ronald Reagan, Senior Bush, Clinton or Junior Bush desired, negotiated, planned or did right or wrong, will be a secret with CIA for all and for all times. It means that President Bush initially in 2001 to 2003 did not know the role played by former US Presidents and secret agents like Kissinger in diplomatic dealings on nuclear proliferation matters relating to friendly or hostile States. If he charged Pakistan of 'clandestine nuclear proliferation' activities in late 2003, his ignorance of past US secret policies would justify or cover his mistake, if any. Similarly, Musharraf in Pakistan came into power in 1999, when Pakistan already had nuclear bomb but badly required a delivery system, supersonic airplanes or missiles capable of hitting targets deep in India, he did not and might not have known the role played by past Pakistani dictators, presidents, army chiefs or prime ministers who worked on the nuclear project in acquiring nuclear capability through black market, barter, exchange or clandestine operations during the years from early 1970s to 30 May 1998 when Pakistan exploded its first test nuclear bomb. A.Q. Khan was a kingpin in this process. The name of A.Q. Khan only emerged to replace Pakistan, rather as a scapegoat, when Libya renounced its nuclear programme and IAEA and US investigators joined in assessing the magnitude of Libya's nuclear progress and how and wherefrom it obtained nuclear know-how.

Thirdly, Pakistan, USA or China never knew in 2003, that fearful of the threats of President Bush's pre-emptive attacks on 'axis of evil', Iran and Libya would foreclose their nuclear research, projects or programme that these had acquired for money, friendliness or deception of nuclear know-how providers or from nuclear black-marketers. The 2003 US leadership perhaps realized or was provided knowledge of the past involvements only in late January or early February 2004.

Fourth, the US investigators immediately joined the IAEA investigators to form one unit. They saw only A.Q. Khan and not Pakistan in the nuclear proliferation racket. Pakistan was also asked or encouraged to go for separate investigations in the matter. Pakistan pledged[92] "to help the international community to unearth and dismantle illicit proliferation networks and said that individual responsibility for it would be dealt with according to law" and Pakistan was glad that President Bush had hailed President Musharraf for his efforts to prevent nuclear proliferation. Pakistani investigators also found that everything in that direction had been done by Khan and not by Pakistan. One by one, all previous Pakistani prime ministers or army chiefs denounced nuclear proliferation and showed official ignorance of A.Q. Khan's activities.

Fifthly, after initially defending himself by charging[93] government and political leaders for basic decisions on Wednesday 4 February 2004, A.Q. Khan melted down and confessed on television on Thursday 5 February 2004, and to the President Musharraf that he was personally responsible for the illicit nuclear proliferation and asked for pardon and mercy. It is reported by media[94]— "I give him pardon", Musharraf told a news conference a day after Khan's televised confession and request for forgiveness. "There's a written appeal from his side and there's a pardon written from my side," Musharraf told reporters. Earlier to the pardon in the day, the cabinet of Pakistan PM Jamali had met and recommended "Musharraf to accept the scientist's mercy petition and forgive him".[95] Subsequently, US Secretary for State, Colin Powell, testifying before the House Foreign Operations Subcommittee on 10 March 2004 clarified that, "The conditional amnesty given to Khan can be reversed if President Musharraf believes cooperation (in nuclear proliferation probe from Khan) is not adequate or he believes another set of actions is appropriate for the (cooperation of) scientist".[96] Thus the curtain has finally fallen on the serious issue of nuclear proliferation during two decades 1980s and 1990s, by Pakistan to Iran, Libya and North Korea.

ENDNOTES

1. Since 11 September 2001 terrorist bombings the Islamic fundamentalism works to oust USA from Arab, North Africa and the Middle East and to end oil diplomacy of the West in the area.
2. 'The Rise of Pakistan's Army', Mahmud Ali, BBC South Asia analyst, *BBC* Wednesday, 24 December 2003.
3. Communist China which attacked India in 1962 was a *de facto* State but not a member of UNO.
4. 'The Rise of Pakistan's Army', Mahmud Ali, BBC South Asia analyst, *BBC* Wednesday, 24 December 2003.
5. *Ibid.*
6. The Soviet Union had in a proxy war occupied Afghanistan in December 1979 and a puppet government was set. A guerrilla war had begun between Afghan *mujahideen* (freedom fighters) and the Soviet forces, and millions of refugees had fled into Pakistan. United States decided to support the guerrilla forces with the active support of Pakistan for canalizing massive arms supplies.
7. (1) In 1958 the Constitution was abrogated and martial law was instituted. A new constitution, promulgated in 1962 by the martial law administrator Ayub Khan. It provided for the election of the president and national and provincial assemblies by an electoral college composed of members of local councils. (2) In April 1973 Pakistan's third Constitution was adopted by the National Assembly and it was suspended in 1977. (3) In March 1981 a Provisional Constitutional Order was promulgated by Zia, that provided a framework for government under martial law. (4) In 1985, a process was initiated for reinstating the Constitution of 1973 by Zia. Under this, in October 1985 a newly elected National Assembly had passed an amended constitution, giving extraordinary powers to the President, including the authority to appoint any member of the National Assembly as prime minister. (5) The Constitution again amended in 1988 provides for a president as head of state and a prime minister as head of government; and, both must be Muslims. The National Assembly, the Senate, and the four provincial assemblies elect the president for a term of five years. The prime minister is elected by the National Assembly. The president acts on the advice of the prime minister whom he can dismiss and form another government.
8. Before being scrapped by the thirteenth amendment in 1997, the power to dismiss the elected governments was exercised four times.
9. P.M. from March 1985 to May 1988.

10. The Fifth Constitution broadly provided for a president as head of State and a prime minister as head of government; and that both must be Muslims. The National Assembly, the Senate, and the four provincial assemblies elect the president for a term of five years. The National Assembly elects the prime minister. The president acts on the advice of the prime minister whom he can dismiss and form another government.
11. The Supreme Court, later on 29 January 1997, upheld the dismissal of Bhutto and the dissolution of National Assembly.
12. The thirteenth amendment, also made it mandatory for the President to seek the advice of Prime Minister in matters relating to the dissolution of National Assembly.
13. 'President Pervez Musharraf' *BBC World Service* Thursday, 25 December 2003.
14. In February 2004, AQ Khan claimed that "Karamat was privy to the details of the barter arrangement through which Pakistan received the missile" in the context of Army's role in N-proliferation in violation of NPT.: 'Musharraf Charged with N-proliferation' PTI news from Washington reporting from the *Washington Post, The Times of India,* Lucknow Ed., dated 4 February 2004.
15. Under these circumstances, later, the only alternative to democracy was extra constitutional military coup and unilateral abrogation of the Constitution and that General Musharraf did in 1999.
16. In February 2004, A.Q. Khan claimed that former Pakistan Prime Minister, Benazir Bhutto, was involved along with others in nuclear proliferation in addition to him: 'Musharraf Charged with N-proliferation' PTI news from Washington reporting from the *Washington Post*, *The Times of India,* Lucknow Ed., dated 4 February 2004.
17. As quoted by US based web portal South Asia Tribune. See "Sharif 'okayed' Kargil Plan: Book": PTI report from New Delhi, *The Times of India*, 29 July 2004.
18. *Pakistan's Drift into Extremism'* authored by a Pakistani officer, Hassan Abbas: "Sharif 'okayed' Kargil Plan: Book" : PTI report from New Delhi, *The Times of India,* 29 July 2004.
19. Strobe Talbott, 'Engaging India–Diplomacy, Democracy and The Bomb' See*: PTI* news commentary on Talbott's book under heading 'Clinton lost it over Sharif bid to link Kashmir & Kargil' *The Times of India*, July 13, 2004.
20. *Ibid.*
21. 'President Pervez Musharraf' *BBC World Service* Thursday, 25 December 2003.

22. The sale of the F-16 fighter planes was suspended in 1990 when the US imposed sanctions on Pakistan after it concluded that Islamabad was producing nuclear weapons. The US sanctions became tougher in 1998 after Pakistan conducted its first nuclear tests. In March 2005, Bush Administration removed the prohibition from the sale of F-16 fighters to Pakistan.
23. Alternatively, Pakistan has acquired hi-tech missile technology and missiles capable of delivering nuclear warheads up to 2000 Km from North Korea, a State included by USA in the 'Axis of Evil'.
24. In 1998, Pakistan also tested its long range missile, the 1,500 km (932 mile) Ghauri missile. The missile was named after a 12th Century Muslim warrior who had conquered part of India. Its technology is believed to have been supplied by North Korea to Pakistan.
25. Owen Bennett-Jones: 'Have nuclear weapons made South Asia Safe?': *BBC* Friday, 9 May 2003.
26. The mountainous area of Kashmir had no approach roads and Indian guardsmen discovered Chinese activities in the region around 1959, after which exchange of diplomatic notes between India and China started. The fact remained that there was no military presence of India in the region while China had regular armies there.
27. 'IANS' news of 22 November 1996 from Washington, "China Transfers 30 M-11 Missiles to Pak: US Study": *The Hindustan Times,* New Delhi, Saturday, 23 November 1996.
28. 'China to Sell Four Frigates to Pakistan': PTI News: *The Hindu*, 20 May 2004.
29. Pakistan became a "frontline state" when the Soviet Union occupied Afghanistan in December 1979. A guerrilla war began between Afghan freedom fighters and the Soviet forces, and millions of refugees fled into Pakistan. The mujahideen (freedom fighters) used a number of refugee camps and other areas inside Pakistan as bases for their activities. The conflict was internationalized after the United States channeled via Pakistan massive arms supplies to the mujahideen. This program included renewed US economic aid to Pakistan of $4.2 billion for the years 1987 to 1992.
30. Both China and Pakistan had not joined NPT.
31. Ahmed Rashid, 'Musharraf's Bin Laden Headache': *BBC World Service* from Lahore, Wednesday, 17 March 2004.
32. The capture of Osama bin Laden and Taliban leader, Mullah Mohammed Omar, is actively being pursued by USA. President Musharraf faced intense pressure from Washington to help US

forces in Afghanistan to capture or kill Bin Laden and other top *Al Qaeda* and Taliban leaders hiding in the Pakistan-Afghanistan border tribal region. Further, Osama bin Laden and the Taliban were created by Pakistan and the US to help fight the Soviets before Cold War ended.

33. After the General Assembly made proliferation of WMD illegal in 1996, it is guessed that the USA used Pakistan to check, or supply or make illegal sales of nuclear technology to various States that were subsequently designated as 'Axis of Evil' by President Bush of USA.
34. 'Rogue nuclear bombs' release lethal radioactivity in a small area.
35. The enouncement was made by the visiting US Secretary of State, Colin Powell, in Islamabad on 18 March 2004, one day after he had left India. B. Muralidhar Reddy "Pakistan will be a 'major non-NATO ally': Powell" *The Hindu*, Friday, 19 March 2004.
36. PTI news "Pak has given 5 airbases, landing rights to US forces" (quoting from *The News*): *The Times of India,* Lucknow Ed., 26 March 2004.
37. According to US Central Command, US had lost to Pakistan over $10 billion since October 2001 for the logistic support to the Action in Afghanistan, Also Pakistan receives "almost $100 million on account".
38. PTI news from Islamabad: "US offers major debt relief to Pak", *The Times of India,* Lucknow Ed., dated 17 July 2004.
39. *Ibid.*
40. The sale of the F-16 fighter planes was suspended in 1990 when the US imposed sanctions on Pakistan after it concluded Islamabad was producing nuclear weapons. The US sanctions became tougher in 1998 after Pakistan conducted its first nuclear tests.
41. Alternatively Pakistan has acquired hi-tech missile technology and missiles capable of delivering nuclear warheads up to 2000 Km from North Korea, a State included by USA in the 'Axis of Evil'.
42. 'Missile test not intended to send political signals: Musharraf': B. Muralidhar Reddy in *The Hindu*, Saturday, 05 June 2004.
43. The US help to Pakistan has been conditioned by its readiness to fight terrorism, particularly from Afghanistan, the stoppage of nuclear proliferation in the context of the scandal involving the transfer of nuclear technology by A.Q. Khan, progress in the operations against *Al Qaeda* and the Taliban and also India-Pakistan relations.

44. By September 2004, the fencing will be completed: Lt. Gen. Mathew Mammen, Engineer-in-Chief of Indian Army:, 'Army to complete J & K fencing by Sept': *Times of India,* dated 11 July 2004.

45. PTI news from Islamabad, "Armitage does Balancing Act–'Terrorists still exist in Pak", *The Times of India*, Lucknow Ed., dated: 16 July 2004.

46. India, on the other hand, maintained that it was a secular State, had constitutional rights for minorities and Kashmir had legally and formally acceded to India and was now its integral part and there was no question of Pakistan claiming sovereignty over Kashmir. All that it had to do was to return Pakistan occupied Kashmir to India or to settle the matter by negotiations under the Simla Agreement of 1974.

47. Owen Bennett-Jones: 'Have nuclear weapons made South Asia Safe?': *BBC,* Friday, 9 May 2003. According to his study on relative armed strength in 2002 was:

Strategic Balance between India and Pakistan

Armed Forces Manpower:	India 1,100,000	Pakistan 550,000
Combat Aircraft:	India 738	Pakistan 353
Nuclear Missiles:*	India 60	Pakistan 25
Surface Warships:	India 27	Pakistan 8
Submarines:	India 16	Pakistan 10
Military Expenditure:	India US$ 15.9 bn	Pakistan US$ 2.7 bn

*Estimated number.

48. Despite the reassurance or confidence that Pakistan gains from having nuclear weapons, at one stage it offered to dismantle its arsenal if India does the same. This offer was made in part, since it was confident that India would never agree to nuclear disarmament in view of its wider zone of conflicts.

49. Owen Bennett-Jones: 'Have nuclear weapons made South Asia Safe?': *BBC,* Friday, 9 May 2003.
[Owen Bennett-Jones is a former BBC correspondent in Islamabad and author of 'Pakistan: Eye of the Storm'].

50. 'Peddling' involves the merchant taking his merchandize to the place of customer instead of the customer visiting the shop.

51. Reference is to period 1990 to 2004.

52. June 2004, both sides have come out with preparations for foreign minister level talks.

53. Quotes are from press talks of President Musharraf with media after emerging from the sanctum sanctorum of the Durgah. With his family President Musharraf visited the Durgah in India on

16 April 2005 to India, while he had come to witness cricket match between Pakistan and India of 17 April 2005 held at New Delhi. Pakistan won the match and the series.

54. 'Agencies' coverage of the meeting of President Musharraf with Indian media, 18 April 2005: *The Times of India*, Lucknow Ed., 19 April, 2005.

55. The US has asserted of a concert between the Iranian government and Al Qaeda, alleging that it has intercepted radio communications emanating from Iran and directed at the perpetrators of the May 12 bombings in Saudi Arabia. According to the US, these intercepts provide proof that an *Al Qaeda* operative named Saef al Adel had, from a base in Iran, masterminded the Riyadh bomb blasts, which killed 34 people.

56. Reference is to Chapter vis-à-vis North Korea, elsewhere.

57. The interception of a significant shipment of components in Italy last fall (2004) led Gaddafi to decide on the elimination of non-conventional weapons programs of Libya, as US officials have said.

58. USA had charged that Iran did have nuclear bombs but just as Iraq it was hiding them.

59. *The Hindu*, 16 February 2004, 'Nuclear Designs Originated in China' by Sridhar Krishnaswami.

60. Interview of President Musharraf to *New York Times* published on Tuesday, 10 February 2004: "US asks Pak to pull up roots of Khan's network", PTI news from Washington: *The Times of India*, Lucknow Ed., 11 February 2004.

61. "US had threatened Pak with Sanctions" by Chidanand Rajghatta, TNN, from Washington, *The Times of India*, Lucknow Ed., 9 February 2004.

62. "N-Proliferation serious issue for Pak: Boucher': PTI news from Washington: *The Times of India*, Lucknow Ed., 6 February 2004. Mr. Richard Boucher is US State Department spokesman.

63. Peter Slevin, John Lancaster and Kamran Khan: 'Nuclear Trafficking Investigation Grows: At least seven nations tied to Pakistani-led smuggling ring', *The Washington Post*, 8 February 2004.

64. Since 1980s and 1990s: 'Pak charges 4 scientists for illegal transfer of N-tech' PTI news from Islamabad, *The Times of India*, Lucknow Ed., 5 February 2004.

65. And has received pardon from Pakistan President.

66. See: "Pakistan Nuclear Father's offer to Saddam—Iraq refused, fearing a US sting operation", by Robert Windrem, Producer, NBC News, *The Washington Post*, 4 February 2004.

67. *The Hindu*: 'A.Q. Khan Visited Uranium-Rich Nations', Tuesday, 20 April 2004, Associated Press News.
68. Peter Slevin, John Lancaster and Kamran Khan, 'Nuclear Trafficking Investigation Grows: At least seven nations tied to Pakistani-led smuggling ring', *The Washington Post*, 8 February 2004.
69. 'Stopping Pak's Black Market Bombs': K. Subramanium, Times News Network, *The Times of India,* Lucknow Ed., dated, 30 January 2004.
70. *Wall Street Journal* report from Kuala Lampur: PTI news from Washington, quoting from the *Wall Street Journal*, *The Times of India*, Lucknow Ed., 11 February 2004.
71. The company is an approved regular supplier of military hardware from international market for Pakistani army, etc.
72. "Khan Nuclear Network an Open Secret: Report": PTI news from Washington, *The Times of India*, Lucknow Ed., 3 March 2004.
73. "Khan's Nuclear smuggling ring tied to 7 Nations": PTI news from Washington, quoting from the *Washington Post*, *Times of India*, Lucknow Ed., 9 February 2004.
74. See: "Pakistan Nuclear Father's offer to Saddam—Iraq refused, fearing a US sting operation", by Robert Windrem, Producer, NBC News, *Washington Post*. 4 February 2004.
75. 'Rashid meets Khan to discuss N-probe Results': PTI news from Islamabad: *Times of India*, Lucknow Ed., 28 January 2004. (President Musharraf reviewed Progress of probe and Prime Minister M.Z. Jamali, while Pak information minister S. Rashid Ahmed met A.Q. Khan in sequence).
76. *Ibid.*
77. A dirty bomb has never been used in a terrorist attack but several terrorist groups, including *Al Qaida*, had professed an interest in building one. Experts said that dirty bombs were attractive to terrorists because technologically simple, yet could cause widespread fear and economic chaos.
78. 'Dirty Bomb could muddy peace in S. Asia: US': PTI news from Washington: *The Times of India*, Lucknow Ed., 30 January 2004.
79. 'I beg to differ, but no nuke transfer in my time': PTI news from New York, *The Times of India*, Lucknow Ed., 29 January 2004.
80. 'On the Trail of the Black Market Bombs': *BBC World News*, Thursday, 12 February, 2004.

81. 'Stopping Pak's Black Market Bombs': by K. Subramanyam, TNN, *The Times of India*, Lucknow Ed., 30 January 2004.
82. 'Army Role in N-transfer being glossed over': PTI news from New York referring to views in New York Times, *The Times of India*, Lucknow Ed., 31 January 2004.
83. "Nuclear Bombshell—The Truth that John Kerry Knows" Times Editorial by K. Subramanyam, *The Times of India,* Lucknow Ed. Monday, 15 March, 2004. All the statements and quotes in the paragraph are from the editorial.
84. *Ibid.*
85. *Ibid.*
86. "Khan Nuclear network an Open Secret: Report": PTI news from Washington, *The Times of India*, Lucknow Ed., 3 March 2004.
87. Peter Slevin, John Lancaster and Kamran Khan, 'Nuclear Trafficking Investigation Grows: At least seven nations tied to Pakistani-led smuggling ring', from Vienna, *The Washington Post*, *ET* 8 February 2004.
88. Pakistan President pardoned A.Q. Khan for his international activities of nuclear proliferation on 5 February 2004.
89. See: "Pakistan Nuclear Father's offer to Saddam—Iraq refused, fearing a U.S. sting operation", By Robert Windrem, Producer, NBC News, *Washington Post. ET* 4 February 2004. It is noted that "If you approach them with an offer of a critical technology and they dismiss your offer, that could mean they have already mastered that technology," said the official, who added that the United States did try some stings during the Gulf War, but that he was not aware of anything like the Khan offer: *Ibid.*
90. 'Pak officials knew modus operandi of Khan: UN': Associated Press report from Vienna, *The Times of India,* Lucknow Ed. Saturday, 9 March 2004.
91. The Bank of Credit and Commerce International owned by a Pakistani, Agha Hasan Abedi, The BCCI handled the banking transactions relating to the Pakistani nuclear programme and the Iran-Contra illegal deals (of US Government) The BCCI collapsed in 1991. See, "Nuclear Bombshell—The Truth that John Kerry Knows" Times Editorial by K. Subramanyam, *The Times of India,* Lucknow Ed. Monday, 15 March 2004.
92. "Pak to tackle N-proliferation": PTI report from Islamabad, *The Times of India,* Lucknow Ed. Saturday, 14 February 2004.
93. 'Musharraf Charged with N-proliferation' PTI news from Washington, reporting from *The Washington Post*, *The Times of*

India, Lucknow Ed., 4 February 2004: In February 2004, A.Q. Khan claimed that "Karamat was privy to the details of the barter arrangement, though which Pakistan received the missile" in the context of Army's role in N-proliferation in violation of NPT and told the Pak investigators that "Musharraf, former premier Benazir Bhutto and ex-army chiefs, Mirza Aslum Beg and Jehangir Karamat, were all involved in nuclear proliferation in addition to him".

94. "I pardon him, Pervez to Khan": PTI news from Islamabad, *The Times of India,* Lucknow Ed., dated 6 February 2004.

95. *Ibid.*

96. "US Talks Tough on Khan, says Amnesty can be withdrawn": PTI report from Washington, *The Times of India,* Lucknow Ed. Friday, 12 March 2004.

9

Nuclear India: A Unique Status

India, the birthplace of pacifism in global human life and human societies, now going all out for ominously devastating nuclear weapons, looks to be a living antithesis of its past. But, the past is also sordid reminder of the historical fact that pacifism has meant political weakness that has attracted invaders on its soil from the West and the North. They always found it easy to conquer and rule Indian territories. The invaders Greeks, Shaka, Huns, Mongols, Muslims and Europeans constitute immediate political and historical past of India of more than two thousand five hundred years. Now, since India regained full independence in 1947, the Indians have had to act to save the only six decades old independence from nuclear status invaders. It is known that both China and Pakistan had become nuclear before India made its first nuclear weapon. It is relevant and interesting that remembering and paying tribute to first successful Muslim invaders of India of eleventh and twelfth century, the Indian neighboring State on its west has proudly christened its nuclear warhead carrying missile as 'Ghauri' and nuclear cruise missile as 'Babar'. Nuclear diplomacy between India and its neighbors is real and complicated.

The history and formation of new State of India in 1947 was fraught with religious, cultural, linguistic strife and divisions. Only Muslims of British India were to live in new State of Pakistan and the rest of religious communities in India. There was mass exchange of population between India and Pakistan. The framers of the constitution of the Indian State preferred a federal, democratic and secular character for the nation. The first decade was full of turmoil with communalism and communism of Chinese origin (Maoist) creating havoc. By the advent of 1960s the West, China and Pakistan particularly were eagerly waiting for Balkanization or disintegration of India into several States. The disintegration of India due to internal divisions was taken to be a matter of time only around 1960. Pakistan had already occupied part of Kashmir in 1950 and it had become aligned to the West in the 'cold war'. China was next, first with hidden occupations and subsequently with overt attack on its northeast frontiers in October 1962 and India had suffered a humiliating defeat in this war. Pakistan became diplomatically friendly with China under the principle of diplomacy that a State "enemy of enemy is friend". There was land route for Pakistan to China through occupied Kashmir and Pakistan had also ceded some occupied Kashmir territory to China while China had secretly built a connecting road to its provinces through Aksai Chin area of Kashmir. Pakistan tried to emulate China in 1965 but in the war it remained unsuccessful and was rather humiliated, since it did not have the same geographical and topographical advantages as China had in the theatre of war. However, the strategic cooperation between the two had continued. China had earned respect of the West by becoming a nuclear power in 1964 and for having boundary disputes with Soviet Russia,[1] a sign of overt conflict between the two communist States. The rapport of Pakistan with China was favorably noticed and was sought for by US President Nixon. Pakistan had become diplomatically important to USA for befriending communist China by 1970s. Conciliation between USA and communist China had followed through efforts of Pakistan and under this process the communist Chinese regime replaced the KMT regime of China in the UNO and its Security Council. India henceforth has viewed the line-up of Pakistan, USA and China as a mortal danger to its existence and security till the end of last century. China was a nuclear power and like Pakistan it had designs on Indian territories; at least China does not want to return to India those territories that are under its *de facto* control. Pakistan has continuously received economic, military and diplomatic support of both the USA and China since 1970s. India under the clouds of hostile nations around signed a treaty of friendship with USSR in 1971 and this diplomatic protection of Soviet Russia had placed restraints on China against any future aggression on India.

Pakistani Attack on India of 1971

Pakistan had rather prematurely gone for a war on India in 1971 trusting friendships of both the USA and China. USA had sent its Seventh Fleet to Bay of Bengal, some days after the start of war, for projected help to Pakistan in the battle taking place in East Pakistan. USA also prompted China to build pressure on Indian north-eastern borders. But, before the alliance of the three could materialize, Pakistan forces had surrendered in East Pakistan to India after the 17-day war. The USA had exerted its pressure on China for action against India but Soviet diplomacy had prevented any Chinese armed action against India. The Soviet Union also exercised its veto several times in the UN Security Council during the war. The USA, it is said by media, had warned India against any further dismemberment of West Pakistan,[2] rather frustratingly, but the warning was seriously taken by India. The war had ended with East Pakistan becoming Bangladesh, an independent State out of Pakistan.

ACQUIRING NUCLEAR EXPERTISE: THE 1970s

Towards Nuclearization

The result of 1971 war of Pakistan on India convinced the West for the good of India that India had a strong self-validating secure presence in South Asia. This gave a new enhanced status to India in international politics and diplomacy. Indian strategic leadership felt that short of a nuclear attack, which could be possible, it had a long era of peace. India had existing strong scientific study centers in the Universities, a Council of Scientific and Industrial Research (CSIR), Defence Research and Development Organization (DRDO) and a hi-tech nuclear science base with self-managed electricity producing nuclear reactors, first going back to late 1950s. The general principles involved in process of nuclear weapon explosions were publicly known world-over. Diplomacy, commercialism and cold war guided the selective proliferation of nuclear technology and science till the NPT came into operation. India had some nuclear reactors that it was operating with the help of other States under agreements and had acquired sufficient know-how for indigenously constructing nuclear reactors. It could manufacture nuclear fuel for uranium and thorium fuel based reactors as well by 1970. Also, nuclear technology and sophisticated dual or multiple use equipments were available in international markets. Metallurgical processes for extracting metals from ores use similar technology and Indian specialists could undertake extraction of uranium from uranium ore easily. The NPT of which India was not a member was in a nascent stage in 1972 and so only a small leap was required to develop nuclear weapon technology indigenously. It may be mentioned that USA, Soviet Russia and France had developed nuclear weapons indigenously. China is regarded to have developed nuclear weapons by spying and by assistance of Soviet Russia. Pakistan developed nuclear technology with the help of China, which became a member of NPT only in 1990, and Pakistan is known to have bartered it to North Korea in exchange for missile technology.

Indian Nuclear Technology Base

India had established the Atomic Energy Commission on 10 August 1948 and Dr. H.J. Bhabha was its chairman. It was later renamed as the Bhabha Atomic Research Centre (BARC) with its centre at Trombay. Its executive arm, the Department of Atomic Energy (DAE), was established in 1954. The Indian Rare Earths Limited (IREL) has since 1950 been engaged in the mining and processing of mineral sands for producing thorium and uranium. The Atomic Minerals Division (AMD) has been engaged in locating reserves and exploring nuclear minerals, particularly uranium, along with the Uranium Corporation of India Limited (UCIL). The latter runs plants to recover uranium from various ores and compounds, though till uranium came under NPT regulations it was cheaper in international markets, since uranium had few purchasers other than laboratories. On the fundamental research and development side, BARC has spearheaded the work of nuclear science and technology. It runs a series of research projects from reactor Apsara to the Phoenix. It has mastered and operated the whole processes of nuclear cycle activities—ranging from exploration, mining and fuel fabrication to designing, construction, operation and maintenance of nuclear power stations, enhancing the life of aging power reactors, fuel reprocessing and radioactive waste management tasks. The last, fuel reprocessing and radioactive waste management has led to the development of Fast Breeder Reactors (FBR). BARC has simultaneously extended research facilities of its research reactors to non-power applications of atomic energy for generation of radioisotopes and radiation technology for cancer therapy, etc. to health-care, agriculture, hydrology and industry. Multipurpose or dual-purpose use technology and products, such as, accelerators, lasers, robotics, special materials and biotechnology have also been developed through the help or guidance of the research establishments of BARC. In addition, two hundred or more young scientists and engineers are admitted to the Training School of BARC every year since 1957 and trained for the jobs; a few of them are also sent abroad under bilateral arrangements for training in specialized areas related to nuclear technology.

Facilities for Nuclear Research and Development

For nuclear advancement, the following plants or facilities constituting nuclear technology infrastructure are in function in India and most of these came into existence before 1974:

(1) Board of Research in Nuclear Sciences (BRNS) is nuclear research funding agency for the country.

(2) Fuel Fabrication Plant at Trombay produces fuel elements for research reactors of the country and also develops new fuels, fuel assemblies such as zircaloy clad uranium oxide and like materials, needed for nuclear reactors.

(3) The Nuclear Fuel Complex (NFC) set up at Hyderabad in 1971 is engaged in production at industrial scale of nuclear fuel assemblies both for Pressurized Heavy

Water Reactors (PHWR) and Boiling Water Reactors (BWR), and also costly sophisticated components needed for reactors such as seamless tubes, instrumentation tubes. Later, it produced the thorium oxide pellets for the new indigenous Fast Breeder Reactors (FBR).[3]

(4) To meet the suspension of foreign supply of fuel for Tarapur reactor, the Advanced Fuel Fabrication Facility (AFFF) component of BARC functions at Tarapur. It fabricated the Mixed Oxide fuel bundles for Tarapur reactor and also the 'carbide fuel' core of mixed uranium-plutonium carbide regularly needed for FBR.

(5) The Indira Gandhi Centre for Atomic Research (IGCAR) established in 1971 is a broad based multidisciplinary project for research and advanced engineering. It has concentrated on the development of sodium cooled FBR for optimum utilization of thorium reserves of the country.

(6) The Variable Energy Cyclotron Centre at Calcutta is a national nuclear research facility that produces nuclear particles for application in research. It produces radioisotopes used for medicinal and agricultural fields.

(7) The Centre for Advanced Technology, 1987, is now an internationally recognized R&D institution that has taken up highly sophisticated technology projects in the areas of lasers, accelerators, cryogenics, superconductivity and ultra-high vacuum, among others.

Nuclear India and International Regulations

First, India has been a founder member of International Atomic Energy Agency (IAEA). It is ever since represented on the Board of Governors as a designated member. The Statute of the International Atomic Energy Agency was approved and adopted on 23 October 1956, by a special International Conference held for adoption of the Statute. This International Conference was held under the patronage of the United Nations[4] at its headquarters. This has meant that India has since 1956 been recognized as one of ten most advanced States in the field of nuclear science and technology. In international forums, India has consistently focused attention on cooperation in promotion of peaceful uses of nuclear energy and for all-encompassing nuclear disarmament. India has hosted several IAEA meetings on a variety of matters and a large number of Indian experts are members of IAEA advisory or technical groups. India trains about 25 IAEA sponsored fellows every year in its nuclear institutions and has donated sophisticated monitoring equipments to IAEA laboratories.

Secondly, India has signed the partial Nuclear Test Ban Treaty of 1963, which professed to be more of humanitarian or environment protection nature by way of saving humanity, flora and fauna from evil effects of nuclear fallout after nuclear test in air, ocean or on ground; but, it did not prohibit underground nuclear tests. At the same time, it made development of nuclear weapons by other States difficult, since nuclear tests in air were in 1960s deemed to be necessary in the development of accurate nuclear explosion technology. India has accordingly made only underground nuclear testing in 1974 and in 1998.

Thirdly, India has not signed and joined the 1970 Treaty on Non-Proliferation of Nuclear Weapons (NPT).[5] The ground taken by India is that this Treaty is discriminatory between the States already possessing nuclear knowledge and capabilities and the non-nuclear weapon States. It does not prevent the former from increasing their stockpile of nuclear weapons or improving these or making new types, so long as prohibited methods of test are not used. Further, the international bodies do not have peremptory rights of disarming nuclear weapon States of their nuclear weapons, paradoxically the possession and use of which remains legal.

Compulsions leading to Indian First Nuclear Test

As mentioned earlier, the configuration of hostile States against India was ominous when Pakistan had committed aggression on India in 1971. Pakistan had lost this war fought with conventional weapons. There had been mass influx of people as refugees into India due to horrifying "genocide" unleashed by the Pak army in the then East Pakistan while the West and USA had adopted a "hands-off" policy in favour of Pakistan. The released old classified State documents of US now reveal the diplomatic hostile encirclement of India, "Nixon instructed: 'Don't squeeze Yahya[6] at this time.'—since US was using Pakistan as a 'secret conduit' to open diplomatic channels with China."[7] During the period of the Pakistan war on India of 1971, according to declassified secret British documents, released in UK on 1 January 2005 it was revealed for the first time that the US suspected that India wanted to dismember Pakistan by splitting not only its Eastern wing but also the West Pakistan. Nixon and his Foreign Policy Adviser, Henry Kissinger, suspected that India's aim was to break up Pakistan and advance towards Pakistan-occupied Kashmir. "The papers also include details of talks of the then Indian Prime Minister, Indira Gandhi, with Mr. Heath in London during which she spoke of the pressures on her from her own Cabinet to occupy Pakistani territory and not return it. Indira Gandhi expressed her apprehensions about an Islamabad-Beijing-Washington nexus building up against India. Pakistan, she said, had already allied itself with China and now Americans were also trying to get close to Beijing. The emerging nexus, she said, made it necessary for India to sign a friendship treaty with Moscow."[8] Also, the nuclear option became a compulsion for India as a lesson from the games of diplomacy being played around.

Post 1971 Pakistan War International Diplomacy

The USA was a nuclear superpower and Pakistan had long-standing defence pacts with USA. President Nixon had ominously for India sent Seventh Fleet, the aircraft carrier USS Enterprise and its escorts were dispatched to the Bay of Bengal near to East Pakistan to "intimidate" India; US had prompted nuclear China to exert military pressure on its border with India in favour of Pakistan.[9] "USA secretly encouraged China to move its military forces towards Indian border. US (even) assured China of protection if the Soviet Union made any move against it for 'menacing India'. Nixon and Kissinger even explored the need to support China's conventional forces if the Soviet Union jumped into the fray. But, as it turned out, China refused to play the ball."[10] The USA had also tried to put pressure on the former USSR to discourage India with the threat that the ongoing US-Soviet detente would otherwise be jeopardized.[11] The explosive international diplomacy of the days was that Nixon had become tired out and angry at China for its inaction: "The Chinese sit there and bullyrag us. They have got to learn, damn right" and he further told Kissinger to "put heat on the Indians who are the aggressors". Kissinger analyzed the result of an escalated conflict for Nixon that the outcome of war would be that "Pakistan is swallowed by India, China is destroyed, defeated, humiliated by Soviet Union, it will be a change in the world balance of power of such a magnitude—that the security of US may be (in danger) forever, certainly for decades—we will have ghastly war in the Middle East".[12] But, fortunately for India the Pakistani military administrator of East Pakistan had surrendered to India before the US Seventh Fleet or China could actively come to the aid of Pakistan. But, there had been as noted some acrimony among US, USSR and China for other reasons and it was feared by USA that Soviet Russia might escalate the war if China stepped into the fray. The declassified US foreign policy documents indicate[13] "complete concurrence of US 'game plan' by Pakistan military ruler Yahya Khan", but others had failed it. Perhaps India took more than thirty-four years to forgive the USA.

For the future, Indian policy makers remained afraid of China-Pakistan military alliance and not of USA. At that time preceding 1971 war China was possessing long-range nuclear warhead missiles capable of hitting targets in India, Soviet Russia and the USA. Its warplanes could have easily targeted nuclear bombs in North India. As such, it was more reasonable assessment that Pakistan would get Chinese nuclear expertise to build nuclear bomb for use against India in case China avoided taking a direct part in a war between India and Pakistan. As a matter of historical corroborative fact, A.Q. Khan, the architect of Pakistani nuclear bomb, had started peddling nuclear bomb technology to other States for profit by the beginning of 1980s. Pakistan also impressed some States of the Middle East and North Africa by asserting its capabilities of making *'Islamic'* nuclear bomb.[14] The USA and UK were signatories of NPT and had not made any transfer of nuclear technology to Pakistan in violation of NPT. China[15] had signed the NPT only in 1992 and if it did transfer nuclear technology to Pakistan it did not violate any international obligations. At the same time, the transfer of this nuclear technology never became an admitted matter and continues to remain a topic of discussions or conjectures.

INDIA ON NUCLEAR PATH

International Diplomacy Compelling 1974 Nuclear Test

Much has been already referred to about the international compulsions, which required India to be strong without external military support. Diplomatically, USSR and India had a treaty of friendship in 1971.This friendship accord helped India by keeping China away from helping Pakistan in its war with India through Soviet pressures on China. Soviet Russia had exercised veto power in favour of India several times during 1971 war to stall any sanctions against India while Pakistan was the aggressor but was loosing the war. But in between 1971 and 1975 the international politics had a highly volatile form:

1. There were direct bilateral talks of détente between USA and USSR, USSR and China had turned competitors in international politics and had boundary disputes that had turned into stalemate.
2. The friendship between USA President Nixon and China brought about by Pakistan had set USSR in a bad mood against Pakistan and led to further creation of distance between USSR and China.
3. China wanted to unite Taiwan by force but USA was ready with nuclear arms to protect Taiwan against any military action by China. By developing friendship with USA and by becoming a veto power member of UN, China could not rely on any support of USSR in a war involving USA on the issue.

4. Pakistan had continued military support of China and USA and was expected to recompense the losses suffered in 1971 war early. Economic packages from USA to Pakistan had improved. The military was keen to level up the humiliation of defeat in 1971 war.
5. India has ever been continuously suspicious of Chinese intentions and capabilities against it, the continuing boundary dispute in which China was using Indian territory in Aksai Chin for road passages to its advantage. The refugee status and asylum granted to Dalai Lama by India was international blot on China.
6. China was a nuclear power and the northern India was within its nuclear targeting zones. India was fortunate that President Nixon had failed to push China to confront India militarily and to help Pakistan in 1971 war, thanks to Soviet diplomacy.
7. It has been noticed in media: "On the day when China became a nuclear weapon power, it became imperative for the Indian policy makers to give serious consideration for the country acquiring nuclear weapons. ... In the wake of China's nuclear threat, Lal Bahadur Shastri was believed to have requested British Prime Minister Harold Wilson for an extended deterrence by Britain during his visit to that country but there was no favorable British response."[16]
8. USA had some sympathies for India after its defeat in October 1962 war with China from 'cold war' angle. But these had come to a naught after the rapprochement between the two brought about by Pakistan. USA had new altered priorities and visions in South Asia. USA was a strong founder-supporter of NPT. "In the light of these developments, there can be no question that the basic factors that triggered the Indian nuclear test in 1974 were the China factor and US nuclear intimidation".[17]

Steps for 18 May 1974 Nuclear Test

Under these above mentioned surrounding pressures of diplomacy and of impending war in which nuclear weapons could be used against it, India made its first Pokhran nuclear underground test on 18 May 1974. India had not exploded a complete nuclear bomb but had only made peaceful nuclear explosion (PNE) experiment that was, of course, also a step necessary to the making of nuclear bomb. This was the starting step for dual nuclear peaceful and military use process. The Indian scientists and nuclear experts had taken up the task of 'breaking the non-nuclear barrier' around 1973 by a carefully planned research and development effort that never conspicuously exhibited the importance of the effort before the test was accomplished. Under the auspices of the DRDO and its 'explosives development and test laboratories', the design of a nuclear device was finally decided upon at some time. BARC accomplished the selection of the team and apportioning the tasks, to test the experimental device in 1973. The selection and identifying the site for the tests had taken six-month field efforts. A precisely calculated 107-metre deep hole was dug in the desert by an engineering regiment. After that, in less than seven days, all the fieldwork for the experimental underground explosion experiment was completed and the device was detonated at 8-10 a.m. on May 18, 1974. The International Data Centre (IDC), Arlington, US, assessed the yield of Pokhran May 1974 test as between 10 and 15 kiloton. India evaluated it as in between 12 and 13 kiloton and this was accepted by leading seismologists in the world. In comparison the maximum yield of the tests done later on May 11, 1998 was 4.5 times the yield of the test done in May 1974, that means, the maximum yield of Pokhran II test was about 50 to 60 kiloton. In 1974 test, there was no radioactive fallout. The entire test operation was carried out without fanfare and foreign intelligence agencies had no clue of the developments. A significant feature of this test, and also of 1998, was the complete secrecy that was successfully managed or maintained. The fact that the explosions were fully successfully contained indicates that the yield was very close to the predicted value. Had the actual yield been even 'slightly above the design value', there would have been a 'radioactive fallout' and the secrecy would have misfired.

International Reactions after the Test

After Pokhran-I, the political fallout from the West was very quick. Sanctions were imposed, supply of critical goods was banned, and access to information for nuclear technology was denied. A worldwide nuclear technology denial regime against the States that refused to sign NPT had developed both against nuclear power generation and nuclear weapon technology equipment acquisition or development. Various hurdles extending to blanket ban were placed so as even to curb India's efforts to make progress in the peaceful applications of nuclear energy. Canada, France and the US went back on their commitments and international agreements. India has gone through a long period of "apartheid" under the arms control agenda of developed and European Union States, called nuclear suppliers group (NSG). National governments and international cartels made rules to isolate India by enforcing discriminatory laws like the NPT. About 200 Indian scientists, research institutions and companies were blacklisted and export restrictions on nuclear fission related materials and technologies were placed. Even the civilian nuclear power reactors were hit by starving them of nuclear fuel that was imported under agreements. By late 1970s, critics started doubting if it was at all a sane or good decision to have gatecrashed into the elite nuclear club. It was a struggle, but by the 1980s, India came out successful, even though bruised, in its effort to expand its nuclear power programme.[18] Accordingly the Indian attitude in 1998 towards the failed or staggered Comprehensive Test Ban Treaty, in the absence of a nuclear international umbrella was uncompromising. India was the lone grumbler and vocal dissenter of CTBT and the real politics or diplomacy required in-built strength of a minimum nuclear deterrence against the obvious could be aggressors. Indian Foreign Minister, Yashwant Sinha, had by taking an overall view of encompassing developments from 1970s to 2004, stated[19] that the argument that the decision of India to develop nuclear weapons was purely political, aimed at enhancing its status in the world by breaking into nuclear club was misplaced. It was a fallacy, that "in a world where weapons of mass destruction are still to be eliminated, nuclear weapons sadly remain the ultimate guarantor of nation's security".... "It was the imposition of an imperfect non-proliferation order, which compelled us to make transition from nuclear abstinence to that of a reluctant nuclear power". In adversely aggressive and isolating diplomacy since 1970s Indian agony was factual, the diplomacy was security oriented and on this he emphasized on the declared 'no first-use' policy of India and a unilateral ban on further nuclear testing. Further, "India has repeatedly reiterated its commitment to a complete and universal elimination of nuclear weapons. Despite attempts to politically isolate and economically weaken India, its response was to engage the leading nations of the world in patient dialogue." Further that "We are not part of Nuclear Non-Proliferation Treaty (NPT). But, we believe in and uphold the broad non-proliferation goals of the Treaty, for its frailties and drawbacks affect India as well.[20] Unlike some other nuclear States, India has no black records of nuclear proliferation and on the other hand its acquisition of nuclear technology is indigenous and is strictly for self-defence set against more than one probable aggressor. India progressed to nuclear weapon technology in the pre-NPT era by way of enrichment for recycling of spent uranium fuel waste of its nuclear power reactors.

Future Decisions on Nuclear Expertise

Prime Minister Rajiv Gandhi had in 1985 "constituted an interdisciplinary committee to discuss the country's nuclear policy in the wake of reports about Sino-Pakistan Nuclear Cooperation" but had settled with an agreement with Pakistan against attacking nuclear installations of each other.[21] In the period 1987 to 1998, Pakistan often talked about its nuclear capabilities, though it had not made any nuclear tests on its soil. There were evidences that Pakistan possessed nuclear weapon grade expertise in 1988. India only drew the attention of US to the Sino-Pakistani collaboration in nuclear weapon development but the US administration remained completely naïve and indifferent to India's concerns and, on the other hand, brought pressure on India to cap its nuclear ambitions. In 1992, the problems posed by the breakdown of Soviet Union and the initiation of the plans for a mandatory CTBT, compelled India to make nuclear weaponization a national security matter and gave it out as the reason for not signing the CTBT. Rather for bringing a kind of negative pressure on India, a clause was added to the CTBT that the Treaty would come into force only after 43 States, including India, signed it. Then, Pakistan obtained a complete Nodsong missile technology from North Korea as a barter agreement for transfer of nuclear technology in April 1998 to complete its nuclear offensive against India, this too with US permissiveness. Pakistan had not exploded nuclear devices but had all the materials and technology to make nuclear bomb and was trading these to non-nuclear States by the end of 1980s. In these backdrop circumstances the National Security Council, advisors and Prime Minister Vajpayee of India gave political approval only around 1998 for 'further' nuclear tests for developing a 'credible nuclear deterrence' system for defence of the country.

Compulsions for Pokhran II (1998) Test

Prime Minister Vajpayee after the test on 27 May 1998 stated[22] in Parliament the core points that had led India to the second nuclear test:

(1) It was a continuation of the national policy on "the path of self-reliance and independence of thought and action" of a sovereign India;

(2) In the decades since 1980, the security environment of India has adversely suffered due to nuclear and missile proliferations;

(3) India is a "victim of externally aided and abetted terrorism, militancy and clandestine war";

(4) The NPT is discriminatory in favour of nuclear State parties and acceding to it would be surrender of nuclear option to Unequal Global Nuclear Bargain (UGNB); more so since the international community

is not taking "decisive and irrevocable steps in moving towards a nuclear weapon-free world";

(5) India has to have nuclear weapons as "weapons of self-defence" that would ensure that India is "not subjected to nuclear threats or coercion". The action taken by Pokhran-II tests is "balanced" since a nuclear deterrence was now "minimum necessary (in order) to maintain what is an irreducible component of our national security calculus".

Faltering International Diplomacy

Truly, the international community of 1990s had been quite preoccupied and concerned with the prevention of proliferation of nuclear technology. The CTBT had been a matter of attention in international conscience. At the same time, Pakistan's undeclared nuclear capabilities were being used by superpowers for sting operations for transfer of nuclear technology for purposes of international diplomacy. North Korea, an underling of China, had made strides by obtaining proliferated nuclear technology from Pakistan in exchange for Nodsong missile technology. While England and France had ratified CTBT, most of other nuclear-capable powers had not.[23] Pakistan had also avoided signing NPT and CTBT, professedly on the ground that it would do so only after India acceded to NPT. While India had to tackle nuclear China also, Pakistan was aligned to it. Pakistan had a diplomatic edge over India and long-lasting military association with US when the latter wanted to have a controlling say in Afghanistan politics. After the Soviet withdrawal from Afghanistan in February 1989, US along with Pakistan became interested in the politics of ousting pro-Soviet government of President Najibullah and nurtured a civil war in Afghanistan. Latter wanted an Islamic State in Afghanistan that had strong dependence on it. Both USA and Pakistan provided moral, military training together with modern arms and logistic support to Taliban, an Islamic fundamentalist youth organization with its foundations in Kandhar. Capital of Afghanistan, Kabul, in 1995 remained besieged by militants:

first by various anti-communist mujaheddin factions and subsequently by Taliban. In September 1996 the Taliban took over Kabul. The Taliban movement provided a pro-West rule in Afghanistan but it also provided a fertile ground for terrorism, training camps for them, arms transfers and drug trafficking which destabilized the whole region, Pakistan and beyond. Pakistan had adopted the diplomacy of mass-scale diverting Taliban irregulars into Kashmir on the same pattern for achieving its objectives in Kashmir. There was real and serious Taliban extension threat to Kashmir since 1996 onwards. This threat had full Pakistan guidance, help and American supplied arms for Taliban that were leftover surplus with Pakistan. The multinational terrorists started to infiltrate into Indian territories with the objective of sabotaging Kashmir peace for annexation. In 1997, Indian military strength was diverted to deal with those of Pakistan and infiltrators threat in Indian territories, particularly Kashmir. The role of USA and China was dubious and the future help from Russia was uncertain. It was clear in 1997 that India had to be *swayam-siddha* (complete, self-sufficient and reliant) in order to survive further humiliations.[24] The Indian government on the advice of its scientists and military strategists took the political decision to perfect nuclear weapons that required few critical underground explosion-tests in May 1998. Prime Minister Vajpayee took the political decision within two months of the assumption of office. Pakistan utilized this event by dramatically conducting five plus one underground nuclear explosions few days later on 28 and 30 May 1998, declaring itself to be nuclear power and challenged India on Kashmir matter. Pakistan ventured the Kargil war in May 1999 against India secretly; it lost the war while its army chief, General Musharraf, was negotiating matters in China. More dramatically, Pakistan again came under military rule with General Musharraf as ruler in October 1999 by the overthrow of Prime Minister Sharif government. These developments in the neighborhood fully justified the pre-emptive action for acquiring a minimum nuclear deterrent taken by India for becoming nuclear State. India sought the status of nuclear State Party in the CTBT.

However, the CTBT was not ratified by USA when on 15 October 1999, the Senate of US Congress failed to approve it with the required majority. The CTBT has gone into limbo since then, saving India from trying or difficult situations. However, international sanctions isolating India economically and particularly in defence sector followed.[25]

The Second Explosive Test at Pokhran

Five tests were conducted by the scientists at Pokhran on 11 and 13 May 1998, four of which were of fission variety and one was thermonuclear. The former used uranium or plutonium, as the principal explosive while the second was a hydrogen fusion device. Of the three tests of 11 May, one was hydrogen bomb of estimated 45-kiloton (Kt) yield; one was fission device of 15 Kt yield and another was experimental sub-Kt fission device of 0.2 Kt yield. The 13 May tests comprised of two more sub-Kt fission bomb devices of 0.5 Kt and 0.3 Kt yield. Each day explosions took place simultaneously at the same time. As compared, at the Pokhran-1 only one peaceful nuclear explosion (PNE) of 12 Kt was made on 18 May 1974. It is claimed that the Pokhran-II tests completed a "planned series of tests" emphasizing that India has a broad-based planned nuclear weaponization programme, meeting both strategic and tactical requirements. At the time, delivery system was warplanes based, as two missiles Prithvi (range upto 1000 km) and Agni (range in excess of 1000 km) both capable of carrying nuclear warheads were under necessary advancements that were to be perfected.

International Censors of Indian Second Nuclear Tests

India has not been formally accepted as a nuclear power since NPT had its cut-off date. But, many States of the world regard India to be a *de facto* member of the small nuclear club. India has, by its new posture, forced the world to take it seriously and has strengthened its diplomatic position. For this, Pakistan is the main cause. There can be an unwanted nuclear war in the region particularly because of the open threats of Pakistan to make any war with India a nuclear war, its support to militants, terrorists and its persistence to ultimately force the Kashmir territory as a battle issue. India is not a party to the NPT and the CTBT had not come into force and was awaiting ratifications. The obligations and restrictions placed on non-nuclear States parties of NPT did not apply on India. It may be recalled that the cut-off date for nuclear power status under the NPT was 1 January 1967. The renewed tests were obviously taken as a failure of NPT that had no enforcement mechanism. Only USA was self-proclaimed sanction enforcer for such States that developed nuclear weapon technology by proliferation processes. India had acquired the nuclear capability indigenously without clandestine procurement from other States. After Pokhran-I test of 1974, some States had imposed sanctions and many of these were in operations which were stifling Indian civil nuclear reactors. After Pokhran-II the 'international pressure' on India was for joining NPT and CTBT immediately and this would have compelled India to roll back its nuclear technology, while some States led by USA proceeded to place wider economic sanctions in addition. The USA had its own compulsions. The US Nuclear Proliferation Prevention Act[26] of 1994 bound the administration to impose stiff penalties on any non-nuclear weapon State that detonated a nuclear device at any time henceforth. Apart from prohibition of any export of nuclear development related hardcore items, which was already existing, the US administration was empowered to cut-off direct foreign aid except humanitarian, withdraw US help to trade deals, work for stopping loans to India from international financial institutions, e.g., World Bank or the IMF, ban sales of military use items and related technology to India, prohibit US banks from lending to designated institutions or government, stop loans or loan guarantees to Indian from federal financial agencies such as US Export-Import Bank. The US administration placed such restrictions against India. The US administration was, however, soft to Pakistan in laying down sanctions, since it was US ally in Afghanistan tangle and thus it was rather discriminatory.

Censor by G-8 States

The USA with incoherent results prompted other States, particularly of the G-8 club, the Nuclear Suppliers Group and the European Union States for taking steps against India. The Indian nuclear tests gave a reason for doubts in several States on the worth and usefulness of NPT as such. While the condemnation of the new nuclear tests syndrome was universal and India was urged strongly to sign NPT and CTBT there was no uniformity in the extent of sanctions to be applied, since this depended on the Indian and the individual State trade collaboration. Only Japan and Canada responded to US call substantially. The G-8, led by Canada, passed a resolution against India. The UN Security Council also censored India and Pakistan for the nuclear tests.[27] Russia, France and Britain came out *against* sanctions for specific reasons and took independent positions. However, as against US and Canadian sanctions India was not much concerned, since these restrictions were already continuing since 1974. The US sponsored sanctions had made Indian economic development slow and more difficult. At the same time, the situation gave incentive for indigenous alternative innovations. Most of developed States wanted to enter fast growing Indian markets for trade. Canada revised its attitude towards India in 2001 to a limited extent and in 2005 further changed its position and decided to resume supplies for civilian nuclear facilities, dual use equipment and technology included, under IAEA safeguards.[28] The US-India Joint Statement or accord of July 2005, is limited to Indian voluntary recognition of IAEA guidelines to civilian nuclear reactors and does not in anyway curtail or regulate military segment of nuclear reactors. Prime Minister had observed in parliament[29] that "there was no compromise on India's fundamental and strategic needs and that 'autonomous' control of nuclear weapons would be retained".... "There is nothing in this Joint Statement that amounts to limiting or inhibiting our strategic nuclear weapons programme over which we retain unrestricted, complete and autonomous control". Prime Minister emphasized in parliament that in pursuance of the Joint Statement India would identify and separate civilian and military nuclear facilities in a phased manner and would take a decision, conditional on US fulfilling its part of condition, to place the civilian nuclear facilities under IAEA safeguards. Later in December, Prime Minister affirmed that the exercise of separating India's civilian and military nuclear facilities in implementation of the nuclear deal with US was at "a fairly advanced stage." Further that for this process "Two groups were set up—one in India and the other in the United States to discuss the implementation of the July, 18, civilian nuclear deal" and the groups were "interacting."[30]

DELIVERY AND TARGETING OF NUCLEAR WEAPONS

Delivery Systems for N-Weapons

Delivery or dropping of nuclear weapons on enemy territory, tactical or strategic, and also safe keeping nuclear weapons before exploding on enemy territory are important part of being a nuclear State. The term 'nuclear capability' includes nuclear weapons as well as effective delivery systems, which are the air force and missiles. According to *Jane's Intelligence Review* (2003), Pakistan has been ahead of India in its nuclear capabilities[31] since "Pakistan did not waste time in developing indigenous delivery systems but acquired tried systems from China and North Korea". Till 2004, the Indian nuclear deterrence had been mainly based on launching or dropping of nuclear weapons from supersonic aircrafts obtained from France, England and Russia, though India was confident of destroying Pakistan even under its 'no first use' doctrine. India had more nuclear weapons that could be launched through warships as well. India developed its missile technology in a slow process and missile based nuclear capability with the development of Agni-II missile sometime after Kargil Conflict of May 1999. Till 2004, India had been inferior to Pakistan in missile sector capabilities.

India—Developing Indigenous Missiles

India has an Integrated Guided Missile Development Programme (IGMDP) [32] started in1983. It has over the years produced two variants of Agni series nuclear warhead capable medium range ballistic missiles (MRBM): Agni-I has a range of 700 to 800 km, while Agni-II has a range of 2000-2500 km. Agni-II is a two stage surface to surface ballistic missile, uses solid propellant and can carry a warhead weighing upto 1000 kg. These two can be fired from mobile launchers also and have been deployed. A nuclear capable ballistic missile of short range is Prithvi,[33] which has a maximum range of 1000 km. Presently in development stage (2005), Agni-III is meant to be intermediate range ballistic missiles (IRBM) with a strike range 3500 to 4000 km. India is also developing (2005) in a joint collaboration with Russia the BrahMos supersonic cruise missile that is meant to attack important surface targets. It can be launched from aircraft, submarines, and ships or even from vehicles. As mentioned earlier, cruise missile is a guided missile with wings and fins, can carry conventional or nuclear warheads and glides to surface targets flying at a low altitude up to 10 metres, that avoids detection by radar. It has a high accuracy and a range of 300 Km. It has not yet (2005) been inducted and deployed for use. Nuclear warheads for BrahMos cruise missiles are optional. It is noted that Pokhran–II exploded nuclear weapon of different caliber, three of which could be for tactical warfare missile systems including BrahMos.

INDIA MANAGING ITS NUCLEAR WEAPONS

India—A Responsible Nuclear State

The West has used the argument that the weapons of mass destruction (WMD) should not fall into 'wrong hands' while taking its stand and action against proliferation of the WMD, particularly nuclear weapons. The emphasis of wrong hands is on irresponsible States, terrorists or 'non-State actors' operating internationally or within a State. India has enacted the Weapons of Mass Destruction and their Delivery Systems (Prohibition of Unlawful Activities) Act, 2005, to this end. The legislation aims for prohibiting possession of WMD related materials by private persons including terrorists, at providing regulatory framework related to control over the export of WMD-usable materials, equipment and technologies, and protection against proliferation of 'sensitive and dual-use nuclear and missile related technologies' into wrong hands. Further, a responsible nuclear power has well-defined imperatives necessary for safe using of nuclear weapons that should be known generally.

India has made it clear, for example, that it has adopted the 'no first use' of nuclear weapons doctrine but that 'a nuclear strike could be ordered if India or its forces anywhere in the world were to be attacked with nuclear, chemical or biological weapons' notwithstanding the doctrine. Thus, a conventional weapon war in which chemical or biological weapons[34] are used will be out of the purview of the doctrine and retaliatory nuclear weapons might eventually be used by India.

Indian Nuclear Command System

The India's Cabinet Committee on Security (CCS) on Saturday 4 January 2003 established and made public the nuclear command structure.[35] At the apex is National Command Authority (NCA) under chosen cabinet ministers as members[36] and Prime Minister at its head. It is the sole authority, a political council, for ordering a nuclear strike; it lays down the guidelines and policy also as to when such orders are to be issued. After this, there is an Executive Council headed by National Security Advisor (NSA).[37] The Executive Council has to arrange all necessary inputs required for decision by NCA and has to oversee the carrying out of the NCA orders. The Executive Council receives inputs from the Chief Staff Committee (CSC) alongwith military advice in general and as related to any threatening situation. In turn, the CSC receives all vital information for planning and decisions from the basic Strategic Force Command (SFC). This command is the custodian of all nuclear weapons and delivery systems and manages and administers all of them. It decides or formulates the placement of nuclear systems both for defence and for retaliation. It also actually fires the nuclear weapons. In working order, it is SFC which gets activitated when there be any nuclear strike on India or when Indian forces are anywhere in the world are attacked by WMD, including chemical or biological weapons. It transmits the information alongwith its advice to the Chief Staff Committee. The latter completes the military viewpoint and assessment and alongwith the inputs received from SFC, it forwards its advice to the Executive Council and the National Security Council. It is for the NSC to seek authorization for retaliatory nuclear attack from the

National Command Authority headed by Prime Minister. As at present, India is committed to 'no first use' of nuclear weapons, so the nuclear arsenal is so far only for retaliatory use after a nuclear attack. Other nuclear States, including Pakistan, have no such doctrine and reserve the right to a first use of nuclear weapons on other States alongwith the right to wage war. Accordingly, India calls its nuclear armory to be a nuclear deterrence. The Indian Defence Minister asserted that India had now a 'credible nuclear deterrence in place' and 'specialized forces were being raised to tackle nuclear threat in all its dimensions'. He further observed, "Whatever is needed to safeguard the country and to ensure effective deterrence, in line with our nuclear doctrine of 'no first use', has been done".

INDIAN ENERGY CRUNCH: NUCLEAR SOLUTION

Developing India with Nuclear Energy

It is now universally recognized that India is, in twenty-first century, developing into an economic giant. India is one of the most populous States and when the per capita income increases even to two-thirds of the level of developed States by the twenties of the century it will be the largest economy alongwith China. For its energy needs, India depends on wood, coal, petroleum along with its products and electricity. Transport is run on petroleum, coal and electricity. Industry depends on coal, diesel oil and electricity for energy needs. Residential and community energy needs are met by wood, coal, electricity and to some extent on liquefied petroleum gas. Vehicular traffic depends on petrol, diesel oil and liquefied petroleum gas (LPG). Thus far, electricity is the most used and sought for energy source for industrial units and community needs. In India, the conventional sources for electricity are hydroelectric power and thermal power stations, both of which have reached their optimum production worth or capacity.[38] Of India's total generated electricity, 25% is by hydro-projects; about 71% is through thermal projects[39] and rest a little more than 3.7% through nuclear reactors. The developed West is now mostly depending on nuclear reactors for generation of electricity, which uses uranium or thorium for fuel. France, Russia and several other States are fully dependent on nuclear reactors.

Energy Options for India

India has to take long term effective steps for meeting the future needs of power as electricity and petrol the chief energy sources are falling short. Petrol needs crude and refineries and distribution system. The price of crude petroleum is rising up staggeringly (more than $75 per barrel in 2005) and its use is becoming cost prohibitive. Petrol is also subject to oil diplomacy and profiteering schemes of world Oil Producing and Exporting Countries (OPEC). All the States are thinking of alternate industrial, vehicular and domestic need fuels. Currently, the matters are looked at with electricity as basic energy source for developing States. It has been estimated that presently (2005) India generates electricity of around 120,000 megawatts level and the addition to generating capacity is negligible when compared to growing demands. Within a decade, it is estimated that energy demands would be double of production of electricity in India. The basic problem is of fuel resources for generating electricity. There is shortage of coal and water resource for generation of electricity. Options under active consideration of the planners are two:

First, augmenting internal exploration and use of natural gas and importing natural gas[40] for direct use both by industrial units, for generation of electricity and for replacing petrol and petroleum-products (diesel and kerosene oils).

Secondly, by increasing the installed capacity of nuclear reactors for more electricity. This means more reactors and better output performance of existing reactors. India has at present 15 nuclear power reactor plants that produce only 3.7% of electricity, about 100,000 mw is produced in India with 40% utilization of nuclear energy generated. Four of these plants operate under IAEA safeguards. India is keen to acquire six more nuclear reactors and hopes to double n-power by 2020.

At a futuristic level, India has worked on research in nuclear fusion 'free from uranium' parallel to the International

Thermonuclear Experimental Reactor (ITER) Project without being its original member.[41] India was made a full partner of this world project only on 6 December 2005. This ITER is a new world effort with seven partner States for peaceful production of nuclear energy, to secure cheap and durable nuclear energy free from uranium fuel. The project will pool together the scientific and financial resources of its members for constructing a fusion reactor.[42] The project has been estimated to cost about $10-12 billion over its complete life of about 20 years. It will use lithium from ground and deuterium from seawater, which are limitless both in quantity and duration of supply. At present the USA, European Union (EU), Russia, South Korea, China, Japan and Switzerland are members of this consortium. The project will take two or three decades in order to become operational. India is now its seventh partner.

Natural Gas Option for India

Liquefied petroleum gas (LPG) is derived from natural gas and it has increasingly replaced coal and firewood in domestic use and is being extended for running road vehicles also. India is also setting up natural gas fired thermal power plants for generation of electricity. It is estimated that over and above its meager domestic production, India will have to import natural gas around 200 million cubic metres per day within a decade. India has had two options for importing natural gas: from Turkmenistan and from Iran but both are subject to illusive Pakistani diplomacy. The first thought-of option was in 1990s when UNOCAL, an American company with headquarters in Texas had blessings of Afghanistan Taliban government. The company had expressed the hope in 1987 that within a decade, the pipeline would extend all the way to Pakistan and then proceed to India and Bangladesh. But, 9/11 event has put the Turkmenistan-Afghanistan-Pakistan-India (TAPI) project of American company in cold storage though it has in May 2006 given some signs of revival. The other additional alternative for import of natural gas is from Iran. Experts say that natural gas from Iran would also be the cheapest available option for India in comparison to the proposed pipelines from Turkmenistan and Qatar[43] via Pakistan. By now a lot of homework has been done on the pipeline from Iran. Countries have concluded that the proposed pipeline should follow the overland route as it was technologically and economically more viable and would sell oil both to Pakistan and India. It has been observed by Indian authorities on merits: "India's enormous energy requirements cannot be met without accessing gas from Iran." But, the initial cost of Iran-Pakistan-India pipeline would be more than $ 3 bn. In totality, Iran said it is a $ 22bn gas deal with India and under the accord, India would import 5m tonnes of liquefied natural gas a year for 25 years.[44] Then, there is Pakistani diplomacy of forcing Kashmir in all kinds of deals and the risk for India of Pakistan using the Iran-Pakistan pipeline as a lever against Indian diplomatic interests. The Indian Prime Minister Manmohan Singh has disclosed in September 2005 to the media, *The Washington Post*, that "the proposed Iran-India gas pipeline was fraught with risks and that no international financial consortium was willing to underwrite the project".[45] It is also known that for various reasons USA is challengingly opposed to any international business deals with Iran. The US administration has been threatening to take punitive action against foreign firms of any country that do business with Iran under the US Iran-Libya Sanctions Act of 1996. Both India and Pakistan would be exposed to this US diplomacy. No doubt, the American pipeline politics in the region which is part of decades old "oil diplomacy" is having an adverse impact on the Iranian economy and energy requirements of several countries particularly those that want to have good relation with USA. It would be thus noticed that import of natural gas is not the forthcoming solution to the energy crunch of India in the foreseeable future. It is also known that petrol and natural gas underground reserves are limited and are likely to be exhausted within a few decades at the present scale of their consumption while nuclear fusion reactors would last unforeseen forever. In nuclear diplomacy, US is against commercial deals with Iran by any nation for any material and this mattered.

More Nuclear Reactors for Electricity

All Indian nuclear power reactors function under Nuclear Power Corporation of India Ltd (NPCIL) and are managed by it. As was mentioned, India has the primary nuclear power reactors that are called Pressurized Heavy Water Reactors (PHWR), which use uranium as fuel. These are of Western design. Then, there are Boiling Water Reactors (BWR) that use recycled spent fuel from PHWR. India has also indigenously built Fast Breeder Reactors (FBR), which use thorium oxide pellets as fuel. Obtaining uranium for existing reactors is a problem. It was reported that natural uranium available in India could support only 10,000 mw PHWR programmes. At present, India has a three-stage nuclear programme.[46] Mainstays of this programme are 13 units[47] of Pressurized Heavy Water Reactors (PHWR), which use natural uranium that contain about 0.7 per cent fissionable isotope (U-235). Since sanctions were imposed on India, the technology for their non-imported fuel has been indigenously developed. The nuclear waste from PHWR is indigenously reprocessed to U-233 to sustain a chain of Fast Breeder Reactors (FBR) by using the vast reserves of thorium (Th-232). The thorium processed U-233, in turn, will fuel the next generation of indigenously designed thermal reactors, such as, the Advanced Heavy Water Reactors (AHWR).

For more installed capacity, import of primary uranium is necessary. The Nuclear Suppliers Group (NSG) sells uranium and nuclear reactors under IAEA and NPT safeguards[48] only. Such an import of uranium to India will be under IAEA safeguards, that is, the imported uranium is in no way to be used for military nuclear weapon use. Russia, a member of NSG, for India is an exception to the extent an agreement made prior to formation of NSG continues. India has been agreeable to the safeguard conditions on import of uranium. Media has reported[49] that for two reactors of Tarapur PHWR the Nuclear Power Corporation of India Limited had imported low-enriched uranium from China in 2000, which lasted for 5 years and from Russia in 2003 that will last upto 2007. India had to find indigenous developed uranium fuel after US and Canada stopped uranium fuel supply to Tarapur nuclear complex and two BWR in Rajasthan and other reactors following sanctions imposed after the 1974 Pokhran nuclear test. Canada has in 2005 agreed to resume supplies of nuclear-related "dual-use items" to Indian civilian facilities under IAEA safeguards.[50]

The Change in IAEA Guidelines Sought

India has at the 49th General Conference of IAEA of September 2005 sought early 'lifting of all nuclear technology restrictions against it' so that India is able to make "rapid growth in nuclear power generation capacity based on full international civilian nuclear cooperation".[51] At the Conference, both France and USA had emphasized on international cooperative approach towards increasing production of nuclear energy for the benefit of nations. India, though not a member of NPT, it was emphasized that it was unique and deserved 'same benefits and advantages' as other nuclear States by "lifting of all restrictions on it" by the IAEA. The reasons given were that (1) India is developing nuclear technologies in a self-reliant manner, (2) It has impeccable record in terms of non-proliferation of WMD and related technologies, and (3) India has on voluntary basis always adhered to all nuclear related IAEA laid safeguards.

US-INDIA 2005 NUCLEAR ACCORD

Significant development from the point of view of international diplomacy, international politics and energy augmentation for India is the accord and understanding reached between US President Bush and Indian Prime Minister Manmohan Singh in July 2005. It is well known that US diplomacy is of bargaining advantages out of any international situation or transaction, it is always transitory and is neither charitable nor idealist in nature; USA has a concept of friendship based on mutual advantages or common interest that change with time. The notable point is that lately USA has softened its attitude against India on civilian use of nuclear energy: away from the wider international restrictions of NPT, of Nuclear Suppliers Group and earlier US unilateral sanctions. The reasons behind this softening of attitudes is also based on realization of the situation that India has energy crunch and the US sanctions against India on its nuclear energy programme are gradually proving meaningless, since other nations are willing to sell nuclear reactors under IAEA safeguards to India. India wants to go ahead for natural gas imports from Iran for meeting its fast growing energy crunch through a Iran-Pakistan-India natural gas pipeline in partnership with Pakistan. This might involve a dilution of US close relationship with Pakistan. Further, the USA recognizes the reshuffling that has taken place on international diplomacy front. The US policies in the Middle East are not paying any dividend; the lessons of unilateralism in Iraq war have reached embarrassing stagnation. Pakistan has not succeeded in capturing Osama bin Laden or in liquidating *Al Qaeda* and continues to be rigidly *Islamic*. Also, China is fast becoming an economic giant and poses no immediate military threat to USA. It is cooperating with USA in disarming and dismantling of nuclear weapons of North Korea as a common cause (2003-2006). India, on the other hand, is economically pro-West and is prospectively a good purchaser of arms and civil and military aircrafts of US, France or British make along with military hardware. It has a counterbalancing presence against China in South Asia. Recognizing these recent changes in international diplomatic balance, freeing India from energy shortage crunch appeared to be sensible and in its own interest to the USA. As a preface to the change, in January 2004, a resolve for expanded cooperation between India and USA had taken place encompassing civilian nuclear activities, civilian space programme and high technology trade including missile defence.[52] Then, as Next Step in Strategic Partnership (NSSP) in April 2005 USA and India had signed the 10-year "New Framework for the US-India Defence Relationship" (NFDR) agreement at ministerial level.[53] The NFDR aims at a broad range of joint military activities that include collaboration in multinational operations as might be 'in their common interest'. This NFDR is to strengthen the capabilities of the two militaries to promote security, defeat terrorism and enhance their capabilities to combat the proliferation of WMD in a cooperative perspective that was not perceived before.

US-India Nuclear Pact

Following these steps in US and India cooperation efforts, a turning point came with 18 July 2005 accord on civilian nuke cooperation reached between US President George W. Bush and Indian Prime Minister Manmohan Singh in Washington. The bilateral pact essentially contemplates the USA to resume under its laws[54] to be suitably amended, the supply of nuclear fuel and technology and reactors to India on various far-reaching conditions. The pact impliedly accepts India a nuclear power with the right of maintaining a minimum nuclear deterrence. India, on its part, is to unilaterally place its civilian nuclear reactors and nuclear materials to be acquired for these from USA within the purview of IAEA new India-specific guidelines; for this, India is to draw a wall of separation between its nuclear defensive deterrence programme and nuclear energy producing reactor system. USA has undertaken to make efforts or good offices to bring the other 44 States of Nuclear Suppliers Group also in line. It has been universally noticed by media and analysts that India is not a signatory of NPT, is both *de facto* nuclear power and *de jure* nuclear state on indigenous development efforts and its case is different from that of Pakistan, North Korea and Iran. The last two are NPT States and have developed or are developing nuclear weapons in violation of NPT while Pakistan is a confirmed proliferated of nuclear weapons and technology. The status of nuclear India is regarded to be unique. As United States Ambassador to India, David C. Mulford, has observed:

> "India can truly be distinguished as *a unique case* and I say that because if you advance that unique case you can do so without violating or compromising *your own* commitment to non-proliferation. The US commitment to non-proliferation and the international architecture is not going to change. And just because we want to find a special way to recognize India's unique position doesn't mean that we are giving up ours and undermining or moving away from it or even that we'll be any less intense in our following the non-proliferation regime."[55]

In essence, the Pact will allow India to acquire nuclear fuel and advanced reactors from the US and other countries under the IAEA new India-specific guidelines to meet the energy crunch. France, Russia and China follow NSG guidelines in the matter and not wider US inhibitions that would now require some US internal legislative changes. The States that come to do such trade with India do not violate their NPT obligations. This pact does not prevent India from obtaining natural gas additionally. An epilogue seems to have been expressed by USA in 2006, when it was observed that the prospect that India "could have civil nuclear energy is one that is welcomed not just by US but also by the other countries of Nuclear Suppliers Group". The good argument taken is that US couldn't have it both ways—telling carbon dependent countries like India that you can't engage in energy relations with a nation like "Iran, but by the way, access to civil nuclear (energy) is closed off to you".[56]

Details of the US-India Nuclear Accord

The text of Indo-US Joint Statement issued after the delegation-level meeting between the Prime Minister, Dr. Manmohan Singh and the US President Mr. George W. Bush, in Washington DC on July 18, 2005 noted the following:

> "The Prime Minister's visit coincides with the completion of the Next Steps in Strategic Partnership (NSSP) initiative, launched in January 2004. The two leaders agree that this provides the basis for expanding bilateral activities and commerce in space, civil nuclear energy and dual-use technology."

Drawing a mutual vision for the US-India relationship, the two leaders agreed on the concepts and mutual interest in "Economy," in "Energy and Environment," in "Democracy and Development", in "Non-Proliferation and Security" and for cooperation in the fields of "High-Technology and Space".

Further: "Building on the strengthened non-proliferation commitments undertaken in the NSSP" and "Recognizing the significance of civilian nuclear energy for meeting growing global energy demands in a cleaner and more efficient manner, the two leaders discussed India's plans to develop its civilian nuclear energy program" leading to the accord.

The Joint Statement recognized the strong commitment of India to preventing WMD proliferation as a responsible State.

President Bush in the Joint Statement stated that India should acquire the same benefits and advantages of advanced nuclear technology as other such States. Continuing the Joint Statement records:

> "The President told the Prime Minister that he would work to achieve full civil nuclear energy cooperation with India as it realizes its goals of promoting nuclear power and achieving energy security. The President would also seek agreement from Congress to adjust US laws and policies, and the United States will work with friends and allies to adjust international regimes to enable full civil nuclear energy cooperation and trade with India, including but not limited to expeditious consideration of fuel supplies for safeguarded nuclear reactors at Tarapur. In the meantime, the United States will encourage its partners to also consider this request expeditiously. India has expressed its interest in ITER and a willingness to contribute. The United States will consult with its partners considering India's participation. The United States will consult with the other participants in the Generation IV International Forum with a view toward India's inclusion."

Further, "The Prime Minister conveyed that for his part, India would reciprocally agree that it would be ready to assume the same responsibilities and practices and acquire the same benefits and advantages as other leading countries with advanced nuclear technology, such as the United States. These responsibilities and practices consist of identifying and separating civilian and military nuclear facilities and programs in a phased manner and filing a declaration regarding its civilians facilities with the International Atomic Energy Agency (IAEA); taking a decision to place voluntarily its civilian nuclear facilities under IAEA safeguards; signing and adhering to an Additional Protocol with respect to civilian nuclear facilities; continuing India's unilateral moratorium on nuclear testing; working with the United States for the conclusion of a multilateral Fissile Material Cut Off Treaty; refraining from transfer of enrichment and reprocessing technologies to states that do not have them and supporting international efforts to limit their spread; and ensuring that the necessary steps have been taken to secure nuclear materials and technology through comprehensive export control legislation and through harmonization and adherence to Missile Technology Control Regime (MTCR) and Nuclear Suppliers Group (NSG) guidelines."

"The President welcomed the Prime Minister's assurance. The two leaders agreed to establish a working group to undertake on a phased basis in the months ahead the necessary actions mentioned above to fulfill these commitments. The President and Prime Minister also agreed that they would review this progress when the President visits India in 2006."

"The two leaders also reiterated their commitment that their countries would play a leading role in international efforts to prevent the proliferation of weapons of mass destruction, including nuclear, chemical, biological and radiological weapons."

As already noted this Joint Statement amounted to an accord different from a treaty or agreement between two sovereign States. The USA is a member of NPT and so are the members of Nuclear Suppliers Group (NSG) but India is not a member of NPT and is a *de jure* nuclear State under international law. The Joint Statement noted through the two statements that US will have to make internal constitutionally valid adjustments while India would be required to surrender some of its sovereign rights in order to receive new nuclear energy reactor units from abroad and fuel for new or existing reactors from the members of NPT.

The Prime Minister of India took into confidence the Parliament of India against the charges of sell-out of the sovereignty of the nation,[57] thus:

> "I rise to inform this august House of the status of discussions with the United States on civil nuclear energy cooperation. Substantive aspects of this are reflected in the Joint Statement of July 18, 2005 that US President Bush and I agreed upon during my visit to Washington DC last year. I would like to use this occasion to outline the

context and core elements of the Joint Statement, before detailing the status of the ongoing negotiations...."

"Hon'ble Members are aware that our effort to reach an understanding with the United States to enable civil nuclear energy cooperation was based on our need to overcome the growing energy deficit that confronts us.... While we have substantial reserves of coal, excessive dependence on coal-based energy has its own implications for our environment. Nuclear technology provides a plentiful and non-polluting source of power to meet our energy needs.... Our nuclear programme is truly unique. Its uniqueness lies in the breadth of its overarching vision of India mastering a three-stage nuclear programme using our vast thorium resources, and mastering more complex processes of the full nuclear fuel cycle...." Consequently, "our civilian and strategic programmes are deeply intertwined across the expanse of the nuclear fuel cycle. Over the years, the maturation of our nuclear programme, including the development of world-class thermal power reactors, has made it possible to contemplate some changes. These are worth considering if benefits include gaining unhindered access to nuclear material, equipment, technology and fuel from international sources...." However, "the Nuclear Suppliers Group (NSG)—an informal group of 45 countries largely determines international trade in nuclear material, equipment and technologies...." "The essence of what was agreed in Washington last July was a shared understanding of our growing energy needs. In recognition of our improved ties, the United States committed itself to a series of steps to enable bilateral and international cooperation in nuclear energy. These include adjusting domestic policies, and working with allies to adjust relevant international regimes. There was also a positive mention of possible fuel supply to the first two nuclear power reactors at Tarapur. US support was also indicated for India's inclusion as a full partner in the International Thermonuclear Experimental Research Project and the Generation IV International Forum."

The Prime Minister continued that the "Joint Statement offered the possibility of decades-old restrictions being set aside to create space for India's emergence as a full member of a new nuclear world order...."

"On our part, as Hon'ble Members may recall from my *suo moto* statement on July 29 last year, we committed ourselves to separating the civilian and strategic programme. "We have amply clarified our objective in pursuing full civil nuclear energy cooperation for our energy security and to reassure them of India's impeccable non-proliferation credentials...."

"At the official level, we have constituted two groups comprising key functionaries concerned with strategic and nuclear matters. They included the Department of Atomic Energy, the Ministry of External Affairs, the Armed Forces and my Office. These two groups were respectively mandated to draw up an acceptable separation plan, and to negotiate on this basis. The directive given to both groups was to ensure that our strategic nuclear programme is not compromised in any way, while striving to enlarge avenues for full civil nuclear energy cooperation with the international community."

"However, this was to be conditional upon, and reciprocal to, the United States fulfilling its side of the understanding...." "There have been discussions with other countries like Russia, UK and France as well. At the political level, I have maintained contact with President Chirac of France, President Putin of Russia, Prime Minister Blair of the UK.... I have also raised this subject with the Heads of State/Government of Norway, Republic of Korea, Netherlands, Czech Republic and Ireland—all members of the NSG. I also met President Bush in New York last September and discussed implementation of the July 18 statement." ... "Hon'ble Members may be assured that in deciding the contours of a separation plan, we have taken into account our current and future strategic needs and programmes after careful deliberation of all relevant factors, consistent with our Nuclear Doctrine. We are among very few countries to adhere to the doctrine of 'No First Use'. Our doctrine envisions a credible minimum nuclear deterrent to inflict unacceptable damage on an adversary indulging in a nuclear first strike. The facilities for this, and the required level of comfort in terms of our strategic resilience have thus been our criterion in drawing up a separation plan.... The Separation Plan that is being outlined is not only consistent with the imperatives of national security, it also protects our vital research and development interests. We have ensured that our three-stage nuclear programme will not be undermined or hindered by external interference...." "We will offer to place under safeguards only those facilities that can be identified as civilian without damaging our deterrence potential or restricting our R&D effort, or in any way compromising our autonomy of developing our three stage nuclear programme. In this process, the Department of Atomic Energy has been involved at every stage, and the separation plan has been drawn up with their inputs."

"Therefore our proposed Separation Plan entails identifying in phases, a number of our thermal nuclear reactors as civilian facilities to be placed under IAEA safeguards, amounting to roughly 65% of the total installed thermal nuclear power capacity, by the end of the separation plan."

"There are complex issues involved. Several aspects of the nuclear programme lend themselves in the public discussions to differing interpretations, such as the Fast Breeder Programme or our fuel-cycle capabilities such as re-processing and enrichment requirements.... Many aspects of the proposed separation plan are currently under negotiation. It is true that certain assurances in the July 18 Statement remain to be fulfilled - the supply of imported fuel for Tarapur I and II, for one. Some elements, such as US support for India's participation in the ITER programme, have materialized. The issue of the nature of safeguards to be applied to facilities designated civilian also remains pending resolution."

On the completion of second round of talks between Prime Minister Manmohan Singh and US President George W. Bush in New Delhi on March 2, 2006, the Joint Statement stated among other matters and reviewed the progress made in deepening the global partnership between the United States and India since their Joint Statement of July 18, 2005, the President and the Prime Minister reaffirmed their commitment to expand even further the growing ties between their two countries. On the item 'For Energy Security and a Clean Environment' they:

1. Welcomed the successful completion of discussions on India's separation plan and looked forward to the full implementation of the commitments in the July 18, 2005 Joint Statement on nuclear cooperation. This historic accomplishment will permit our countries to move forward towards our common objective of full civil nuclear energy cooperation between India and the United States and between India and the international community as a whole.
2. Welcomed the participation of India in the ITER initiative on fusion energy as an important further step towards the common goal of full nuclear energy cooperation.
3. Agreed on India's participation in Future Gen, an international public-private partnership to develop new, commercially viable technology for a clean coal near-zero emission power project. India will contribute funding to the project and participate in the Government Steering Committee of this initiative.

The Prime Minister of India made a statement[58] in Parliament on the 'Discussions on Civil Nuclear Energy Cooperation with the US' on India's Separation Plan of nuclear reactors of military and civil character, thus:

"Our discussions covered the expansion of our ties in the fields of agriculture, economic and trade cooperation, energy security and clean environment, strengthening innovation and the knowledge economy, issues relating to global safety and security and on deepening democracy. Expanded cooperation in each of these areas will have a significant impact on India's social and economic development.... India will identify and separate its civilian and military nuclear facilities and place its civilian nuclear facilities under IAEA safeguards. I would like to outline some salient elements of the Separation Plan:

(i) India will identify and offer for IAEA safeguards 14 thermal power reactors between 2006-14. There are 22 thermal power reactors in operation or currently under construction in the country. Fourteen of these will be placed under safeguards by 2014 in a phased manner. This would raise the total installed thermal power capacity in Megawatts under safeguards from 19% at present to 65% by 2014. I wish to emphasize that the choice of specific nuclear reactors and the phases in which they would be placed under safeguards is an Indian decision. We are preparing a list of 14 reactors that would be offered for safeguards between 2006-14.

(ii) We have conveyed that India will not accept safeguards on the Prototype Fast Breeder Reactor (PFBR) and the Fast Breeder Test Reactor (FBTR), both located at Kalpakkam. The Fast Breeder Programme is at the R&D stage. This technology will take time to mature and reach an advanced stage of development. We do not wish to place any encumbrances on our Fast Breeder programme, and this has been fully ensured in the Separation Plan.

(iii) India has decided to place under safeguards all future civilian thermal power reactors and civilian breeder reactors, and the Government of India retains the sole right to determine such reactors as civilian. This means that India will not be constrained in any way in building future nuclear facilities, whether civilian or military, as per our national requirements.

(iv) India has decided to permanently shut down the CIRCUS reactor, in 2010. The fuel core of the Apsara reactor was purchased from France, and we are prepared to shift it from its present location and make it available for placing under safeguards in 2010. Both CIRCUS and Apsara are located at the Bhabha Atomic Research Centre. We have decided to take these steps rather than allow intrusive inspections in a nuclear facility of high national security importance. We are determined that such steps will not hinder ongoing Research and Development.

(v) Reprocessing and enrichment capabilities and other facilities associated with the fuel cycle for our strategic programme have been kept out of the Separation Plan.

(vi) One of the major points addressed in the Separation Plan was the need to ensure reliability of fuel supplies, given our unfortunate past experience with regard to interruption in supply of fuel for Tarapur. We have received commitments from the United States for the reliable supply of fuel to India for reactors that will be offered for safeguards. The United States has also reaffirmed its assurance to create the necessary conditions for India to have assured and full access to fuel for such reactors. Under the July 18 Joint Statement, the United States is committed to seeking agreement from its Congress to amend domestic laws and to work with friends and allies to adjust the practices of the Nuclear Suppliers Group to create the necessary conditions for India to obtain full access to the international market for nuclear fuel, including reliable, uninterrupted and continual access to fuel supplies from firms in several nations. This has been reflected in the formal understandings reached during the visit and included in the Separation Plan.

(vii) To further guard against any disruption of fuel supplies for India, the United States is prepared to take other additional steps, such as:

(a) Incorporating assurances regarding fuel supply in a bilateral US-India agreement on peaceful uses of nuclear energy which would be negotiated.

(b) The United States will join India in seeking to negotiate with the IAEA an India-specific fuel supply agreement.

(c) The United States will support an Indian effort to develop a strategic reserve of nuclear fuel to guard against any disruption of supply over the lifetime of India's reactors.

(d) If despite these arrangements, a disruption of fuel supplies to India occurs, the United States and India would jointly convene a group of friendly supplier countries to include countries such as Russia, France and the United Kingdom to pursue such measures as would restore fuel supply to India.... In light of the above understandings with the United States, an India-specific safeguards agreement will be negotiated between India and the IAEA. In essence, an India-specific safeguards agreement would provide: on the one hand safeguards against withdrawal of safeguarded nuclear material from civilian use at any time, and on the other permit India to take corrective measures to ensure uninterrupted operation of its civilian nuclear reactors in the event of disruption of foreign fuel supplies. Taking this into account, India will place its civilian nuclear facilities under India-specific safeguards in perpetuity and negotiate an appropriate safeguards agreement to this end with the IAEA. In the terms of the Separation plan, there is hence assurance of uninterrupted supply of fuel to reactors that would be placed under safeguards together with India's right to take corrective measures in the event fuel supplies are interrupted.... The House can rest assured that India retains its sovereign right to take all appropriate measures to fully safeguard its interests....

No constraint has been placed on our right to construct new facilities for strategic purposes. The integrity of our Nuclear Doctrine and our ability to sustain a Minimum Credible Nuclear Deterrent is adequately protected. Our nuclear policy will continue to be guided by the principles of restraint and responsibility....

The Fast Breeder Test Reactor and the Prototype Fast Breeder Reactor remain outside safeguards. We have agreed, however, that future civilian Thermal Power Reactors and civilian Fast Breeder Reactors would be placed under safeguards, but the determination of what is civilian is solely an Indian decision.... The accord also ensures India's participation as a full partner in cutting edge multilateral scientific effort in the nuclear field such as ITER and Generation IV Initiative.

Reactions and Fears

Indian scientists have had many of their technical concerns pacified and taken care of. But political opposition in India emphasized repeatedly that India must resist US pressure to link the nuclear deal to any wider strategic realignment. That is, the nuclear civil use future facilities should not come in the way of defence preparedness. It is to be remembered first, that Next Steps in Strategic Partnership (NSSP) initiative was launched in January 2004. Then, in April 2005 USA and India had signed the 10-year "New Framework for the US-India Defence Relationship" (NFDR) agreement at ministerial level by the Government ruled by political parties that formed the parliamentary 'Opposition' in July 2005. Therefore both the Government and the 'Opposition' had little to differ and President Bush was common factor between the two Governments of India. Secondly, that under the so-called accord based on Joint Statements there is no curtailment of Indian defence present or future projects or initiatives. India is to decide on the quality or quantum of 'minimum credible nuclear deterrence' both presently and in future. Thirdly, there is reciprocity of efforts and achievements before the accord might materialize. The US has to obtain constitutional sanction of the Congress and persuade NSG for supplying nuclear fuel to India, while India completes separation of military and civil nuclear facilities. This separation would be worthwhile and affordable even if the accord fails to materialize.

It would be difficult for President Bush to get the approval of Senate. There are some objections for American diehard conservative politicians that President Bush has to tackle. For example:

Will the US-India civil nuclear cooperation deal accelerate the nuclear arms race in South Asia?

Will this initiative effectively recognize India as a nuclear weapons State contrary to NPT?

Will the accord succeed in placing a desired curb on India on production of nuclear weapons and on existing nuclear arsenal?

Will this initiative create a charge of double standard against US and encourage rogue nations like North Korea and Iran to continue to pursue nuclear weapons programs?

Will this initiative not weaken or demolish by creating exception in the global non-proliferation regime for which US has so ardently worked?

Keeping in view the projected emergence of India as a giant economic power and its self-dependence on nuclear weapons against threat from neighbors, President Bush is offering the nuclear accord to the US Congress as an achievement for the benefit of and in the overall interest of USA and Nuclear Suppliers Group.

Post Script on Status of Accord

The US India Nuclear Accord envisages a radical change in the perspectives of NPT obligations of its members; the NSG and IAEA Guidelines for trade in nuclear fuels and technology with India. As leader and super nuclear power USA has in the context of changed international political and diplomatic values and relations undertaken to make India-specific moderation in world approach to energy needs of India through nuclear technology. The policy makers of USA have their own constitutional restraints on its President. These restraints come from US Atomic Energy Act of 1954, US Arms Export Control Act and the US Nuclear Proliferation Prevention Act, 1994. The House of Representative of US Congress adopted on 26 July 2006 by 359 to 68 votes the 'United States and India Nuclear Cooperation Promotion Act of 2006' that is to make constitutional empowerment of US President to help out India through its energy crunch by going for more nuclear energy civilian reactors from international market.[59]

Significantly, the "*Statement of Administrative Policy*" issued by the Executive Office of the President[60] for this proposed Act, addressed the members of the House thus:

> "The Administration strongly supports House passage of H.R. 5682, the United States and India Nuclear Cooperation Promotion Act of 2006, and appreciates the House International Relations Committee's endorsement of this historic initiative. The legislation will facilitate nuclear energy cooperation between the world's two largest democracies. It is part of a profound transformation in the way the United States and India are partnering to promote energy, security, prosperity, democracy, stability, and peace in the region and around the world."
>
> "The Administration is pleased that the bill grants the President authorities related to the Atomic Energy Act of 1954, consistent with the Joint Statement of President Bush and Indian Prime Minister Singh in July 2005. An important feature of this legislation is the procedure for a joint resolution of approval that ensures an up-or-down vote without amendment on a proposed nuclear energy cooperation agreement with India."
>
> ....
>
> "The Administration would oppose any amendment that would require renegotiation of what was agreed to in the July 18, 2005 Joint Statement, such as, requiring India to cap its production of fissile material before cooperation could occur. The United States should not hold up the significant non-proliferation gains afforded by this Initiative in order to seek a fissile material cap to which India has indicated it cannot agree, absent a similar undertaking by Pakistan and China. Moreover, the United States and India are engaged in discussions on a multilateral Fissile

Material Cutoff Treaty, to be negotiated in the Conference on Disarmament, and the United States is pressing for substantial progress in that context."

"The Administration would also oppose any amendment conditioning cooperation with India upon India's policies toward Iran, which would be beyond the scope of our July 2005 commitments. India has agreed to support international efforts to limit the spread of enrichment and reprocessing technologies including to States such as Iran. As a responsible member of the international community, India has supported our efforts to address Iran's nuclear program, voting twice in the International Atomic Energy Agency (IAEA) Board of Governors to find Iran in non-compliance with IAEA safeguards and to report the issue to the UN Security Council. India has made the decision that it is in its own national security interest to oppose the development of Iran's nuclear weapons program."

Now the US Act is to be passed by the Senate of US Congress followed by the assent of the US President in order to empower the President to operate the Accord.

The Prime Minister of India clarified in Parliament (Council of States) on 27 July 2006 that the US constitutional process is active and "Let it be completed. Once it is completed we will then determine whether there are elements which go beyond what we have committed in July 18 (agreement) last year". Further at present "All that I can say is if the US legislative process leads to an end product which is not consistent with what we have committed that would be the determining factor of what we can do".[61]

The changes in IAEA guidelines are part of the Accord but are essentially a matter between India and the IAEA. This will empower the members of NPT to export nuclear fuel and technology to India as takes place among its own members. The inspections and monitoring of Indian civil nuclear reactors by IAEA under the Accord is an exclusive and singular process which does not entitle other States to substitute them for IAEA functions. As required in the Joint Statement, India has already moved the IAEA for evolving India-specific safeguards pursuant to the civil and military nuclear reactors separation plan accepted in the Accord in March and spelt out in detail in May by the Prime Minister. In March 2006 the Indian Department of Atomic Energy (DAE), had submitted the separation plan to the IAEA and initiated the process of negotiating safeguards on the declared civilian facilities. Subsequently, on 8 July the safeguards negotiating team of the IAEA visited India to pursue further the negotiations.

The USA placed a proposal at NSG Consultative Group meeting of March 2006, for making an exception to NSG Guidelines for nuclear related exports to and trade with India. The U.S. officials briefed the NSG on the developments on the Indo-U.S. nuclear deal and the nature of exception that the U.S. is proposing to make in its domestic law to forge nuclear cooperation and commerce with India. However, NSG nations in May preferred to defer action till US Congress takes a positive action on the Accord. Of course, other members of NSG might have to make their own constitutional empowerment changes after NSG makes India-specific relaxations and it is for the USA to make the move under the Joint Accord. It is surmised that in NSG meet China, Sweden, Japan and Germany may have to be tackled for their reluctances.

ENDNOTES

1. In March 1969, Sino-Soviet relations had exploded into a series of border clashes.
2. Further discussed, below.
3. Fast Breeder Reactors, which use plutonium, are called so because they have no moderator (heavy water or light water) and breed more fuel than they consume.
4. The resolutions of the United Nations General Assembly had made calls for the conclusion of an agreement on the prevention of wider dissemination of nuclear weapons.
5. The NPT was signed on 1 July 1968 and it entered into force in 1970.
6. The military ruler of Pakistan.

7. 'Indians are so treacherous': Report from Washington by Rajat Pandit/TNN, *The Times of India,* Lucknow Ed. 18 June 2005, p. 7.
8. Hasan Suroor 'Secret Papers Throw New Light on Indo-Pak War [1971]': from London: *The Hindu*, New Delhi, 2 January 2005.
9. These US policy facts have now been made public through the declassified US State documents. US Department of State in June 2005, in normal course released the old official records of US foreign policy around the 1971 Pakistan war based on President Nixon and his national security advisor Kissinger's White House tape recordings. These are now declassified documents.
10. 'Indians are so treacherous': Report from Washington by Rajat Pandit/TNN , *The Times of India,* Lucknow Ed. 18 June 2005, p. 7; PTI report from Washington: "Nixon wanted to brand India naked aggressor": *The Times of India,* Lucknow Ed. 2 July 2005.
11. *Ibid.*
12. PTI report from Washington: "Nixon wanted to brand India naked aggressor": *The Times of India,* Lucknow Ed. 2 July 2005.
13. PTI report from Washington: "Nixon wanted to brand India naked aggressor": *The Times of India,* Lucknow Ed. 2 July 2005.
14. One fallout of making of 'Islamic bomb' was that Pakistan feared pre-emptive destructive air attack from Israel: B.Muralidhar Reddy from Islamabad "Pakistan established contacts with Israel to ascertain the veracity of speculation that Tel Aviv was planning pre-emptive strikes on its nuclear installations. Pakistan feared Israeli raid on nuclear sites" in 'Pakistan feared Israeli raid on Nuclear Sites' *The Hindu*, 26 September 2005.
15. Communist government of China had replaced Formosan Nationalist (KMT) government of China in UNO in 1971 and China joined NPT only in 1992.
16. K. Subrahmanyam, *Nuclear India.*: Cited in 'Indian PMs Supported N-weaponization', PTI reported, in *The Hindustan Times,* New Delhi Ed., 18 August 1998. K. Subrahmanyam is a former Director of Institute for Defence Studies and Analyses.
17. K. Subrahmanyam, *Nuclear India.*: Cited in 'Indian PMs Supported N-weaponization', PTI reported, in *The Hindustan Times,* New Delhi Ed., 18 August 1998. Also, K. Subrahmanyam, "Fragmented View: Focus on Future Nuclear Policy", *The Times of India,* Lucknow Ed. 11 November 1998.
18. T.S. Subramanian: 'Key Players in Pokhran [1998]', *Frontline,* Vol. 15, No. 11 (1988).

19. Yashwant Sinha, "India is Mature Nuclear Power": Speaking on '*Geopolitics: What it takes to be a World Power*' at 'India Today Conclave 2004', New Delhi: *The Times of India,* Lucknow Ed. 13 March 2004.
20. *Ibid.*
21. 'Indian PMs Supported N-weaponization': PTI report, *The Hindustan Times,* New Delhi Ed., 18 August 1998.
22. Summary of the statement in Parliament alongwith a tabled nine-page note, entitled "Evolution of India's Nuclear Policy".
23. The US Senate ultimately on 14 October 1999 decisively voted out CTBT. The reasons given by US Senate for rejecting CTBT—that US sovereignty could not be subject to international regulations—had put a big question mark on future of CTBT itself. The US had the "Stockpile Stewardship Programme" under which US existing nuclear weapons were to remain safe and reliable in the absence of further testing.
24. See, K. Subrahmanyam: Write-ups (1) "Fragmented View: Focus on Future Nuclear Policy", *The Times of India,* Lucknow Ed. 11 November 1998, and (2) "Western Doublespeak: Overlooking India's Nuclear Reality" *The Times of India,* Lucknow Ed. 1 March 2004.
25. Discussed earlier in this Chapter.
26. This Act is called Glenn Amendment to the Arms Export Control Act of USA.
27. UN Security Council Resolution 1172.
28. "Canada to Resume N-exports', TNN/Indrani Bagchi reporting from New Delhi, *The Times of India,* Lucknow Ed. 28 September 2005.
29. Report of PM's Statement in Parliament of India on 29 July 2005: see "No Sellout to US; N-key in India's Hand", *The Times of India,* Lucknow Ed. 30 July 2005.
30. "*Work on Separation of Nuclear Facilities at Advanced Stage*" Amit Baruah reporting from Kuala Lampur, *The Hindu,* 12 December 2005.
31. Pakistan had nuclear weapons since late 1980s, depending on limited range US make F-16 warplanes for targeting Indian sites. It exploded six nuclear devices on 28 & 30 May 2005 in Chagai hills in north-west of Baluchistan province. Pakistan under Prime Minister Nawaz Sharif of Kashmiri origin, claimed that the 'fission' (not 'thermonuclear') tests had "boosted the morale of the Pakistani nation by giving it honorable position in the nuclear world" and

had "validated scientific theory, design and previous results from cold tests." Also, that the "devices tested correspond to weapon configuration, compatibility with delivery systems". Pakistan had already tested 1500 Km Ghauri missile in April 1998.

32. Prime Minister Indira Gandhi initiated this Programme. The basic document was prepared by three: Venkataraman, V.S. Arunachalam and A.P.J. Abdul Kalam. The IGMDP was to design and develop simultaneously five missile systems along with pilotless or remotely piloted vehicle (RPV) for a "comprehensive missile-based defence umbrella" for the country within 10 years.
Non-Nuclear Missiles: 1. Short-range surface to air missile 'Trishul'; 2. Medium-range surface-to-air missile 'Ákash'; 3. Anti-tank guided-missile 'Nag'; 4. Short-range surface-to-surface missile 'Prithvi', and intermediate-range ballistic missile 'Agni'. All these were conceived for delivering conventional warheads but 'Prithvi' and 'Agni' missiles are now since 2003 nuclear warhead capable also. The army, navy and air force use 'Trishul' in its three configurations. 'Prithvi' is designed to hit large enemy concentrations, ammunition dumps, air-bases and similar targets with accuracy. "Trishul" is powered by a two-stage solid propellant system, has a target range of nine km, has a 'radar command-to-line-of-sight guidance system' and is deployed by army, navy and air force against enemy to destroy aircraft or helicopters.

33. An extended version of Prithvi primitive missile for air force has been tested fired in March 2004. It has a payload of one tonne, has an advanced guiding computerized inertial navigation system, has a range of 150 to 200 km and is very fast—moves at 150 km in 300 seconds.

34. India is a signatory of Chemical and Biological Weapons Convention.

35. "India's N-Command in Place": Vishal Thappar/Jay Raina in *Hindustan Times,* New Delhi, 5 January 2003. The contents of this para are in general based on this news/report.

36. The Home Minister, Defence Minister, Foreign Minister and Defence Minister are its members.

37. Brajesh Mishra was the first Indian NSA.

38. Thermal power generators run on coal are not environment or eco-friendly. Processed coal from coalmines needs regular transportation in large quantities to long distances to power stations that is inconvenient and costly process. Indian railways are over-burdened already. The natural gas as substitute for coal is in formative stage as supply of natural gas depends on petroleum refineries where it is a byproduct.

39. The State-run NTPC has installed capacity of 24,250 MW and operates 13 coal/fired and 7 gas fired power generating units.

40. Natural gas is both a byproduct in the process of crude petroleum refinement and a product directly extracted from natural-gas wells drilled into the earth that discharge only the gas and not crude petrol. The natural gas is mainly composed of methane gas, mixed with volatile hydrocarbons, such as propane and butane, and water vapour, carbon dioxide, hydrogen sulfide, other sulfur compounds. It needs processing that extracts methane gas. For use, it is transported in compressed gas form through pipeline or is liquefied by cooling down to minus 160°C and transported in tankers. Major natural-gas deposits have been found in Western Europe, Russia, North Africa, Middle East, China and Burma. Since oil crisis of 1970s natural gas is increasingly being exploited in America, Russia Turkmenistan, Myanmar and other countries for domestic and industrial fuel and also as basic chemical feedstock.

41. The Indian programme called Aditya for experiments on "magnetically confined plasmas" for production of energy had begun in 1982, when the design and construction of India's first 'Tokamak' was undertaken. Aditya was commissioned in 1989 and 'Tokamak' based experiments began to be carried out. In 1995, it was decided to build a second-generation super conducting Steady-State Tokamak (SST-1) involving a high investment of about Rs. 350 crores. This research project was envisaged under the Department of Atomic Energy.

42. Nuclear fusion reactor would be based on a technique that would be a replication of the Sun or a hydrogen bomb. The project will be clean, since it would not leave any radioactive waste as fission nuclear reactors do.

43. The could-be 'Qatar to Pakistan pipeline' natural gas option mooted by Pakistan was not pursued by India.

44. "Iran denies shift in India ties" *BBC World News*: Wednesday, 28 September 2005.

45. John Cherian "Deals and Doubts" *Frontline,* Volume 22-Issue 16, 30 July 2005.

46. Ramachandran 'Behind the Bargain' *Frontline*, Volume 22-Issue 16, 30 July-12 August 2005.

47. These 13 units have a total installed capacity of 2,990 MW.

48. The NSG guidelines are tougher than those of the NPT; they additionally prohibit the transfer of certain dual-use materials and items to countries such as India that do not have full-scope International Atomic Energy Agency (IAEA) safeguards.

49. "India to Import Natural Uranium if Supply is Assured: Kakodkar": PTI news from Mumbai, *Times of India,* Lucknow Ed., 29 August 2005, p. 9.
50. PTI news from Ottawa: 'Canada to Resume Supply', *The Hindu,* New Delhi, On-line, 28 September 2005: A joint statement, issued after talks between visiting External Affairs Minister K. Natwar Singh, and his Canadian counterpart, Pierre Pettigrew, said that Canada agreed to "allow the supply of nuclear-related dual-use items to Indian civilian nuclear facilities under International Atomic Energy Agency safeguards, in accordance with the requirements of the Nuclear Suppliers Group's dual-use guidelines." *Ibid*; "Canada to Resume N-exports', TNN / Indrani Bagchi reporting from New Delhi, *The Times of India*, Lucknow Ed., 28 September 2005.
51. PTI report from Vienna of the speech of Chairman of Indian Atomic Energy Commission and leader of Indian Delegation, Anil Kakodkar, on 28 September 2005.
52. Identical statements were issued by US President George W. Bush and Indian Prime Minister Atal Bihari Vajpayee: This "will include expanded engagement on nuclear regulator and safety issues and missile defence, ways to enhance cooperation in peaceful uses of space technology and steps to create the appropriate environment for successful high technology commerce". It further added: "These cooperative efforts will be undertaken in accordance with our respective national laws and international obligations" and the new 'relationship between India and USA was based increasingly on common values and interests': PTI from New Delhi *The Times of India,* Lucknow Ed., 14 January 2004.
53. US Defence Secretary Donald Rumsfeld and Indian Defence Minister Pranab Mukherjee made the agreement in Washington See, "India, US Ink Defence Pact", Chidanand Rajghatta/ TNN reporting from Washington, *The Times of India*, Lucknow, Ed., 30 April 2005.
54. U.S. Nuclear Non-Proliferation Act (NNPA) of 1978.
55. Report by Kesava Menon & Nirupama Subramaniam entitled, 'Nuclear issue: "India is a unique case"', vide, *The Hindu*, Online edition, 28 September 2005.
56. PTI report from Washington "Rice endorses India's Quest to Acquire N-Tech": *The Times of India,* Lucknow Ed. 7 January 2006. Ms Condoleezza Rice is currently US Secretary of State. Discussed further in section *Postscript.*
57. *Suo Moto* Statement in Parliament on 27 February 2006 made before the visit of President Bush in India, 1 to 3 March 2006.
58. Statement was made *suo moto* on 7 March 2006.

59. For the constitutional intricacies of US administration initiatives implementing promises to bring out necessary constitutional and legal amendments which are fraught with dangers of failure for President George Bush: See R. Ramchandran, (India and US) 'Cooperation and Hurdles' *The Frontline*, Vol. 23 Issue 15 (29 July—11 August 2006).
60. Cited on *On-line Edition of The Hind*, 2 August 2006 (Box item).
61. PTI news, 'End Product Matters': *The Times of India*, Ed., Lucknow 26 July 2006.

10

Iraq – The Nuclear Obsessions

Did Iraq possess nuclear bombs or nuclear technology in the year 2002? This has been a world history-making question. It is the history of the rise and fall of President Saddam Hussein of Iraq in his lifetime like Napoleon or Hitler. It could also be an important chapter of a book if one writes on world oil diplomacy. This question could have proved to be a cause of the silent shelving of the United Nations in the catalogue of dormant international organizations, like the earlier League of Nations after Italy invaded Ethiopia in 1935. There is a history of power politics of States in which the UN collective security system for securing State boundaries replaced the geopolitics of empires by extending the principle of self-determination to its utmost limits. Now since 2004, a new kind of nuclear strength based unilateralism in world politics and international law has lifted up its head, sidelining the United Nations that appears to be breathing for its reputation and credibility among power conscious States in a silent way in this first decade of this century. The Nuclear Test Ban Treaty of 1963 is getting sidelined in absence of nuclear umbrella for non-nuclear States and the growing unilateralism in international diplomacy and politics.

The unilateral armed action by USA and UK led alliance in Iraq in 2003 has its own geopolitical diplomatic history. At the outbreak of First World War Iraq was a part of Ottoman Empire that touched the Shi'ite Iran on way to north-eastern Turkmenistan province of the empire. All these areas were border areas with the Russian Czar Empire. Since Crimean War of 1850s, under a new international politics against Czar

Empire, the Ottoman Empire had come under protection of Britain and France. The First World War brought the end of Ottoman empire, it was broken and its separated parts were placed under the mandate system of the League of Nations system. Turkey became a small one State and several mandated and protected areas, viz., Egypt, Syria, Lebanon, Iraq, Iran, particularly in the Middle East, gradually evolved into sovereign States. This development was coupled with vigorous oil diplomacy that had vigorously started with the onset of last century. At present, 80% of petrol needed by USA, France, Germany, England, Japan and various other countries is met by the oil fields of the Middle East and of Persian Gulf States. Oil diplomacy in earlier times meant occupying by conquest when necessary those States that were rich in oil resources. Now under the Charter of United Nations when the State boundaries against conquest are secure, the oil diplomacy means controlling or keeping in check the price and quantum of oil production set by the Organization of Oil Producing and Exporting Countries (OPEC) in the interest of consumers, apart from maintaining and ensuring the commercial and political stakes of foreign oil companies owned or operated by Western States world over. For about first two decades of 'cold war' under the fear of Soviet expansion, Iraq and Iran had felt secure by joining Baghdad Pact and by lending their territories for airbases against Soviet Russia and thereby these indirectly submitted to the oil diplomacy of the West. However, oil diplomacy has inflicted heavy blows on the economies and political systems of Iran and Iraq, particularly as and when these States have acted to nationalize their oil industry as a move that hit the interests of companies of French, British or US origin. The desire to go for nuclear weapons has been occasioned for Iraq in order to work for Arab cause against nuclear capable Israel and for the deterrence it provides against other nuclear States, discussed earlier. For a clear assessment of international problems of Iraq a purposeful insight into its international and national socio-politics is necessary. The net result in first decade of this century has been devastated, politically and economically unstable Iraq and Iran as States.

These States have also committed diplomatic and legal mistakes, which often gave chances to their adversaries to play the cards of oil diplomacy.

IRAQ: A CONFUSING GENESIS

Socio-Politics of Iraq

Modern Iraq was once undemarcated part first of Persian Empire and later of the Ottoman Empire. Since League of Nations 1919, the State of Turkey, Iraq and Iran, all of which were parts of the Ottoman Empire at one time or other, are now independent States. Modern Iraq has territories, religions, tribes and people whose affinity fades into or is common with both Turkey and Iran. While Turkey since 1856 is accepted as a *de facto* European State, Iraq associates itself with Arab culture, aspirations and Islamic polity.

A Look Back of Iraq

Modern Iraq State has had the names Persian Iraq and Ottoman Iraq that form its political history. It does not take inspirations for having been part of Ottoman Empire or for having ethnic closeness with Iran. Any ethnic or political past does not back its present boundaries. This situation, like that of Pakistan, reflects in its quest for nuclear status. The relevant historical antecedents of modern Iraq for a sociological or anatomical look hard glance are thus:

(1) From c 300 to 1055 AD, present Iraq was a province of the Persian *Sasanian* Empire. The western quarter of *Sasanian* Empire, called Khvarvaran, included most of modern Iraq. It was probably the most populous and wealthy legendry area, of famous 'Arabian Nights' fables, situated in the Middle East of Asia and having cultural or business links with India. It had intensive irrigated agriculture in the basin of the lower Tigris and Euphrates rivers and of their tributaries, Diyala and Karun. This Persian Iraq formed the main economic resource base of the *Sasanian* monarchy of Persia. On western side of Persian Empire was Iraqi land of Ottoman Empire but there were no clearly defined borders of the two Empires. Southward, Persian Iraq extended to somewhere in the 'sands of the Syrian

and Arabian deserts' and touched the eastern side of the Ottoman territories of Syria and Anatolia. The Persian Iraq had no specific name and defined boundaries as such.

(2) The Persian Iraq was at some point of time conquered by Ottoman Empire (1534–1918) and such position continued till the end of the First World War. For administrative purposes, Ottoman Iraq was divided into six districts called province of Mosul, Baghdad, Basra, Shahrizor, Tigris, and Al-Hasa, extending to the coasts of Persian Gulf. These provinces roughly reflected the linguistic, and religious divisions of Ottoman Iraq. Most of the inhabitants of Mosul and Shahrizor in the north and north-east were and are Kurds and some other non-Arab tribes. On the other hand, the central and southern plains of Persian Iraq were a belt of irrigated farmlands bounded by desert and merging into the marshlands around the Persian Gulf and were inhabited mostly by Arabs. In the countryside, as much as half of the Arab and Kurdish population was nomadic or semi nomadic. Their social organization and personal allegiances were primarily tribal going back into several generations of tribal ties. Baghdad, situated near the geographic center of Iraq, is predominantly Shia and continues to be capital of Shi'ite Muslim sect of the whole world. Shi'ite Islam covers south while north is largely Sunnite. Iraq's Non-Muslim communities in south Iraq were modest in size, the Jew dominated commercial and financial elements in Baghdad. Assyrian Christians mostly inhabited in Mosul, Anatolia[1] and Syria. In the 17th and 18th centuries, central government at the capital Istanbul of Ottoman Empire had become weak and fragile and was obliged to concede extensive autonomy to the governors, including that of Iraq, and some areas remained beyond the reach of Ottoman authority for long periods. During this era, few people only in outskirts of Baghdad, Kirkuk, and some other lesser towns and their suburbs spoke Turkish language. Centuries of political upheavals, invasions, wars, and general insecurity had taken their toll on Iraq's population, especially in the urban centers.

(3) In the 19th century, when administrative centralization and reorganization was undertaken by the Ottoman government

as part of a comprehensive reform and modernization program, the arrangements were also extended to Iraq. In internal relations, Iraq territory served as a buffer zone that protected part of Anatolia in Ottoman and Syria against aggressiveness of the tribes of Iran, of the Arabia and of Kurd. Modern Iraq has inherited all the tribal animosities and aggressiveness of the wide area around.

(4) The Caliphate under Ottoman Empire with dynastic features comprised and had held the supreme leadership of the Sunnite Muslim world. In area now called Iraq, Ottoman rule represented the religious domination of Sunnis, although the Shi'ite notables of southern Iraq bordering Persia continued to enjoy considerable local influence and prestige, but they rather identified themselves with Shi'ite Iran and resented the Sunnite-dominated Ottoman administration and were often suppressed.

MODERN IRAQ SINCE 1918

The New Iraq State

After the construction of Suez Canal, the Black Sea, East Mediterranean Sea and the Ottoman territories around in Africa and Asia had become matters of intense diplomacy due to the new trade route as the twentieth century emerged. Also, most of the Ottoman territories were rich in oil but oil production technology was controlled and given for operation to France and England. The 'oil diplomacy', relevant to the present nuclear issues, took shape after the First World War and till then empire building or dismemberment spirit had dominated. France and England had joined in the venture of destruction by dismemberment of Ottoman Turkey. The fact that Turkey had sided with Germany and Italy during the First World War and was enemy of England and France hastened the divisive decisions on this aspect. The Allied Powers first supported anti-Turkish Pan-Arab rebellion for breaking Turkey. Emir Hussein of the Hejaz, was promised British aid for creating a united Arab State by a Treaty of 24 October 1915. When this rebellion plan did not succeed Britain and France partitioned between themselves by the 'secret Sykes-Picot Agreement'[2] of 1916 all the Asian and African possessions of

Turkey leaving much-limited international boundary north of Arabia for a Turkey State. Under the Treaty of Versailles 1919, this agreement was imposed upon Turkey after it had surrendered to the allied powers. Iraq and Palestine[3] were separated and made mandate territories under Article 22 of the Covenant of the League of Nations.[4] The boundaries of the 20th-century Iraq State were drawn by allied powers which had no resemblance to those of the province of Ottoman Iraq; the three provinces of Mosul, Baghdad, and Basra were merged into one new political entity that came to be called Mesopotamia and later renamed Iraq.

British Mandate on Iraq

The British started to rule Mesopotamia or Iraq with a military government that had to reconcile with upsurge of nationalism. This nationalism had been inspired by the allied powers against Ottoman rule but which persisted after British mandate had been established in Iraq. British were confused as administrator and suggested "indigenous regime under British supervision" and control.

(1) The nationalists in Iraq were demanding independence. To compromise with the political situation in 1921, Britain offered the Iraqi throne to emir Faysal, who had led revolt against Ottoman earlier, along with the establishment of an Arab government under British mandate. Faysal wanted to accept the throne only if the Iraqi people offered it to him. He also suggested the replacement of the mandate by a treaty of alliance. The British government accepted these proposals. A plebiscite confirmed this and Faysal was formally crowned King of Iraq on 23 August 1921. It was deemed necessary that a treaty should define relations between Iraq and Britain. A treaty was signed on 10 October 1922, which reproduced most of the provisions of the mandate. Iraq undertook to respect religious freedom and missionary enterprises and the rights of foreigners, to treat all States equally, and to cooperate with the League of Nations. Britain was by the treaty put under an obligation[5] to offer advice on foreign and some domestic matters of military, judicial, and financial nature. By a protocol

of 30 April 1923 the period of the treaty was reduced from 20 to 4 years. The king signed a constitution on March 21, 1925. It provided for a constitutional monarchy, a parliamentary government, and a bicameral legislature. The legislature was composed of an elected lower House of Representatives along with a nominated Senate. The lower house was to be elected every four years by a 'male only' free suffrage. The first Parliament of Iraq met in 1925.

(2) A new treaty was signed with Britain on June 30, 1930. It provided for the establishment of a "close alliance" between Britain and Iraq with full and frank consultation between them on all matters of foreign policy that may affect their common interests. Iraq was to maintain internal order and Britain was to support Iraq against any foreign aggression. Iraq was made independent in 1932 and was admitted as a member of the League of Nations. King Faysal died in September 1933 and was succeeded by his son, King Ghazi (1912–39). In 1939, shortly before the outbreak of World War II, King Ghazi was killed in a car accident, and his four years old son Faysal II ascended the throne. His uncle, Emir 'Abd al-Ilah, was appointed regent and served in this capacity for the next 14 years.

(3) The army gradually dominated the political scene and it became the ultimate deciding factor in more than 50 Cabinet changes from 1936 onwards. The army while it remained in background had continued to dominate the political scene from 1936. Ten general elections were held before the downfall of the monarchy in 1954. Iraq recognized that the maintenance and protection of essential British run communications was in the interest of both parties. Airbase sites for British troops were accordingly maintained near Basra and west of the Euphrates, but these bilateral arrangements were to be in no way taken to prejudice the sovereign rights of Iraq. During World War II, British army had virtually taken over the administration. After the war, the existence and influence of Monarchy had gradually faded out and the military strongmen ruled through civilian governments. The Iraqi military strongman, Abd al Qarim

Qassem, came to power as military ruler after the overthrow of the monarchy around 1955.

International Influences on Iraq

Iraq has always maintained strong trans-border tribal ties extending into Turkey, Iran, Saudi Arabia, Syria or Jordan. It had joined the "Arab League" formed in January 1946, with headquarters in Cairo, of which Egypt, Saudi Arabia, Yemen, Syria, Lebanon and Palestine were other members. As a link, the international Baath Party, formed in the 1950s with pan-Arab ideology, had its Iraqi wing of small grouping of Iraqis, many of them hailing from the town of Tikrit. The Baath Party had a widespread support all over the Arab world. At the same time, Iraq already had strong military link with Britain. Since 1930s, its economy had become dependant on the oil royalties received from British oil companies who had been given concessions by favorable governments.

The close of the Second World War, brought the Cold War on Iraqi doorsteps. The Government of Iraq had before the fall of monarchy joined the Baghdad Pact, which like NATO was set against expansion of Soviet communism in country. This had brought a new kind of pro-West and pro-Soviet division both in the military and administration of Iraq, along with divisions of loyalties also in Arab League and Baath Party. In the 1950s and 1960s, the pro-Soviet Communist Party was a popular political party in Iraq, while the Iraqi wing of the Baath Party, also popular, had a deeply rooted anti-communist leanings. In this context after the overthrow of monarchy the fact that the military ruler Abd al Qarim Qassem, had an active relationship with the Communist Party of Iraq proved to be an important factor for the future events of Iraq. The Americans keen on their anti Soviet planning and oil diplomacy preferred the Baathist Party to Qassem and the Communist Party in Iraq during the Cold War and the Baathists continued to plot ouster of Qassem. Saddam Hussein a low-cadre Baathist leader, alleged to have links with US States Central Intelligence Agency (CIA) at that time and later became President of Iraq, participated in a messed up attempt to assassinate Qassem in

1959, he escaped and found sanctuary in Egypt, where he lived under the patronage of President Nasser of Egypt. Qassem was overthrown in 1963 by a military coup. The new military regime under Abd al Salam Aref took over. He was hostile to Baathist Party and the party was suppressed. The Baath Party staged a counter coup with help from sections of the Army in 1968, ousted Abd al Salam Aref and came to power. Saddam Hussein, on returning in 1964 from exile in Cairo following an ideological split had acquired a leading position in the Baathist Party, and he was the main architect of the coup of 1968. Hassan al-Bakr, became the new President while Saddam Hussein became the main power wielder. The new regime started a modernizing process, banned the Communist Party, and land reforms were mooted that eliminated landlordism and all these were strictly implemented. At the same time in order to boost economy of Iraq the oil sector was nationalized, earning Iraq the enmity of the West in consequence and also a break in relations with USA. In the reaction against land reform process, some tribes, Kurds and sections of Shia population, tried to destabilize the government by making demands of secession. The West and Iran were blamed for this reaction by the government and in the turmoil Saddam Hussein took over the rule from Hassan al-Bakr who had resigned on July 16, 1979, and Saddam Hussein formally became President of Iraq. However, the future diplomacy of USA was very much influenced by this political upheaval in Iraq.

IRAQ OF NEW ERA

US Interest in Iraq

From 1979, perhaps the two most important complicating factors having close bearing on later misfortunes of Iraq were decision of Egyptian President Anwar el-Sadat to make peace with Israel in 1977 and the bid of President Hafiz al-Assad of Syria for economic, military and political union with Iraq. These two events were related to Arab unity had been a long-standing goal of the Baath Party in both Syria and Iraq. These two events, coupled with other factors, led to a redefined and rigid international stance both of the West and Soviet towards Iraq. Americans saw designs against Israel and problems for their oil interests in the region, while Soviet Russia found that its friends were getting separated. The 1980s saw nationalization of American oil interests in Iran and the USA used Iraq for a military showdown of Iran.

The Beginning of Nuclear Diplomacy

Iraq had discussed acquisition of nuclear weapons in late 1980s and was also secretly offered nuclear weapon technology in violation of NPT by Pakistani A.Q. Khan, which was taken to be an American 'sting operation' move by President Saddam Hussein and was therefore refused. Iraq received US, French and Soviet arms but the 8-year war expenses brought it down to poor conditions. All this was followed by Iraqi tiff with Kuwait on oil drilling, by which time it had lost support of Soviet Russia in the Security Council because of its changed diplomacy.

Iraq and Iran

Several elements have been at stake leading to arms race that included nuclear weapons between Iraq and Iran: The pro-American Baath Party, Iraqi access to Persian Gulf for oil export outlet, cross-border Shia-Sunni and tribal affinity or rivalry, Anglo-American oil diplomacy, which placed the two States at crossroads and the choosing by them of differing loyalties in the cold war. The hatred for Israel and successful nationalization of oil industry have been matter of competition rather than of cooperation between the two. Relations of Iraq with Iran became strained after the Shah of Iran, friend of West was overthrown by a religious leader Ayatollah Ruhollah Khomeini, in 1979. Iraq recognized new Shi'ite Islamic Government of Iran, but the Iranian leaders were highly inimical of American backed Baath party. They adopted a policy of "exporting the Islamic revolution," and Iraq was placed on the list of countries whose governments were to be overthrown and replaced on the pattern of the Islamic regime in Iran, that meant ouster of President Saddam, who was not an Islamic fanatic. Further, a treaty of 1975 on Iran-Iraq border adjustment had been made but Iran still occupied three territories that were to be transferred to Iraq. In 1979 and 1980, border clashes took place on Iran-Iraq border in sequence.

Iraq-Iran War

Saddam Hussein announced on 17 September 1980, that he was abrogating the 1975 agreements because these had been violated by Iran. On 22 September 1980, Iraqi forces entered Iran and Iraq bombed Iranian airbases and other strategic targets. On 28 September 1980, the UN Security Council called for a ceasefire and appealed both Iran and Iraq to "settle their dispute by peaceful means." The response of Iran to the resolution of UN Security Council was, however, negative since it claimed to be a victim of aggression. But, the West took note of the defiance of Security Council by Iran only. Further, mediation efforts of 1980 and 1981 were also rejected by Iran. This war continued in favour of Iraq and in succeeding years it spread to the Persian Gulf area. Iraq had bombed and destroyed Iranian oil terminals in the Gulf, including the one on Kharg Island, leading to threats to oil outflow from Iran and that invited foreign intervention. The Iraqi advances into Iran continued till November 1980. Thereafter Iran mustered a series of successful counter offensives and by May 1982 the Iraqi troops had been successfully cleared from most of the territory of Iran. Iranian forces began to penetrate into Basra province of Iraq during 1983–86, they occupied Majnun Island and threatened the city of Basra. In the north-eastern provinces, Iraqi Kurds joined Iranian forces on the basis of tribal affinity and vast areas of Iraq were threatened. Iraq used chemical weapons on the Kurds. This was noted as an illegal international act or event in international law. Both sides suffered heavy casualties before forces regained regular border. The Iranian attacks on Basra were repulsed with heavy casualties on both sides. The gain of Iran was occupation of Majnun Island and of Fao peninsula and its continuing threats to Basra. In 1987, Iraq received significant arms aid from France and the Soviet Union since it had backing of UN Security Council resolution. Iraq already had both diplomatic and military support of the United States at the United Nations. In October 1987 and April 1988 the US forces had attacked Iranian ships and oil platforms in Persian Gulf for their own reasons. On 20 July 1987, the UN Security Council unanimously passed Resolution 598, which urged Iraq and Iran to accept a ceasefire, withdraw their forces to internationally recognized boundaries, and settle their frontier disputes by negotiations under the auspices of the United Nations. Iran, however, without rejecting the resolution demanded amendments that would condemn Iraq as the aggressor in the war and declared that all foreign navies should leave the Gulf. After a brief halt, the military operations in the Gulf were resumed. Iraq recaptured its Fao peninsula and the districts of Salamcha and Majnun. After making comprehensive assessment of internal and external situation, Iran formally accepted Security Council Resolution 598 on 20 August 1988, and thereafter a ceasefire ensued. Gradually meeting under the UN Resolution 598 in 1990 both Iraq and Iran finally agreed to settle their boundaries, etc. on the basis of the earlier 1975 agreement. The eight-year-long war with Iran had devastated the Iraqi economy and killed more than a million Iraqis. Iraq sought material help from Saudi Arabia and Kuwait, which it did not receive. Historically, this war will be recorded as a failure of collective security system of United Nations since latter had no means of enforcing the Security Council decisions considering the uncertain nature of interests of superpowers involved in the region.

Iraq and Kuwait

Iraq had often repeated its claim that Kuwait is Iraqi territory since 1923 and ultimately there was the Kuwait War of 1991, after which Kuwait was occupied by Iraq for about eight months. The question involved was: Could Kuwait be regarded as a separated part of Iraq? The origin of the city of Kuwait and of the State of Kuwait in desolate area took place only at the beginning of the 18th century. The Bani 'Utub, a group of families of the 'Anizah tribe' living in the interior of the Arabian Peninsula had migrated to the area and had settled there for better pastures. An autonomous sheikhdom of Kuwait came into existence in 1756, the first Sheikh was from the Arab Saabah family. Kuwait developed as a thriving, independent trading center in the 19th century. Toward the end of the 19th century, Kuwait came closer to the Ottoman Empire, though it did not become part of Ottoman. But, Ottoman threats to annex Kuwait prompted its ruler Sheikh Mubarak to cultivate a close relationship with Britain. By a treaty of 1899 Britain was given control of Kuwait's foreign affairs and on the outbreak of the World War I, Turkey being at war against Britain, Kuwait became a British protectorate. At the 1922 Conference of Al-Uqayr, Britain negotiated the Kuwait-Saudi border, and handed over substantial territory of Kuwait to Saudi Arabia. Iraq had also claimed Kuwait with a memorandum in 1923 based on a unratified 1913 convention. When in 1938, oil was discovered in the sheikhdom first full Iraqi claim to Kuwait was made and there was an unsuccessful Iraq prompted uprising 'majlis movement' against the Sheikh. Iraq continued to put forth a claim to Kuwait then only to a part of it comprising of strategic islands of Bubiyan and Al-Warbah. On June 19, 1961, Britain recognized Kuwait as independent State and its independence was ensured first by British and then by Arab League forces. In October 1963 the Iraqi regime formally recognized Kuwait as independent State and also its borders, but continued to press for 'right to access' to the islands Bubiyan and Al-Warbah of Kuwait.

The relation between Iraq and Kuwait came under cloud by end of 1980s. After the war of Iraq with Iran that had practically ended inconclusively by 1988, Kuwait had refused to bail out Saddam from its economic collapse. Further, since the underground oil floor was common to Iraq and Kuwait oil wells, there was an agreement between the two for proportionate drilling of oil. Kuwait was caught and charged for fraudulent "slide drilling", that is, for pumping Iraqi oil from the Kuwait side of the border. Then, Iraq wanted higher oil pricing through a controlled oil production by the Organization of Petroleum Exporting Countries (OPEC) of which it was a member. Kuwait broke quota fixed by the OPEC and sold such oil cheap in the international market causing loss to Iraqi revenues.

Peeved and upset Iraq committed the blunder of invading Kuwait on 2 August 1990, claiming it to be its part historically. The occupation of Kuwait was quick; Iraq formally annexed Kuwait on 8 August 1990 and it was declared to be a province of Iraq. This was an act of aggression under Chapter VII of the Charter of United Nations and sanctions from UN Security Council followed. The Resolution 661 (1990) Security Council had established international economic sanctions against Iraq in response to Iraq's invasion of Kuwait. Both Soviet Russia and USA ignored their earlier friendship with Iraq in order to uphold the Charter of United Nations. The USA undertook to end the aggression and occupation while Japan, Germany and Saudi Arabia promised to bear expenses. UN forces were organized under USA, France, Egypt, Syria and several other Arab nations joined the anti-Iraq coalition known as Operation Desert Shield by contributing forces. Saudi Arabia declared that it feared attack from Iraq forces that resulted in US and NATO ally troops to rush into Saudi Arabia. The UN Security Council authorized the use of force on 29 November 1990 against Iraq and set 15 January 1991 as deadline for the voluntary end of Iraqi occupation of Kuwait. Next day, the Persian Gulf War started with a massive US led air bombardment offensive against Iraq. A massive Allied ground offensive was launched on Kuwait and Iraq territories on 24 February and within three days Arab and US forces had freed Kuwait City. Simultaneously, the main US armored thrust drove into Iraq from the rear of Kuwait. By end of February, these forces had destroyed most of Iraq's elite army units south of Basra in southeastern Iraq. Kuwait's independence was restored when ceasefire came into effect on 28 February 1991. The United Nations Compensation Commission (UNCC) was created immediately as a subsidiary organ of the UN Security Council with the mandate to process claims and pay compensation for losses and damage suffered as a direct result of Iraq's unlawful invasion and occupation of Kuwait. Further, taking note of the fears and charges of nuclear programme of Iraq mandates for the United Nations Special Commission (UNSCOM) and the IAEA for Monitoring and Verification

Plans along with demolition of the WMD programmes in Iraq were established.[6] Iraq was made liable to pay for the costs of the operation of these two mandated authorities.[7]

UN Panel Award against Iraq

After working for twelve long years, the UN Compensation Commission[8] processed claims totaling $52.5 billions against Iraq. Of this (a) over $2.68 million is to be paid to individuals, governments and companies and (b) over $366 millions is to be paid to successful State claimants, including the Governments of Iran, Jordan, Kuwait and Saudi Arabia, which had claimed compensation for damage caused by Iraq to their natural resources.[9] Rest of $52.5 billion would go to Kuwait. Money to pay the claims is to come from Iraqi oil sales: the Security Council has decided that the claims would be funded by 5 per cent of Iraqi oil sales. Iraqi officials have expressed their displeasure with the level of the payments, but did not by July 2005 make an official request to lower it. It is expected to take years to pay all the claims, with big oil companies having to wait until the end. Iraq has suggested that payments be temporarily suspended until an international conference could be convened to discuss the matter further.[10]

War Consequences and UN Sanctions on Iraq

By the time of ceasefire, Iraqi army set-up and military resistance to UN forces had completely collapsed but the UN-sanctioned trade embargo on Iraq continued to remain in force after the end of war. After the war, Iraq had only formal international existence and Saddam Hussein survived as its President. The State had no industry and no economy left and the people were on starvation precipice. It was imperative for the UN bodies to take note of the lack of jobs, health and medicare services, industries, and starvation in the wake of international trade restrictions on Iraq when the main revenues of the State depended on oil exports. Humanitarian grounds compelled United Nations to supplement State efforts of public good, which it did but subject to Iraq not obstructing the ongoing Monitoring and Verification Plan submitted by the IAEA. The Security Council[11] established the organized system of oil sales and exports by Iraq for funds for humanitarian purposes, also known as "oil-for-food program" and subsequent resolutions have extended this programme from time to time. Later, it established[12] import/export-monitoring mechanism with a bi-monthly sanctions reviews and submission to it of consolidated periodic reports required under its previous resolutions.[13] The exports/imports were reviewed for genuineness of humanitarian requirements of Iraq. This humanitarian mechanism came under stress whenever Iraq did not cooperate with UN Special Commission in its assigned task, e.g., in 1998 the Security Council condemned[14] Iraq for suspending full cooperation with inspection process and suspended the bi-monthly sanctions reviews, expressed intent to revise UNSCR 986 (1995) arrangements for sale of goods and commodities to Iraq or adopted a system of "Goods Review List (GRL)" and procedures of application for implementation beginning from 30 May 2002. The oil-for-food programme was closed[15] by 2003 when Iraq came under fresh clouds for alleged encouragement to terrorism after 9/11 bombings. After the US and UK unilateral military action for tracing WMD in Iraq of 2003, a Humanitarian Coordinator for Iraq (HIC) was established by the United Nations Office for the Coordination of Humanitarian Affairs (UNOCHA), and this office operates under the UN Office of the Humanitarian Coordinator for Iraq (UNOHCI). The United Nations Assistance Mission for Iraq (UNAMI) was created on 21 November 2003 by the Security Council[16] as a one-year follow-through mission in the wake of the Oil-for-Food programme closure. The new arrangements by the UN took into account the diplomacy of not endorsing of US and UK led military action in Iraq but at the same time of continuing its humanitarian efforts for saving people of Iraq from starvation, malnutrition and ill health.

TRACING AND DISMANTLING OF WMD IN IRAQ

No Nuclear Weapons Recovered

What is significant is that even after Kuwait regained its independence, the IAEA and UN Special Commission continued the task of tracking down and dismantling any remnants from

Iraq's weapons of mass destruction (WMD) programme, destruction of medium-range missiles and Iraqi chemical and nuclear weapons research facilities. Nuclear weapons were not found, though it was believed on the basis of intelligence reports both of USA and UK that Iraq did possess some in imperfect stages of development. These weapons were presumed to have been cleverly and successfully concealed. The US intelligence worked on the presumption that A.Q. Khan, the main architect of nuclear weapon program of Pakistan had offered to Iraq 'critical nuclear weapons technology and components' few months before the Gulf War 1991, which the UN inspectors had found memorialized in an Iraqi intelligence document dated 6 October 1990 seized in 1995. The inspectors found the document in 1995 after being tipped by Hussein Kamel, head of the WMD program of Iraq. Kamel had defected that year and had provided a great deal of intelligence about nuclear weapons programs of Iraq both to the United States intelligence officials and to UN Inspectors. In 1995, it was believed by both that the offers of nuclear deals were real and came from A.Q. Khan of Pakistan. The inference drawn by the inspectors[17] was logically possible: "If you approach them with an offer of a critical technology and they dismiss your offer, that could mean they have already mastered that technology." Another, a new set of United Nations weapons inspectors, conducted later detailed investigations into the correctness of the charge that Iraq possessed nuclear weapons in 2002. 'Under the threat of military action by the United States and pressure from the Arab states, Iraq agreed to admit United Nations weapons inspectors without conditions.' Iraq has assessed that the return of the nuclear inspectors after inspection would lead as soon as possible to the lifting of sanctions and normalizing of the situation for the country.[18]

The UN Special Commission (UNSCOM)

As discussed, the UN sponsored armed action in November 1990 against Iraq for illegal annexation of Kuwait was accompanied after taking note of the fears and charges of nuclear programme of Iraq with mandates for the United Nations Special Commission and for the IAEA for Monitoring and Verification Plans along with demolition of the WMD programmes in Iraq.[19] The United Nations Security Council had established the terms and conditions for the formal cease-fire between Iraq and the coalition of Member States that were fighting for regaining the independence of Kuwait by its resolution 687 of 3 April, 1991. Section C of this resolution[20] had called for the elimination, under international supervision, of Iraq's weapons of mass destruction and ballistic missiles having a range greater than 150 km, together with related items and production facilities. It had also called for measures to ensure for future that the acquisition and production of prohibited items were not resumed by Iraq. This was an obvious limitation on the sovereign rights of Iraq to which it was said that Iraq had agreed as part of the creasefire. The International Atomic Energy Agency (IAEA) was to perform this task in the nuclear areas or sector while the United Nations Special Commission (UNSCOM) was set up to implement the non-nuclear parts of the resolution in close coordination with the IAEA. The precise terms of this assignment were laid out in paragraphs 7 to 13 of the resolution. On 17 June, 1991, the Security Council confirmed[21] that the Special Commission and the IAEA would have a continuing authority to conduct activities under section C of resolution 687 (1991). It was also made clear[22] that Iraq shall "accept unconditionally the inspectors and all other personnel designated by the Special Commission". The Secretary-General had at first appointed Rolf Ekéus of Sweden as the Executive Chairman of the Special Commission and on 1 May 1991, the Secretary-General appointed 20 other members of the Commission that came from Australia, Austria, Belgium, Canada, China, the Czech Republic, Finland, France, Germany, Indonesia, Italy, Japan, the Netherlands, Nigeria, Norway, Poland, the Russian Federation, the United Kingdom, the United States and Venezuela. Richard Butler of Australia replaced Rolf Ekéus as the second Executive Chairman on 1 July 1997. In the end Deputy Executive Chairman, Mr. Charles Duelfer of United States functioned as officer-in-charge from 1 July 1999 to 17 December 1999. After this date by a decision of the UN Security Council[23] the United Nations Monitoring, Verification and Inspection Commission (UNMOVIC) had replaced the UNSCOM. Detailed sessions of the members of the UNSCOM were held periodically, approximately twice yearly in New York, to discuss policy issues and to assess the results of the operations. The last such meeting of the Commission members was held in October 1998.

The Work Tryst of UNSCOM in Iraq

The Security Council had affirmed[24] that it was for UNSCOM alone to determine which items are to be destroyed under its Resolution 687. During July 1992 UNSCOM began the destruction of large quantities of Iraq's chemical weapons and production facilities and continued with the destruction of large quantities of chemical warfare agents and precursors and their production equipment by June 1994. Iraq had repeatedly made accusations that UN weapons inspectors were exceeding their brief and that the inspecting teams had gathered intelligence on many aspects of national security apparatus of Iraq that often went beyond the WMD and missile programmes. Obstructions and objections to the reach of inspectors to various sites were made by Iraq to which the Security Council reacted with threats of stringent economic sanctions. It again and again reiterated that the Special Commission and the IAEA had a continuing authority to conduct activities under section C of resolution 687 (1991). It was the prerogative of the Commission to judge of the definition of documents or materials to be subject of inspection, to choose the sites for inspection and to install monitoring devices at chosen places. Iraq was not allowed to escape inspection on grounds of 'sensitive areas' or sovereign places. UNSCOM and IAEA Action Team worked in close unison for monitoring and verification commitment and professed to exercise their rights and privileges in a manner that respected the legitimate concerns of Iraq regarding sovereignty, independence, security and dignity. As a result of investigations by UNSCOM and in the light of irrefutable evidence, Iraq, for the first time, admitted on 1 July 1995 the existence of an offensive biological weapon 'programme' but it denied any 'weaponization'. In November 1995 Iraq provided a full, final and complete disclosure of its prohibited missile programme to UNSCOM. In 1996, UNSCOM further conducted an investigation, which confirmed that Iraqi authorities and missile facilities have been involved in the acquisition of sophisticated guidance and control components for proscribed missiles. Divergence of views between the two sides started from March, 1996 onwards when the UNSCOM teams were denied immediate access to five sites designated for inspection of missile by Iraq. However, in May-June of 1996 UNSCOM supervised the destruction of Al-Hakam, the main facility of Iraq for the production of biological warfare agents. Iraq again blocked from 21 June 1997 teams of UNSCOM from entering certain sites, which had been designated by UNSCOM for inspection and that lead to reaction from Security Council which demanded[25] from Iraq immediate, unconditional and unrestricted access to any sites for inspection and officials for interviews by UNSCOM. In July 1996 Iraq had provided another, the third 'Full, Final and Complete Disclosure' of its prohibited missile programme but in November 1996 Iraq without success disputed for three months the right of UNSCOM of removing outside Iraq the remnants of missile engines for in-depth analysis.

In September 1997, there were tiffs over the inspection of unauthorized movement of Iraqi vehicles inside a site that was declared by Iraq to be "sensitive" or were "presidential sites", but were designated for inspection by UNSCOM. Iraq unsuccessfully resisted the destruction of large quantities of chemical weapons related equipment and precursor chemicals. Iraq had denied any intention of using these for making chemical weapons. In November 1997 Iraq asked the UNSCOM that the personnel of United States nationality working for it should leave Iraq immediately. The Executive Chairman of the UNSCOM in reaction decided for temporary withdrawal of majority of the UNSCOM personnel from Iraq; only a skeleton staff remained in Baghdad to maintain premises and equipment of UNSCOM. This development led to serious arguments, condemnation and discussions in the UN Security Council.

The impasse continued further when Iraq announced in January 1998 that it would not cooperate with the inspection teams on the ground that these had too many individuals of US or UK nationality. The dissentions took greater dimensions when on 5 August 1998, the Revolutionary Command Council and the Baath Party Command decided to halt cooperation with UNSCOM and the IAEA pending Security Council agreement to lift the oil embargo on Iraq altogether, reorganization of the UNSCOM and moving it to either Geneva or Vienna. In the interim period, Iraq said that it would permit monitoring to be done under resolution 715 (1991) on its territory only on its own terms. Security Council unanimously condemned[26] the decision of Iraq to suspend cooperation with UNSCOM, termed such actions as a totally unacceptable and to be in contravention of Iraq's obligations; demanded Iraq to rescind its decision and as punitive sanction decided not to conduct the periodic 60-day reviews of export/import embargo until Iraq did so abide and the Commission reported to the Security Council that it has been able to exercise its full range of activities, including inspections to its full satisfaction. Iraq did not give in and on 31 October 1998, it announced that it would cease all forms of interaction with UNSCOM and its chairman and to halt all activities of UNSCOM, including monitoring inside Iraq. The Security Council reacted without success and on 16 December 1998 the UN Special Commission withdrew its staff from Iraq. The UNSCOM had submitted its last semi-annual report[27] to the Security Council on 8 October 1999 and in the meantime the last Executive Chairman of UNSCOM Richard Butler had completed his two year tenure on 30 June 1999. The Security Council replaced[28] UNSCOM by a new United Nations Monitoring Verification and Inspection Commission (UNMOVIC) on 17 December 1999. This was a temporarily successful diplomacy of USA and UK over Iraq.

The UNMOVIC

The new system for Monitoring Verification and Inspection of WMD in Iraq had a past of a series of protests and involuntary or forced cooperation of Iraq in the functioning of

UNSCOM on its territory. UN weapons inspectors were understood by Iraq to be continually exceeding their assigned brief. Iraq had several times charged that the inspecting teams had gathered intelligence on many aspects of Iraq's national security apparatus that often was beyond the scrutiny of its WMD and missile programmes. Also, Iraqis had complained that inspections were at times and at certain places were carried out in a manner that was calculated to injure their national dignity, when the inspectors had demanded access to all kinds of sites. At many times, Iraq had obtained support from Russia, China, France and some other members of the European Union in favour of its objections against untrammeled inspections by the UN inspectors and most of whom were of US and UK nationality. In this background when Iraq firmly refused to cooperate with UNSCOM, the United Nations Monitoring, Verification and Inspection Commission (UNMOVIC) was created by Security Council through a Resolution[29] on 17 December 1999 and the continuity of mandate for IAEA was also confirmed. UNMOVIC replaced the former UN Special Commission (UNSCOM) and continued with the mandate to verify compliance by Iraq with its obligation under the resolutions of Security Council and to dismantle its weapons of mass destruction which included chemical or biological weapons and missiles with a range of more than 150 km, and to operate the system of ongoing monitoring and verification operating "to ascertain that Iraq does not reacquire the same weapons prohibited for it by the Security Council".[30] The Secretary-General of the United Nations appointed Dr. Hans Blix of Sweden to be the Commission's Executive Chairman,[31] with 16 others forming the College of Commissioners of UNMOVIC which provided advice to the Executive Chairman in the execution of his duties. The staff of Commission included weapons specialists, analysts, scientists, engineers and operational planners. The staff of UNMOVIC is employees of the United Nations unlike its predecessor, UNSCOM. The UNMOVIC was composed of four additional divisions, viz, Planning and Operations, Analysis and Assessment, Information, Technical Support and Training as well as an administrative service unit. The Commission had its headquarters at the United Nations in New York. The Executive Chairman was required to report to the Security Council on the activities of UNMOVIC every three months. For this, the Executive Chairman had to consult the College of Commissioners on his written reports to the Council. The College of Commissioners of UNMOVIC held at least four sessions every year to discuss the report and other organizational and operational activities. When the US-UK led military action took place in March 2003 its inspectors were withdrawn from Iraq. The UNMOVIC had maintained a degree of preparedness to resume work in Iraq after that. After the chaotic unilateral action of two superpowers in Iraq, UNO had withdrawn its work from Iraq except for the humanitarian work. The US President Bush and British Prime Minister Blair asserted that Iraq did possess nuclear and other prohibited weapons of mass destruction and took over the task of discovering weapons of mass destruction supposed to be in the armory of Iraq which UNMOVIC and IEAE had been unable to unearth. UNMOVIC inspectors had after a break returned to Iraq in November 2002; they had destroyed some Iraqi Al Samoud 2 missiles and warheads, some launchers, shells filled with chemical weapons precursors and other arms.

Nuclear Verifications by IAEA

The IAEA had been given mandate[32] in Iraq for monitoring and verification, removal and destruction of all weapon-grade nuclear material, like, highly enriched uranium and plutonium. It started this activity through Iraq Action Team, and later Iraq Nuclear Verification Office (INVO) conducted this task. It is now recorded that through these agencies, IAEA has "successfully removed from Iraq; has taken custody of all known remaining uranium compounds; has destroyed and rendered harmless all known dedicated facilities and associated equipment, and has monitored all known dual-use equipment" in Iraq. The overall goal of ongoing monitoring and verification in Iraq was to provide reaffirmation that its clandestine nuclear programme has been neutralized and is not being revised or reconstituted. The OMV plan was designed to "provide timely detection of indications of any attempt by Iraq to reconstitute its clandestine nuclear program, or more specifically, to give assurance of the absence of prohibited equipment, materials and activities." The INVO staff also "reviewed contract applications to ensure no nuclear related or duel use items were sold to Iraq." It is noted that during the period between the inception of the programme and its completion in March 2003 the IAEA had reviewed nearly 10,000 contract applications. The IAEA continuously monitored the situation in Iraq against nuclearization; that was continuously "monitored through the analysis of satellite imagery, the collection and analysis of open source information, and contact with Member States."[33]

IRAQ IN HELL

Iraq Under Occupation: The Reasons

Now with the retrospective circumspection of international events and diplomacy of the last two decades it is possible to unzip the reasons which brought Iraq under occupation and the shadow of Hell in the years since 2002. First, there was continuing oil-diplomacy under which Iraq, Iran, Kuwait and Gulf States are economic targets of industrial States and superpowers of the world; these Middle East areas meet their more than 80% heavy oil requirements. The West did want to maintain steady oil outflow from this region. Secondly, the President Saddam Hussein of Iraq was not responding to the games of the West, he was hitting the oil interests of the West and was trying to be leader of Arab States with anti-Israel stand. He had been a cruel and ruthless ruler of Iraq with pro-Soviet attitudes. His presence in international politics was a severe monstrosity for USA and UK and an obstruction in maintaining their hegemony in the Middle East. He had at a time wanted Iraq to become a nuclear power. Thirdly, Iraq had already committed the mistake and illegality of annexing Kuwait in 1990 and was under a punitive syndrome, had a limping economy, restricted international status and had been ex-communicated by most of Arab States. Fourthly, Saddam

Hussein was linked with terrorism; the UN had noted disapprovingly the reports alleging that Saddam Hussein had rewarded Palestinian suicide bombers with money and this money he had received through kickbacks from contractors, illegal smuggling or side oil deals in breach of the economic sanctions imposed on it by the Security Council since 1991. As a consequence, the United Nations had been led to the negotiating of the International Convention for the Suppression of the Financing of Terrorism, which has the aim to prevent the type of activity that Saddam Hussein had allegedly committed. The United Nations had acted against Osama bin Laden, *Al Qaeda* and the Taliban also. These had been declared international outlaws by it after the 1998 terrorist bombings of United States embassies in Nairobi, Kenya, and Dar-es-Salaam and Tanzania. By the fear generated by 9/11 terrorist bombings in USA of 2001, through anti-US attitude of *Al Qaeda* in common, Iraq was suspected and feared to be a springboard for future *Al Qaeda* terrorism on US soil.

Post 9/11 Attitudes

The USA prompted the international community in 2002 for adopting tougher sanctions against Iraq in order to suppress Iraq from indulging in State terrorism and USA coupled the sanctions with resumption of nuclear and WMD inspections. The last phase of inspections were carried out under the terms of an agreement between the Iraqi government and the UN Secretary-General. The Bush administration indicated in 2002 that it would not put up with time-consuming negotiations between Iraq and the Secretary-General before inspections can be resumed. It hinted again and again on unilateralist US action in March 2002 unless there was unconditional return of UN weapon inspectors to Iraq to track down and dismantle any remnants from Iraq's weapons of mass destruction (WMD) programme. The nature of the rights of inspectors and sanctions in the face of objections of Iraq remained matters of discussion. At the same time, President Bush did make it clear that his diplomacy included a change of regime in Iraq. The Security Council was apparently not united behind US plans and probable Arab reaction was also a matter of concern for US policy makers. However, from strategic point of view as Iraq had regular military establishment, it was easily vulnerable to US missiles and satellite imagery by way of a pre-emptive military strike against Iraq. The US President, George W. Bush, in a speech to General Assembly[34] challenged the United Nations to confront the threat from Iraq "deliberately and decisively". He emphasized at length on Baghdad's alleged efforts "to acquire weapons of mass destruction, including nuclear weapons and its refusal to account for as many as 600 missing nationals in Kuwait from 1991". "The conduct of the Iraqi regime is a threat to the authority of the United Nations and a threat to peace".

Submission by Humiliated Iraq

Under the threat of military action by the United States and pressure from the Arab States, Iraq agreed to admit United Nations weapons inspectors without conditions.[35] However, US did not accept that Iraq meant business in a real search for weapons of mass destruction. It went on with the preparations for unilateral action against Iraq. By solid majority, the United States Congress approved the use of military force against Iraq and its leader, Saddam Hussein. The resolution authorized President George W. Bush to use military force, if necessary, to compel Iraq to get rid of its biological and chemical weapons and to disband its nuclear weapons program. This was done by the US Congress against the argument that "completely bypassing the UN would set a dangerous precedent that would undoubtedly be used by other countries in the future to our and the world's detriment".[36] Rather to ward off a military action by USA, the Security Council unanimously voted on a tough new Iraq resolution that warned the Iraqi leader, Saddam Hussein, that he must disarm or face "serious consequences".[37] The Security Council transferred the onus fully on Iraq and its leader to adhere to the terms and conditions of the new resolution. Ahead of the resolution, President Bush had set 15 November 2002 as the last date for final decision by Iraq. On 13 November, Iraq said that it was accepting the new United Nations Security Council Resolution 1441 on weapons inspections. The weapons inspectors' team was headed by the chief inspector, Hans Blix, who, with a technical and communications team, landed on the ground of Iraq by the end of November. The Blix team was made in-charge of biological and chemical weapon inspections while the International Atomic Energy Agency was to continue with nuclear inspections. Iraq made a declaration of 7 December 2002, stating and clarifying the material position of involved weapons on the matter.

The Unilateral Action over Iraq

In January, 2003, media reported that the US President, George Bush, has signed a top secret directive authorizing pre-emptive strikes against nations close to acquiring nuclear weapons.[38] This was at that time linked to North Korean problem but Iraq was also in the "axis of evil". The USA and UK made vehement statements in Security Council meeting of 5 February 2003, dismissing the repeated denials of Iraq that it has no weapons of mass destruction as nothing more than a "web of lies", asserted that there was "irrefutable and undeniable" evidence that the Iraq was indeed concealing weapons and programmes of mass destruction, and that Iraq was in "deeper" material breach of Resolution 1441 that would justify military action by UN. However, Russia, China and France, veto power holders, cautioned against any hasty decision against Iraq involving sanctions of UN.[39] The top United Nations weapons inspector, Hans Blix, stated[40] in the Security Council:

> "Conditions had improved for weapons inspectors in Iraq and that inspections had found no weapons of mass destruction.
>
> But even while stressing the positive elements of the inspection process, he maintained that many prohibited weapons had not been accounted for, a finding of 'great significance'.
>
> 'One must not jump to the conclusion that they exist. However, that possibility is also not excluded. If they exist, they should be presented for destruction. If they do not exist, credible evidence to that effect should be presented'."

This meeting of Security Council convinced USA and UK negatively that these two will have to take unilateral action against Iraq and to begin a new intensive process to get something definitive and conclusive. The Bush administration apparently wanted the Security Council to go on record that Iraq has not disarmed and, therefore, it has to face "serious consequences". After the UN failed to agree to a second resolution on 20 March 2003, the USA-led missile strikes and thus started the historic war on Iraq. The UNO was sidelined in this process. A US-led Coalition Provisional Authority (CPA) was created and US appointed the Iraqi Governing Council to decipher the future of Iraq and unilaterally enforce international law on it. The coalition authorities restarted the tracking for nuclear revamping by Iraq and presumed presence of WMDs on its territory. An Iraq Survey Group (ISG) for hunting WMD was established; 1400 American, British and Australian military experts had arrived in Iraq on 5 June 2003 to pursue the unfinished task.[41]

The War Gamble

On 2 May 2003 George Bush had formally declared victory in war on Iraq. The war was won, whole of Iraq came under occupation of US-UK led coalition, the constitutional government was dissolved by occupation command and President Saddam Hussein in hiding was arrested[42] about eight months after he had fled Baghdad and is yet to face trial for punishment. The occupation command could not find any WMD or nuclear weapons on Iraqi territory, which was the reason for military action that had bypassed the Charter of United Nations. Both President Bush of USA and Prime Minister Blair of Britain took the stand that they had twin objectives for the war: First, tracking and destruction of WMD and nuclear weapons of Iraq, and secondly, the ouster of tyrannical regime of Saddam Hussein. The successful achievement of second objective was good enough and in case the first reason could not be substantiated, this would not belittle the war or make it illegal. But for the question mark remained on USA and UK who had misled the international community on the basis of intelligence reports, might be in order to pursue their oil or regional hegemony diplomacy. In the process, a unilateral military action was undertaken and the UNO was placed on a shelf.

The Report of Iraq Survey Group (ISG) on WMD

Iraq Survey Group interim report of October 2003 said that it had drawn a blank in search for WMD, though significant amounts of equipment and weapons related activities had been discovered all of which were concealed from United Nations inspectors. However, definitive conclusions on the worth of this development remained to be worked out. The ISG chief David Kay resigned on 24 January 2004, saying that he does not believe Iraq had large stockpiles of chemical or biological weapons. The Iraq Survey Group hunting for banned weapons inside postwar Iraq in its final report of 6 October 2004 said it had found no chemical, biological or nuclear weapons in postwar Iraq. Its Chief Inspector Charles Duelfer reported that he doubted Iraq had any "militarily significant" WMD stocks. The ISG report had made significant conclusions the main points of which could be summarized thus:

(1) Iraq's weapons of mass destruction were "essentially" destroyed in 1991, but that Saddam Hussein wanted to recreate them after sanctions were removed.

(2) The motivation of Saddam Hussein for developing these weapons was his enmity with Iran, with which Iraq fought an eight-year war in the 1980s. His secondary goals were to oppose Israel and raise his status in the Arab world.[43]

(3) Iraq ended its nuclear programme in 1991 after the Gulf War, and there was no evidence to suggest existence of any concerted efforts to restart it. However, Senior Iraqi officials believed Saddam would restart a nuclear programme if UN sanctions imposed after the end of the Gulf War were halted.

(4) Iraq did undertake a variety of measures to conceal key elements of its former nuclear programme from successive UN inspectors, and specific directions from

Saddam Hussein were to hide and preserve relevant documents. The regime prevented scientists from the former nuclear programme from either, leaving their jobs or Iraq. In the late 1990s, key personnel were given significant pay rises in a bid to retain them. The regime also undertook new investments in research at university level to ensure that Iraq retained technical knowledge.

(5) Iraq had abandoned its biological weapons programme in late 1995 out of fear it would be discovered by victors and such a discovery would have made it harder for Iraq to free itself of UN sanctions. There was no interest in biological weapons after 1996.

(6) Iraq had unilaterally destroyed its hidden chemical weapons stockpile in 1991, and there is no credible evidence that Iraq ever resumed production of such weapons. However, the regime had reorganized its chemical industry after the mid-1990s and had allowed it to conserve the knowledge-base of a chemical weapons programme.

The Ghost of WMD and Nuclear Weaponry

Was the Iraq war legal? The answer to this question depends on result of an inquiry whether Iraq possessed nuclear weapons and other WMD in early 2003 or since 1991, which US-UK claimed. Former President of Iraq, in captivity, denied[44] that his government had possessed WMD. This question has been haunting international politics and diplomacy like a ghost ever since. The statesmen of the world and top officials of USA, UK and UN have been skeptics on the point.[45] A former US Treasury Secretary Paul O'Neill is reported by media as alleging that during his tensure for 23 months he never saw in the 'intelligence' anything that could be characterized as direct evidence of weapons of mass destruction being present in Iraq.[46] Further,[47] "US Secretary of State, Colin Powell, has held out the possibility that pre-war Iraq may not have possessed weapons of mass destruction. Powell was asked about comments last week by David Kay, the outgoing leader of a US weapons search team in Iraq, that he did not believe

Iraq had large quantities of chemical or biological weapons." Even people of UK have questioned the credibility of statements of their Prime Minister on the matter. It was reported by media[48] that British military was adamant on not leaving for Iraq without prior assurance of Attorney General over the legality of the campaign. Sir Michael Boyce, the then Chief of Defence Staff, raised concerns. The former Cabinet Minister, Clare Short, is quoted to have said "I was told at the highest level in the department (Department for International Development) that the military were saying they wouldn't go, whatever the PM said, without the Attorney General's advice." The Attorney General Lord Peter Goldsmith was "sitting on the fence" until the very last minute and his advice, even two weeks before the war was evasive. The revelations increased pressures on Prime Minister Blair for reports of Butler Inquiry, which was set-up earlier for investigation into the intelligence fiasco and failure that had led to the run-up of UK to the war in March 2002.[49]

Post-mortem Investigations

Bush had set-up a seven member independent bipartisan commission[50] to investigate pre-war intelligence about Iraq's weapons of mass destruction over which US went to war and related 21st century threats. Commission co-chaired by Senator and Governor, Chuck Robb, and retired Judge, Laurence Silberman, to compare the reports of Iraq Survey Group with prior US Intelligence reports. The Congress had also set up its committees to make inquiries into possible abuse of intelligence about alleged Iraqi WMD. The public opinion of UK led to embarrassment to Prime Minister Blair, suicide of David Kelly and the establishment of the Hutton Inquiry. Commons Foreign Affairs Committee of Members of Parliament had been formed that looked into how ministers made the case for war in Iraq. Both President Bush of USA and Prime Minister Blair of UK, on their part, have accepted that there was error of judgment while going to war but have claimed that it was failure of the input of intelligence reports which prompted them to take the recourse of war and that they had not misled their people.

At the War End

The US-UK led nuclear diplomacy resulted in ouster of the constitutional government of President Saddam Hussein for internal tyranny and for violating UN mandate on inspection of nuclear weapons and other WMD. It also pointed to the imperfections and irrelevance of UN Charter on peace and security system, which has shaken the existence of United Nations. Later, the UN satisfied itself vicariously by hopes for return of democratic rule in Iraq in near future and by rendering humanitarian services to starving, physically bruised and under-nourished population of Iraq. The country Iraq only witnessed a change in government of democratic polity on the basis of religion, Shi'ites replacing Sunni, or a change involving one tribe replacing another tribe in formation of government on the basis of votes. President Bush has stated on 13 December 2005 in reply to questions after his speech at World Affairs Council of Philadelphia[51] that Iraqis have paid high price in their 'push for democracy'; he asserted that 30,000, more or less, Iraqis "have lost their lives since the beginning of the war as a result of initial incursions and the ongoing violence" and that "We've lost about 2,140 of our own troops in Iraq". Followers of Saddam Hussein are now terrorists menacingly and persistently targeting both the local administration personnel and foreign troops. Only the elements of tussle in Iraq under foreign influence have altered. Oil diplomacy remains at the same place.

ENDNOTES

1. Also, known as Asia minor; geographically, it is the western half portion of Turkey proper.
2. F. Schuman, *International Politics*, p. 322.
3. Palestine included the Trans-Jordan and Israel territories along Saudi Arabia border. Jordan was separated from Palestine and made independent by British in January 1946 under King Emir Abdullah while Israel was made a new State for Jews, providing the Jews of the world a homeland.
4. The League of Nations introduced 'Mandate' system and it placed all Asian and African territories detached from Germany and Turkey under the power of governance of either Britain or France,

the power of mandate was *ad hoc* arrangement, annexation of territory was not their aim in the war under their Armistice declaration (5 November 1918). Turkish ruled Syria and Lebanon in Asia went to France. Mandated territories were grouped as Class A, B, or C on the basis of their location and their level of political and economic development. All Class A mandates had reached full independence by 1949 with puppet governments under Kings or Emirs installed in these new States by Britain and France.

5. These were defined in separate and subsidiary agreements between Iraq and Britain.
6. Resolution 687 (1991); while Resolution 707 (1991) repeated the demand that Iraq comply with the provisions of previous UNSC resolutions and declared Iraq in material breach of UNSCR 687.
7. Resolution 699 (1991).
8. *The Hindu,* dated, 2 July 2005; The panel consists of the 15 permanent and other UN Security Council members.
9. "Jordan received the biggest award of $162 millions. A further $25.9 millions went to Palestinians who lived in Kuwait or owned small businesses there at the time of the invasion, while the remainder was awarded to individuals and governments from other countries". "The panel is paying out about $200 millions every three months, with individuals receiving priority. The next payment is scheduled for mid-July 2005."
   "The overall amount released for individuals, companies and governments is now $19.2 billions, the commission said. It is expected to take years to pay all the claims, with big oil companies having to wait until the end.", *Ibid.*
10. "$52.5 billions compensation for Iraq's invasion of Kuwait": AP news from Geneva: *The Hindu,* 2 July 2005.
11. Security Council Resolution: 986 (1991).
12. Security Council Resolution: 1051 (1996).
13. Security Council Resolutions: 699 & 715.
14. Security Council Resolutions: 1194 (1998); 1352 (2001); 1382 (2001).
15. Security Council Resolution: 1447 (2002).
16. Security Council Resolution 1500 adopted on 14 August 2003.
17. NBC News, "Pakistan Nuclear Offer to Saddam: Iraq refused, fearing a U.S. Sting Operation", by Robert Windrem. *Newsweek,* 04 February 2004.
18. AP news from United Nations "Iraq agrees to unconditional weapons inspections": *The Hindu,* 17 September 2002.

19. Resolution 687 of 3 April 1991; while Resolution 699 (1991) established Iraq's liability for the costs of the Special Commission and the IAEA and Resolution 707 (1991) repeated the demand that Iraq comply with the provisions of previous UNSC resolutions and declared Iraq in material breach of UNSCR 687.
20. SC Resolution 687 (1991) Section C, laid down that "Iraq shall unconditionally accept, under international supervision, the destruction, removal or rendering harmless of its weapons of mass destruction, ballistic missiles with a range over 150 kilometers, and related production facilities and equipment". It also provides for "establishment of a system of ongoing monitoring and verification of Iraq's compliance with the ban on these weapons and missiles". The Resolution required Iraq to make a declaration, within 15 days, of the location, amounts and types of all such items, to which it in due course agreed and submitted.
21. Resolution 699 (1991).
22. Security Council Resolution 715 of 11 October 1991.
23. Security Council Resolution 1284 of 17 December 1999.
24. Statement of President of the Security Council, upon receipt of the special Commission's report, on 28 February 1992.
25. Security Council Resolution 1115 of 21 June 1997.
26. Security Council Resolution 1194 of 9 September 1998.
27. Document: S/1999/1037.
28. Security Council Resolution 1284.
29. Security Council Resolution 1284.
30. The Security Council by another Resolution 1441 in 2002 reiterated that IAEA and UNMOVIC have clear mandate in Iraq, with full and explicit authority, for unrestricted inspections.
31. He served from 1 March 2000 to 30 June 2003 and in 2004-2005 he became otherwise famous for his statements that Iraq War was illegal. Also footnote 45.
32. Security Council Resolutions: 687, 707, 715, 1051, 1284 and 1441.
33. Quotations are as per a UN Document.
34. "Bush wants UN to confront Iraq", Report from United Nations 12 September 2002. by Sridhar Krishnaswami, *The Hindu*, 13 September 2002.
35. "Iraq agrees to unconditional weapons inspections": News from United Nations: *The Hindu*, 18 September 2002.
36. "Congress grants Bush war powers" Report from Washington by Sridhar Krishnaswami, *The Hindu*, dated, 12 October 2002.

37. "U.N. votes tough resolution on Iraq" Resolution 1441 of 8 November 2002, Report from Washington by Sridhar Krishnaswami, *The Hindu*, 9 November 2002.
38. *Times* magazine based report: PTI news from Washington dated 26 January 2003: *The Hindu*, 27 January 2003.
39. "Powell presents irrefutable proof against Iraq in U.N." report by Sridhar Krishnaswami from Washington: *The Hindu*, 6 February 2003.
40. "We have not found weapons of mass destruction: Blix"; Security Council proceeding of 14 February 2003: Report by Sridhar Krishnaswami from United Nations; *The Hindu*, 15 February 2003.
41. The Reports if ISG refered to later, blow.
42. International media reported that Saddam Hussein came out of a makeshift hideout in a pit near the town of Tikrit, reacting as if he was still holding power as ruler of Iraq. He is quoted as saying to Major Brian Reed of the Fourth Infantry Division which captured him: "I'm Saddam Hussein, I'm the President of Iraq and I am willing to negotiate" and is reported to have added that "Americans dreamt up Iraq's weapon threat as an excuse to invade." Obviously, his was not a case of unconditional surrender to enemy under the laws of war.
43. The Report does not suggest he sought the weapons to oppose the US or to give weapons to terrorists.
44. "Saddam denies his Govt. Possessed WMDs", PTI reporting from New York: *The Times of India,* Lucknow Ed., 17 December 2003.
45. The former chief UN weapons inspector, Hans Blix, held that the invasion of Iraq was not legal: *BBC World News*: Friday, 5 March 2004.
46. "Never any Evidence of WMD in Iraq", PTI reporting from Washington: *The Times of India,* Lucknow Ed., 13 January 2004.
47. "Iraq may not have had WMDs: Powell" AP reporting from Tiblisi (Georgia): *The Times of India,* Lucknow Ed., 26 January 2004.
48. "Sure Short: UK Army had doubts on Iraq War", PTI reporting from London: *The Times of India,* Lucknow Ed., 1 March 2004.
49. *Ibid.*
50. "Bush sets up seven-member panel", PTI report from Washington, *The Times of India,* Lucknow Ed., 8 February 2004.
51. "30,000 Iraqis Died in War, reveals Bush": Agencies reporting from Philadelphia, *The Times of India,* Lucknow Ed. of 13 December 2005, p. 10.

Index